INCORRECT ENTERTAINMENT

or

Trash From The Past:

A history of political incorrectness and bad taste in 20th century American popular culture

Anthony Slide

INCORRECT ENTERTAINMENT OR TRASH FROM THE PAST:
A HISTORY OF POLITICAL INCORRECTNESS AND BAD TASTE
IN 20TH CENTURY AMERICAN POPULAR CULTURE

© 2007 Anthony Slide

All rights reserved.
No part of this book may be reproduced in any form or by any means, electronic, mechanical, digital, photocopying or recording, except for the inclusion in a review, without permission in writing from the publisher.

www.Bearmanormedia.com
1-800-566-1251 (Order line only)

ISBN10: 1-59393-093-3
ISBN13: 978-1-59393-093-6

Printed in the United States

Book Cover Design by Sue Slutzky
Book Design and Typesetting by SUN Editing & Book Design

Published in the USA by Bear Manor Media
PO Box 71426
Albany, GA 31708

Contents

Introduction 1
Chapter One: Camp 11
Chapter Two: Apart from That Mrs. Lincoln, How Did You Enjoy the Play? 25
Chapter Three: War 41
Chapter Four: Religious Ecstasy 53
Chapter Five: "This Race Business" 69
Chapter Six: Bad Taste and the Motion Picture 85
Chapter Seven: Bodily Functions and Dysfunctions 93
Chapter Eight: Sex 107
Chapter Nine: "Ain't It Grand to Be Blooming Well Dead" 123
Chapter Ten: Bimbos in History 139
Chapter Eleven: The Male Body on Display 151
Chapter Twelve: Substance Abuse 161
Chapter Thirteen: The Songs of a Nation 181
Chapter Fourteen: Hollywood's Fascist Follies 191
Chapter Fifteen: Hedda Hopper's Hollywood 205
Chapter Sixteen: The Porky's Trilogy 217
Chapter Seventeen: Icons of Political Incorrectness 221
Bibliography 231
Index 241

Introduction

If good taste is defined as an appreciation and presentation of the beautiful and sublime in nature and art, then bad taste, it might be claimed, is represented by the obvious and the ugly. It was once considered bad taste to discuss bodily functions, ranging from eating to death. It was bad manners, if not bad taste, to discuss politics or religion. The problem in defining bad taste—and its significant other, political incorrectness—is that it is often neither deliberately offensive nor deliberately unattractive to its audience. It is bad taste to enjoy racist humor or racial stereotypes, but there is no question that both are appealing to a substantial number of Americans—quite a few of whom should know better. When singer Anita Bryant denigrates the gay community is she offensive or merely a sad, deluded lady? Because she was the spokesperson for the orange growers of Florida are they guilty of homophobia by association? Can the depiction of urination on the motion picture screen be defined as vulgarity or as nothing more than a presentation of life in the raw, a realistic showing of a very natural, and normal, bodily function?

As with bad taste and good taste, political incorrectness has ebbed and flowed with the decades and with the centuries. Pets become animal companions, and owners become guardians of those companions in the quest for political correctness—but this is a "safe" enough area for comedians to ensure continued jokes on the subject. Negroes become blacks and then become African Americans, but this is no laughing matter. A century ago, "coon" songs were performed on the vaudeville stage both by African Americans and major white performers in blackface. In today's society, the "n" word may neither be written nor spoken—except, of course, in hip-hop and rap, where it became popular, often as a term of endearment, in the 1990s. Niggaz Wit' Attitude was the name of one 1990s group of California rappers. As in so many other modern arenas, the "n" word is politically incorrect, except when used by those who would take offense at being so-called by any other group. Jewish humor is OK, but only when offered by Jews (or, to be politically correct, Jewish persons).

Fat humor is a subject confined only to those comedians who are "big-boned" or "possessing an alternative body image." Only the mature, the seasoned or the chronologically gifted should consider telling jokes at the expense of the aged. As for humor involving the female sex, one can only quote a classic comment (which actually has a popular 1905 song as its origin) translated into politically correct terms: "A woman is a only a woman, but a good cigar is a smoke, which should, of course, be enjoyed only in areas set aside for tobacco users, observed the comedian whose concern for the health of others was, regrettably, not matched by a sensitivity to wimmin's issues."

America has become a nation of the humorless, the culturally deprived or dispossessed in the terminology of the politically incorrect. Across the Atlantic, the British publisher of one of the most popular series of 1950s children's books, *Noddy*, by Enid Blyton, denounced them as sexist and racist in the summer of 1990 and had each rewritten. References to the inhabitants of Noddy's home of Toytown being "gay" disappeared, along with Noddy's feeling "queer." In a cowardly bow to multi-culturalism, Toytown's citizens were no longer all blond and Caucasian, but now black, Asian, Chinese and Eskimo. The little girl who had previously announced, "I'm frightened, will you look after me," now says, "I'm not frightened but I know you'll look after me anyway."

As mainstream culture adopted the politically correct nomenclature of dominant culture, so did the political stage of popular culture change. As it was acceptable to ridicule right-wing values in the 20th century, it became the norm to dishonor left-wing ideology in the 21st. Of course, one might argue that much of the often vitriolic humor directed against the left-wing is justified in view of its obsession with political correctness.

At what period of time did bad taste become camp? Certainly, long before Susan Sontag's famed essay on the subject. Despite becoming a mainstay of public television, and, therefore, a part of the entertainment establishment, the BBC sitcom, *Are You Being Served?*, remains camp. The "sissies" of the 1930s, including Franklin Pangborn, Eric Blore and Edward Everett Horton, are defiantly camp. Cary Grant wearing a frilly, woman's dressing gown in *Bringing Up Baby* (1939) is camp, but Jack Benny and Bob Hope in drag are not. Joan Crawford, Bette Davis and Mae West are camp because there is a pronounced masculine quality to their femininity. The early Barbara Stanwyck is not camp, but the later, "butch," performances by the actress are.

What is the dividing line between bad taste and art? If the slicing of an eyeball in Luis Buñuel's *Un Chien Andalou/An Andalusian Dog* (1928) is art then what does one make of the scene in *Carrie* (1976) in which Sissy Spacek is doused in a blend of blood and pigs' livers? When does straight reporting become bad taste? When *Daily Variety* (October 8, 1986) carried the story of producer Hal Wallis' funeral, it concluded the piece by noting that the ceremony was attended by wife Martha Hyer, son Brent, secretary Marge Giddens, "and his Chinese help." Does the ethnicity of the help deny it the right of a name in *Daily Variety*?

When bad taste is deliberate, self-centered and self-congratulatory, as with Howard Stern on radio, *Beavis and Butt-Head* on television, *National Lampoon's Animal House* on the cinema screen, or the Red Hot Chili Peppers (naked except for socks covering their genitalia), the Beastie Boys and the Sex Pistols in popular music, then it is not worthy of consideration on any critical level. There is no virtue in the planned and the obvious. A self-proclaimed "shock jock," such as Howard Stern, is anything but. Comedian Don Rickles does not represent bad taste; all his jokes are carefully manufactured. Rickles' comedy is as sanitized as a show on basic cable television, promising sex and nudity, but with every shot of breast and buttock cleavage digitally blurred. Anyone is capable of predetermined bad taste. Few are virtuous enough to aim for the heights but to sink innocently and without premeditation to the depths of bad taste.

As it has matured—I use the word very loosely—American television has aimed for the outrageous, for shock appeal and political incorrectness with just about anything on MTV, much on E! Entertainment Television, and in sitcoms such as *Will & Grace* and *Married ... With Children*. The last might be crass and vulgar, and even been the subject of a 1989 campaign against its blatant lewdness by Michigan housewife Terry Rakolta, but everything about its production was politically correct. One of the creators, Michael Moye, is African American; the other, Ron Leavitt, is Jewish, while co-star, and sometime director, Amanda Bearse is openly lesbian. In other words, there can be no complaints from minority groups as to its storyline or gags in that every prominent (i.e., given to complaining) minority group is strongly represented in the production.

The Internet in the 21st Century is more than just a superhighway to knowledge. It also provides the entire world, or at least the Westernized portions of it owning computers, with a potential outlet for bad taste. What a century earlier was the result of happenstance or sheer ignorance is now nothing more than a wanton lust to be clever — or stupid. Again, bad taste is never original if deliberately created. As internet outlets such as Amazon.com permit readers to write their own reviews, regardless of credentials, so does bad taste and political incorrectness become the domain of the ignorant masses rather than the ignorant few.

The problem facing 21st century entertainers is that, in terms of bad taste, there is nothing very original left to accomplish. Scatology is about the only subject relatively ignored in 20th century popular culture, but even here there was Butthole Surfers, a Texas band specializing in scatological humor, resulting in a Capitol Records contract in 1991. Even spit has become rather commonplace ever since director Todd Haynes used it as an exercise in humiliation in his 1991 film *Poison*, and Dutch filmmaker Paul Verhoeven provided the wettest, most spit-laden kiss of all time — and between two men — in his 1983 production *The Fourth Man*. It might be childishly amusing to use four letters words on stage or screen, but swearing is far from a novelty. As early as 1905, George Totten Smith and Harry von Tilzer wrote a song titled "The Whole Dam Family." The American public was so enthusiastic in its embrace of the use of the previously censored swear word "damn" that the song became a popular hit, and was the basis for two 1905 comedy shorts produced by the Edison Mfg. Company, *The Whole Dam Family and the Dam Dog* and *I. B. Dam and the Whole Dam Family*. Harry von Tilzer, along with Vincent Bryan, was also responsible for the suggestive song, "Cows May Come and Cows May Go But the Bull Goes on Forever." And World War I provided John O'Brien and Theodore F. Morse with a 1917 anti-German risqué hit, "We'll Knock the Heligo into Helio out of Heligoland!" In her 1930s' recordings, Sophie Tucker made casual use of a remarkable number of "Hells" and "Damns," and in one of her English recordings, she hints at rhyming her last name with a word not used in polite society. Today's rap songs have lyrics far less suggestive than Dirty Red's recording from the 1940s of "Mother Fuyer."

In the 21st century, it is easy enough to aim for the puerile and thus embrace bad taste with almost intellectual justification. The best bad taste changes with the decades. In 1925, the Ku Klux Klan could march down Washington's Pennsylvania Avenue with impunity. In the 1930s, anti-Semitism was pretty much OK if it came from the mouth of a Catholic priest such as Father Coughlin. During World War II, there was no outrage at songs about "The Jap and the Wop and the Hun."

Similarly, political correctness has ebbed and flowed with the decades and with the transition from the left to the right wing in national government. The American motion picture industry endorsed alcohol abuse and cigarette smoking for decades without one word of protest. Onscreen and off, war hero Audie Murphy killed large numbers of German soldiers—and the American public applauded. In the late 20th century, political correctness was the domain of the leftwing and utilized to attack right-wing broadcasters such as Morton Downey, Jr. and popular Christian writers such as Frank E. Peretti. In the 21st century, political correctness is still under liberal control, but, with the right-wing having the upper hand in all areas of the media, it is the left-wing that is made to look ridiculous while under fierce attack. More and more, it is political correctness itself that has become the joke.

Tattoo art, which was once the province of the "lower levels" of society and thus emblematic of bad taste, was taken up by a "higher" order at the end of the millennium. Tattoos that were once only to be found on the bodies of sailors and bikers were suddenly mainstream. The Tattoo Association has been holding annual shows since 1980. *Tattoo Time* (first published in 1985), which also celebrates body piercing, likens the ritual of the tattoo to a religious experience, while competitor *Tattoo* (first published in 1989) guarantees a healthy readership by featuring female nudity.

Television evangelism has become big business. And for those viewers needing a respite from the Trinity Broadcasting Network and its like, there are always the consumer channels of the Home Shopping Network (founded in 1985) and QVC (founded in 1986), or the infomercials, which first began airing in the mid-1980s. The American cable television viewer now has the opportunity to spend his or her money on salvation or a tacky piece of jewelry created by Joan Rivers or Suzanne Somers.

In the 1990s, American television sought to capture new audiences with talk shows that encouraged audience participation and outrage, notably those hosted by Maury Povich, Sally Jessie Raphael, Geraldo Rivera, and Jerry Springer. In 1995, one man killed another after both had been on *The Jenny Jones Show*. Academic Richard Keller Simon compares this incident to the fatal shooting at the conclusion of Luigi Pirandello's *Six Characters in Search of an Author*, and proudly proclaims that the "confessional talk show does for real" what Pirandello can only pretend. In other, less academic, terms, reality talk shows take the magic and innate good taste out of the theatrical experience. It is better that life imitates art rather than the reverse.

Jerry Springer, which first aired on September 20, 1991, has had the most lasting influence on American popular culture, and has even been the basis for the highly popular *Jerry Springer — The Opera*, presented at London's National Theatre in 2003. Reality talk shows such as this break down cultural barriers and inhibitions, but at the same time, they are all so carefully and obviously stage-managed. Indeed, if the concepts and conflicts that they discuss are as widespread as one might be led to believe, they offer nothing new to the average American television viewer. "Chicks with dicks," a favorite Jerry Springer topic, are everywhere in the United States; they may be more commonplace today, but American audiences seventy or eighty years ago were long familiar with "chicks with dicks" in the form of female impersonators and transvestites as staples of vaudeville bills.

The corporate America that controls the nation's airwaves likes the non-controversial controversy of political incorrectness, drawing publicity and the inquisitive. But it no longer cares for the reality of those who are politically incorrect. In April 1996, radio talk-show host Bob Grant, who had been outraging listeners for twenty-five years, was finally taken off the air by WABC-New York. Grant's crime was that he had been "spewing ugly hate talk," as the Rev. Jesse Jackson described it. Grant had described welfare mothers as "brood sows" and African Americans as "savages." The real crime was not Grant's outrageous comments, but the new ownership of ABC by the Walt Disney Co. that was more than merely uncomfortable with controversy. Mickey Mouse could not share corporate life with a Bob Grant.

A prominent British academic, Jeffrey Richards, has noted, "That wise man Mr. Chips, after a lifetime of teaching boys, observed that if a boy had a sense of humor and sense of proportion he was fit for anything. Once that philosophy prevails again, we shall rediscover the value of good taste."

Happily, very few of us have any sense of proportion and our humor is more often perverse rather than clean. We may deplore pedophilia, but we get secret enjoyment and satisfaction from the thought that perhaps James Hilton's title character in *Goodbye, Mr. Chips* is molesting and filling his young charges with something more than righteousness. It is that inner humor that dare not speak its name that provides us with an innate appreciation of bad taste and political incorrectness.

Think of English schoolteachers and one thinks of spankings and canings. In fact, think of English critic Kenneth Tynan, and we also think of spankings and canings. Malcolm McDowell in *if...* (1968) and Rupert Everett in *Another Country* (1984) are just two British actors who assumed the position on screen—and thus titillated an audience that should, but doesn't know better. It's all very naughty, and all in very bad taste. But, then, as British Judge Bertrand Richards remarked in August 1975, "Buttocks were ordained by nature for the purpose."

When we see a Coca-Cola-dispensing machine, how many of us think of comedian Roscoe "Fatty" Arbuckle and the 1922 rape-murder of Virginia Rappe, in which a Coca-Cola bottle was the bladder-rupturing weapon of choice? Perhaps not so many of us, because we don't know who Roscoe "Fatty" Arbuckle was. But if we did, we would—and we would relish our own bad taste.

We may not need to cultivate bad taste and political incorrectness, but we do need to preserve it for posterity. We cannot lose it to the MTV generation that seeks to provide it with a corporate identity and thereby correct its incorrectness. It needs to be there, lying in wait under the surface, rather than held up for immediate recognition and ridicule.

The reality is that nothing is as shocking or original in popular entertainment today compared to the culture of America's immediate past. No ethnic group was spared racial stereotyping. Hollywood producers as diverse as Hal Roach and Walter Wanger embraced fascism. Wife beating was glorified in song, as were the pleasures of cocaine and opium addiction. Novelist Thomas Dixon, whose works form the basis for D.W. Griffith's *The Birth of a Nation*, advocated the deportation of the Negro race back to Africa. The Southern legacy was very much alive as evidenced by the song, "Save Your Confederate Money, Boys (The South Shall Rise Again)," by Larry Markes, Hank Fort and Justin Stone. John Wayne glorified the war in Vietnam. Helen Keller appeared on the vaudeville stage, billed as "Deaf But Not Dumb." Peg Leg Bates and others danced on wooden legs to the delight of full-legged audiences. There was not a disability beyond humor.

Women were vamps, tramps and sex objects long before they became bimbos. Children once played with "gollywogs," and, in 1908, Charles Gounod composed the "Gollywog Cake Walk." Phallic symbolism and the discussion of the penis did not begin with

INCORRECT ENTERTAINMENT

Robert Mapplethorpe or John Wayne Bobbitt. There was scandal over pissing long before Andres Serrano and his photograph of "Piss Christ." There have been jokes about Jews, mothers-in-law and gays decades prior to the O.J. Simpson trial captured the imaginations of stand-up comedians. The Ku Klux Klan was raised on a pedestal as saviors of the white race in *The Birth of a Nation*, applauded in song, and once sued a major Hollywood studio for libel.

There were few subjects that were off-limits in 20th century American popular culture. All aspects of life, from eating and urinating to sex and dying, were subjected to scrutiny. Substance abuse — legal or illegal — was fair game, as were religion and racism. It might be bad taste or politically incorrect, but it found a ready and appreciative audience in a variety of media.

Bad taste or political incorrectness might be offensive, but it was never boring or lacking in outrage. For many, popular entertainment in the 20th century was a land in which the postmodern theorist was unwelcome and the Newspeak of George Orwell's *1984* had yet to be adopted. The first major example of bad taste in 21st century television owes its origin to Orwell's phrase "Big Brother" from *1984*. And to a large extent, the motion picture, the theatre, television and popular music, along with their exponents, which entertained us with political incorrectness and bad taste in the 20th century, were in every respect pre-*1984*.

CHAPTER ONE

Camp

What is camp? Just as if one has to ask the price of an item in an expensive store, one cannot afford it. So, if you have to ask "what is camp," you will never know what it is. Susan Sontag wrote a famous essay on the subject. "The essence of Camp is its love of the unnatural: of artifice and exaggeration," noted Sontag. Expanding on her subject, and probably losing most of her readership (certainly the camp ones), she continued, "Camp is a certain mode of aestheticism. It is one way of seeing the world as an aesthetic phenomenon. That way, the way of Camp, is not in terms of beauty, but in terms of the degree of artifice, of stylization." In more amusing, and camp, fashion, Philip Core offered a number of definitions, including that camp "was a prison for an illegal minority; now it is a holiday for consenting adults."

Susan Sontag's essay "Notes on Camp" was first published in *Partisan Review* (vol. XXXI, no. 4, 1964), and later reprinted in her 1966 book of essays, *Against Interpretation*. The piece proved tremendously important to Sontag, not because of what it had to say, but because it was picked up by *Time* (December 11, 1964), which devoted a five-paragraph article to the subject and made Susan Sontag an intellectual celebrity. What neither the essay nor the recognition in *Time* did was make the writer camp. She is too boring, too academic ever to be that. Far closer to camp, but still removed from the label, is gay writer Christopher Isherwood, whom Sontag dismissively notes in her essay had provided a "two-page sketch" of the subject in his 1954 novel, *The World in the Evening*.

In fact, the "sketch" is little more than one paragraph in length, but it is far from the "lazy" commentary as described by Sontag. Isherwood has the character of a gay doctor, Charles Kennedy, argue that there is both low camp and high camp. The former is represented by "a swishy little boy with peroxided hair, dressed in a picture hat and a feather boa, pretending to be Marlene Dietrich." High camp "is the whole emotional basis of the ballet, for example, and of course of baroque art." Mozart, El Greco and Dostoevski are representative of high camp, and, therefore, inappropriate to the theorization that camp and bad taste are inter-related. Arguably, low camp is pure camp, while high camp borders on the intellectual and creates a passion that can be linked to a camp audience but also can be instilled in the non-camp and the non-gay. The "private code," of which Sontag writes in regard to camp recognition, can only be broken by the gay and the gay-friendly.

In reality, camp in the gay sense would appear to date back almost to the start of the 20th century. The indispensable *Historical Dictionary of American Slang* notes that as early as 1909, one reference work defines camp as "Actions and gestures of exaggerated emphasis ... Used chiefly by persons of exceptional want of character. 'How very camp he is.'" The October 5, 1931 issue of *New Broadway Brevities* makes reference to "Boys and men with painted faces and dyed hair flaunt[ing] themselves camping and whoopsing for hours each night."

Political correctness is not a part of the camp equation. Camp is above political correctness, and, equally, it transcends bad taste. They who are camp and it that is camp would never acknowledge that camp, to be what it is, must always cross the borderline of good taste. As Susan Sontag acknowledges, in order to be good, camp must be awful — and sometimes awfully good.

Camp is gay. It is also very British and very European. The classic camp musical of stage and screen, *The Rocky Horror Picture Show*, is not American, but a British product, replete with very English references. The language of camp was developed back in the 1960s on a British radio series titled *Round the Horne*; it was called "campalare" and included such words as "bona," meaning good, "paloni," meaning women, and "omipaloni," meaning homosexual men. The *Carry On* films, which have only enjoyed a modicum of success in the United States, are very camp, in large part thanks to the presence of comedians Charles Hawtrey and Kenneth Williams and a big-bosomed blonde named Barbara Windsor. Among the greatest of God's camp creations are photographer Cecil Beaton, novelist E.F. Benson, novelist Barbara Cartland, surrealist Jean Cocteau, megastar Dame Edna Everage, novelist Ronald Firbank, composer Ivor Novello, aristocratic siblings Edith, Osbert and Sacheverell Sitwell, and, of course, writer Oscar Wilde, his illustrator Aubrey Beardsley and his lover Lord Alfred Douglas. Sadly, none of them belong in this book. They are all non-Americans, and their fame is in no way affected by their popularity — or sometimes lack of it — in the United States.

Americans are very nervous of camp behavior. They can just about tolerate eccentricity in others because foreigners, and particularly the English, are notably eccentric — and, by extension, probably gay. That is generally why gays define camp and straights fail to acknowledge its existence. Gays can convert camp into a verb — and camp it up — but heterosexuals cannot. The typical Los Angeles businessman saw nothing odd in eating at the Brown Derby on Wilshire Boulevard, enjoying his cobb salad inside a gigantic male hat. The gay man immediately recognized that it was pure camp. The average American housewife standing in the checkout line at the supermarket glances through the *National Enquirer* and similar publications and ponders the deviant sexual behavior of the rich and famous. The gay man in the same line sniggers and jokes with his companion at the ludicrous nature of the stories.

Arguably, camp reached its zenith in the 20th century. It is just too good for the 21st. It flowers only in the right environment and at the right time in history. One can, of course, argue that camp goes back well beyond the late 19th century, but, to all extents and purposes, it began with Oscar Wilde, and faded away with *Absolutely Fabulous*. Creator Jennifer Saunders was hard pressed to write a new series for the beginning of the 21st century, and Roseanne, who had acquired the U.S. rights, quietly dropped her plans for an Americanized version.

In between these two British happenings — after all, Oscar Wilde was born in a city that in 1854 was part of the British Empire — there was some camp activity in the United States, primarily centered around Alla Nazimova in the film industry's silent era, a group of Hollywood actresses of the 1930s and later, a bevy of simpering gay comedians in supporting roles, and Andy Warhol.

There is one American novelist who, while not camp himself, is responsible for the best in American camp, and that is Thorne Smith (1893-1934). This remarkable man, who was only forty when he died, began his writing career as editor of the Naval service newspaper, *Broadside*, during World War I. His three greatest novels have all been filmed and all, at their publication, were hailed as brilliant comedic reactions to the era of prohibition: *Topper: An Improbable Adventure* (McBride, 1926), *The Night Life of the Gods* (Doubleday, 1931) and *Turnabout* (Doubleday, 1931).

The Night Life of the God was the first Thorne Smith novel to be filmed — in 1934 — and involves a scientific experiment that can turn statues into flesh and blood. Various statues of gods and goddesses at New York's Metropolitan Museum of Modern Art, including an armless Venus de Milo, are thus brought back to life, check into the Waldorf-Astoria Hotel and experience modern city life. Unfortunately, it is not comparable to the "old days," with Bacchus complaining of a lack of decent alcohol under Prohibition, and Venus unable to find a lover. The gods and goddesses agree to return to stone but in new poses.

On the printed page, the story works better than on the screen, in large part because nude statues cannot be nude when played by Hollywood actors and actresses. There was, however, something a little kinky about the filming of *Night Life of the Gods*; *The Hollywood Reporter* (September 15, 1934) noted that it was so hot on the set that director Lowell Sherman decided to strip down to his underwear during shooting. A modern remake might be quite entertaining, although it is doubtful yet again that Hollywood's acting community will respond with the appropriate nudity. At its initial release, producer Universal realized the film was out-of-the ordinary and tacked on a foreword reading, "Once upon a time, a famous author named Thorne Smith wrote a book, conceived in a moment of delicious delirium, and written in a cuckoo clock. The first chapters convinced us he was crazy. The ensuing left no doubt that possibly we were. So we leave you to enjoy this new and completely mad type of whimsical humor on the screen. Stop rattling cellophane! Take Sonny's shoes off! Park your gum under the seat where it belongs, and let's all go crazy together."

Turnabout is concerned with physical transformation, as were other of Thorne Smith's novels, and may have its origins in the works of Ovid and Apuleius, as well as English writer F. Anstey, whose *Vice Versa* concerns a father and son exchanging bodies. (He was also responsible for *One Touch of Venus*, both a play and a film, in which a statue of Venus comes to life.) What makes *Turnabout* pure camp is that the transformation concerns a husband and wife. Not only does the husband learn of the insults women must contend with but also experiences the humiliation and discomfort of child birth.

The latter is only suggested in the 1940 Hal Roach production, as a result of objections from both the Production Code Administration and the Legion of Decency, but just about every potential area of gay-oriented humor is covered. *Turnabout* provides Franklin Pangborn with a golden opportunity in the role of Mr. Pingborn, an irate client who is placated when the wife (Carole Landis), now transformed into her husband (John Hubbard), swishes around the office. "They've kept us apart too long," he tells him/her. Not surprisingly, the Production Code Administration noted an "inference of sex perversion here," and informed the producer, "The characterization of Mr. Pingborn as a 'pansy' is absolutely unacceptable."

The stars of *Turnabout* are shown cross-dressed in a publicity photograph for the film, but do not switch clothes on screen. It was OK to be outrageous on the printed page but not on the movie screen. There was neither cross-dressing nor Franklin Pangborn to save a miserable, short-lived 1979 NBC television series based on the novel.

Turnabout was not the first Hollywood film to deal with male-female role reversal. A few years earlier—back in 1933—Fox released *The Warrior's Husband,* in which the Amazonian women, led by Elissa Landi, did the fighting, while their husbands stayed home. A lot of gay men in the Hollywood community—and there always have been a lot of gay men in the Hollywood community—were enlisted for the production, which is based on a 1932 Broadway play by Julian Thompson, and *Variety* reported on some of the antics at the studio under the heading "Boys will be girls!" However, *The Warrior's Husband* is nothing more than a weary Hollywood film, and the presence of a gay ensemble here, as anywhere else, does not make a film camp.

Suggesting a male-female reversal, and definitely camp, is Iowa-born society hostess Elsa Maxwell (1883-1963). Sadly little-remembered today, Maxwell was best known as a party-giver. She had no real talent, and apparently no money, but she did have an ebullient personality. As her few films—including *Elsa Maxwell's Hotel for Women* (1939) and *Elsa Maxwell's Public Deb No. 1* (1940)—indicate, she was famous for being Elsa Maxwell, a one-time nobody taken up by the social set led by Elsie de Wolfe/Lady Mendl. Like her benefactor, Elsa Maxwell was a lesbian, but unlike the slim and vivacious Lady Mendl, Maxwell was obese and very masculine in appearance. She would often don male attire in public, and in 1962, photographer Cecil Beaton (another representative of camp) photographed her as the Balkan Count Korsetz in Quail in Aspic, a comic photographic essay, spoofing royal memoirs. In his 1961 diary, Beaton described Elsa Maxwell as "that pillar of all that is decadent," and he would often describe Truman Capote as the Elsa Maxwell of his day.

So non-feminine was Elsa Maxwell's appearance that in 1997, Bob Kingdom presented a one-man show in which he emphasized the similarity in looks between Maxwell and J. Edgar Hoover. Hoover was the transvestite who became Elsa Maxwell, "the oaken bucket in the well of loneliness."

Russian-born and British-educated George Sanders (1906-1972) is the cynical epitome of camp in American films from 1937 until his death. In a magnificent screen adaptation of Wilde's *The Picture of Dorian Gray* (1945), it is difficult to know what is the most camp, the film itself, the Technicolor insert of the painting in a black-and-white film, Hurd Hatfield's performance in the title role, Angela Lansbury trying to be cockney music hall performer Sibyl Vane, or George Sanders as Lord Henry Wotton. Everything about Sanders' life was camp: his marriage to Zsa Zsa Gabor and her sister Magda, and his bored-with-life suicide. He once asked actress Mary Brian to marry him, and when she declined, Sanders demanded in mock outrage, "But I have fired my mistress, and who is now going to iron my shirts?"

As a runner-up to George Sanders there is the American-born Clifton Webb (1891-1966), a model of sophisticated sexual perversity in films such as *Laura* (1944), and a waspish, highly dubious bachelor in *Sitting Pretty* (1948), *Mr. Belvedere Goes to College* (1949) and *Mr. Belvedere Rings the Bell* (1951). It was not so much that Webb cultivated camp, but he really was that way inclined, a gay man who lived his entire life with his beloved mother, Maybelle. As he explained to gossip columnist Hedda Hopper in 1948, "Maybelle has been so much a part of my career, so thoroughly the *gay companion* of my work and travels." (The italics are mine.) When Maybelle died at the age of ninety, a desolated Webb telephoned Noel Coward, who pointed out to him that at his age it was rather late to be orphaned.

Actor-turned-novelist Thomas Tryon based the homosexual actor in *Crowned Heads*, who is murdered by two young men, not on Ramon Novarro, as might be thought, but on Clifton Webb (who died in his sleep). As was Webb, the character in the novel is besotted with a woman whom the killers believe to be his wife but who, in reality, is his mother.

Clifton Webb was one in a long line of Hollywood Mama's Boys, beginning with J. Warren Kerrigan (1879-1947), whose film career lasted from 1910 through 1924, and who told the *Denver Times* in May 1917 that he would not go off to fight in World War I, because "I think that first they should take the great mass of men who aren't good for anything else, or are good only for the lower grades of work. Actors, musicians, great writers, artists or every kind — isn't it a pity when people are sacrificed who are capable of such things — of adding to the beauty of the world." "The Beautiful Slacker," as Kerrigan was dubbed, lived until her death with his mother, and dedicated his 1914 autobiography to her.

The archetypal screen fusspot was Edward Everett Horton (1886-1970), who appeared in more than 120 films between 1922 and 1971. He was usually the leading man's sophisticated sidekick or valet who generally showed no interest in either men or women. He could be effeminate as in *The Front Page* (1931) or *Lost Horizon* (1937) but he was more an old maid than an old lecher. Horton is perhaps at his most camp in the risqué 1931 feature *Reaching for the Moon*. Here, he is the manservant of Douglas Fairbanks, Sr. and gives his master a lesson in the art of lovemaking, with Fairbanks playing the female role. The two are spotted by a workman whom Horton imperiously calls, "My man," and to whom he hastens to explain "what's what." The workman responds, "I'm not your man, and I know what's what."

By modern standards, the sequence is clichéd. But, it is precisely this type of banter that made for camp seventy or more years ago. On one level, there is the humorous bad taste, obvious to the majority of American filmgoers. On another level, the camp level, this is comedy for the initiated. All members of the audiences are laughing, but only a privileged few are laughing because of the gay sexual innuendo.

Horton and his mother were inseparable. When he called his 98-year-old mother, to alert her he was going to an after-theatre party, she warned him, "That's fine, Edward, but don't eat too much and don't talk about yourself." Unlike his contemporary Webb, who never knew how to unbend, Horton was always a very loveable camp character, often displaying all the mannerisms of a frustrated lover. He never achieved the bitchiness or the unpleasant underside of Webb and Sanders — and he probably never wanted to.

Along with Eric Blore, the quintessential English butler on screen, Edward Everett Horton is the more restrained of the gay, supporting comedic actors of the 1930s and later, whose most outrageous member is Franklin Pangborn (1889-1958). The latter's performance in *Turnabout* is relatively staid compared to other roles, particularly those in the films of W.C. Fields. In *International House* (1933), Fields has arrived in a hotel garden in China rather than, as he believes, Kansas City. Of hotel manager Pangborn, the comedian asks, "Hey, Charlie, where am I?" "Wu-Hu," replies Pangborn. Taking the flower from his buttonhole, Fields comments, "Don't let the pansy fool you." Pangborn plays a film producer in *Never Give a Sucker an Even Break* (1941), and the Production Code Administration was forced to remind Universal, "If Pangborn plays his role in any way suggestive of a 'pansy,' we cannot approve any scenes." Pangborn did—and got away with it.

Franklin Pangborn and his fellow "sissy" performers seldom, if ever, appeared in drag. Had they so done, it would in no way have made them more camp, because female impersonation as and of itself is not camp. The play and films of *Charley's Aunt* are about drag, but are not camp. Apart from Milton Berle, who was born to wear a dress, most American mainstream comedians are not camp in drag. Some of the great female impersonators of the vaudeville stage, including Bert Savoy, Francis Renault, Karyl Norman, and Barbette, are camp. Julian Eltinge was the greatest of all female impersonators, a star of vaudeville, musical comedy and revue, and with a theater named in his honor. Yet, he is not camp. He took himself and his art too seriously. When a detractor would accuse him of being effeminate or gay, Eltinge would not hesitate to use his fists on the offender. For that reason alone, an inability to appreciate his sexuality, a defense mechanism to protect his image and that forced him to live a lifetime of lies, Julian Eltinge fails to gain the label of camp.

Of the later female impersonators, Charles Pierce is camp, but T.C. Jones, Craig Russell, Michael Greer and Jim Bailey are not. With T.C. Jones, it is perhaps the denial of his being gay, but with the others it is simply a lack of a camp quality in their performances. They embrace their "art" too seriously. At the opposite end of the spectrum is Barry Humphries, a boring heterosexual, who is responsible for the outgoing Dame Edna Everage, who takes her mega-stardom very seriously—and is undeniably camp. Full feminine attire is not a necessity in camp. One of the classic camp moments on screen involves minor feminine attire as, for example, when Cary Grant appears in Katharine Hepburn's negligee in *Bringing Up Baby* (1938). When questioned as to his costume by May Robson, Grant leaps in the air and announces, "I just went gay ... all of a sudden!" While the use of the word "gay" may not have a homosexual connotation, gay historians have pointed to Grant's next line, "I'm sitting in the middle of 42nd Street, waiting for a bus!" as evidence of exactly that. 42nd Street was notorious as a gay pickup and cruising area. "And the gags!" wrote Frank S. Nugent of *Bringing Up Baby* in the *New York Times* (March 4, 1938). "Or the one about the man wearing a woman's negligee?"

Drag is, of course, a masculine trait. The word derives from the "drag" of a dress on the ground, and, thus, cannot be used in reference to a woman in male attire. At the same time, there is a small coterie of female stars who are impersonated by drag queens, and who themselves might well be female impersonators. They are the "fag hags" of the screen — the legendary stars who have become gay icons because they are camp and because in their screen personae they would appear to be reaching out to a gay audience. Just as camp is only camp to those in the know, so do these actresses exude a camp quality identifiable only to a special, loving group.

Marlene Dietrich is an obvious and early example, camp in old age because she is so desperately trying to cling to her youth like so many aging homosexual men, and camp in her golden years because of a penchant for male attire. There is nothing more camp than Marlene Dietrich in her tuxedo, singing of a dying love, while smoking a cigarette and kissing the lips of a young woman in her audience in *Morocco* (1930). Here, she exudes bisexuality. Two years later, in *Blonde Venus*, she appears in an ape suit, singing of "Hot Voodoo," and suddenly suggests bestiality.

Stars such as Joan Crawford and Bette Davis had to wait until they reached old age before becoming true daughters of camp. In the former's case, it was a matter of her daughter publishing a tell-all biography, *Mommie Dearest*, and then Faye Dunaway camping it up as Joan Crawford in the 1981 movie version. A reference to "no wire hangers," from which Christina Crawford was to hang her clothes, has become one of the better-known lines in gay mythology, while female impersonators no longer play Joan Crawford but rather Faye Dunaway as Joan Crawford.

Similarly, Gloria Swanson was not camp at the height of her fame. It was only after starring in *Sunset Blvd.* (1950) that she gained camp status. As a glamorous silent star of the 1920s, Gloria Swanson was not Norma Desmond. But from the 1950s onwards, with her rather eccentric eating habits and her garish makeup, she became and remained Norma Desmond.

Tallulah Bankhead comes closer to Marlene Dietrich than either Crawford or Davis in the camp hierarchy. Like Dietrich, she is presumably bisexual. Unlike all three, she was never a major movie star. Her theatre work is probably unknown to her gay followers. The husky voice, the scandals real or imagined, the later friendship with fellow Southerner Tennessee Williams—these are what made her the darling of the gay community. It is the double entendres. It is what she might have said that makes Tallulah what she is. Did she really tell a lover that if she did not arrive on time, he was to start without her? When told by MGM studio head Louis B. Mayer that she must end her lesbian affairs, did she really express puzzlement as to what was lesbianism, and then, in realization, ask, did he mean what Greta Garbo did with young girls? Did she really respond to the statement that cocaine was addictive with "Nonsense, I've been taking it for years"?

As a star, Tallulah Bankhead found her true—and gay—audience after she had died. She is better in retrospect and dead than when she was alive. Her appeal on stage and on screen was limited. She first made a national impact with the general public in 1952 and 1953, hosting NBC's *All Star Revue*. "And my name dahlings, is Tallulah Bankhead," she would tell an audience that had come to laugh at what was really a caricature of what the actress had been.

Before Dietrich, before Crawford and Davis, and around the same time that Bankhead was making her mark on stage, there was Alla Nazimova (1879-1945). A distinguished member of the Russian theatre, Nazimova came to Hollywood in the late 'teens, and appeared in 22 films between 1916 and 1944. Her leading man in eight, and her whilom director, was Charles Bryant, to whom the actress claimed to be married. In 1922, she produced and starred in the greatest camp achievement of the American silent cinema, *Salome*, playing the title role requiring a white wig from which hung what appear to be Christmas tree ornaments. It wasn't enough that a pouting Nazimova looks far too old for the role—and she was—but she looks positively bizarre. The costumes obviously make up for the limitations of the sets, which are minimal. Adding to the overall effect is what appears to be a cast of lascivious and often overweight gay men, and an emaciated actor named Nigel de Brulier playing John the Baptist. Oscar Wilde would have been thrilled with the production, but critics and the public were not. Some were kind; one wrote that Nazimova was "like a dove that has strayed; like a narcissus quivering in the wind." *The New York Times* (January 1, 1923) opined, "It is different but does not depend upon mere difference for its attraction." Yes, *Salome* was different—it was camp.

Here is what might definitely be termed a "limp-wristed" production. One title introduces "Greeks with painted eyes and painted cheeks," followed by a shot of three very camp-looking, aging Hollywood queens—perhaps the most outrageous shot in an outrageous film.

While working on *Salome*, Nazimova was living with cinematographer Paul Ivano, Rudolph Valentino and Natacha Rambova, who was to become the latter's wife. While Valentino may have been bisexual, it is doubtful that Rambova was gay, but rather she was attracted to the gay chic that Nazimova and her crowd represented. With her art direction of *Salome*, Rambova certainly deserves the title of camp—and to confirm it, she later made a film concurrent with her divorce from Valentino in 1926 titled *When Love Grows Cold*. Is Valentino camp? A little more so, perhaps, than his rival in the Latin Lover category, Ramon Novarro, who is a bit too flabby to be camp, but only when dressed in outlandish period costume as in *The Young Rajah* (1922) and *Monsieur Beaucaire* (1924).

Written in French and illustrated with drawings by Aubrey Beardsley, *Salome* was banned in Britain until 1905. Its reputation, however, was substantial, and as early as 1907, there were two Salomes appearing in the *Ziegfeld Follies*, the one who sang, Helene Gordon, and one who danced, Mlle. Dazie. In 1910, Maud Allan, wearing a see-through costume and barefooted, brought her "The Vision of Salome" from the United Kingdom to the United States, but she had already been bested by Gertrude Hoffman, who performed a "cooch" (or sexually suggestive) dance with the same title as early as 1908. There were any number of Salomes performing on the vaudeville stage in the first decade of the 20th century, including at least one black performer, Laura Bowman. Female impersonator Malcolm Scott appeared as Salome with his object of desire not John the Baptist's head but a bottle of whiskey. Vulgarian Eva Tanguay, "The I Don't Care Girl," also performed a parody of "The Vision of Salome" in 1908.

Nazimova's *Salome* might be the purest form of camp, but in vulgar and unadulterated form *Salome* had been camp for as long as it had been performed in one manner or another on the American stage.

From the camp of Oscar Wilde and *Salome*, the 20th century progressed to a conclusion with the camp of Andy Warhol and the Factory. Warhol (1928-1982) was the "father" of pop art in the 1960s, whose factory of devotees, hangers-on, filmmakers, and performers embraced drugs, homosexuality and camp. It was a world as manufactured as the Campbell's soup cans and the portraits of Marilyn Monroe and Elizabeth Taylor, representative of Warhol's artwork. Andy Warhol was a camp celebrity who became a camp legend, who understood celebrity, be it Coca-Cola or Elvis Presley. His work owes much to the influence of two European camp artists, Man Ray and Marcel Duchamp, and Andy Warhol was given camp's old world seal of approval when Cecil Beaton photographed him in 1969.

The Warhol Factory was popular culture at its most accessible and with a new, late 20th century camp sensibility. Warhol's young assistant, Gerard Malanga, one of his "Most Beautiful Boys," along with artist-poet Charles Henri Ford, helped the artist acquire his first movie camera in 1963. And Warhol used it initially, that same year, to make a six-and-a-half-hour silent film of John Giorno sleeping. Sleep established Warhol as a voyeur. The most famous "actor" among those upon whom Warhol turned his camera was Joe Dallesandro, long-haired and sulky "Little Joe," flashing his penis, and enthusing the gay crowd with *Flesh* (1968), *Lonesome Cowboys* (1969), *Andy Warhol's*

Frankenstein (1973), and others. There was bleached-blond rent boy Paul America, starring in *My Hustler* (1965). Drag queen Candy Darling was the transsexual superstar of the factory, while Edie Sedgewick was all-woman—all that is of her, which was not much. Warhol endorsed Lou Reed and the Velvet Underground, who personified degeneracy on the concert stage.

Warhol was a major influence on Robert Mapplethorpe. The photographer "adapted" a childhood image of Warhol in 1971, photographed him in 1987, and also photographed Candy Darling (on the telephone) in 1973. In that the Mapplethorpe images are blatantly homosexual, sadomasochistic and often derivative, he can hardly be designated camp, although certainly his most famous self-portrait, naked and with the handle of a whip shoved up his rectum, endorses his claim as a major, late 20th century purveyor of bad taste.

The "campest" of all camp Warhol films is *Lonesome Cowboys* (1969), which features not only Joe Dallesandro, but also such other famous Warhol luminaries as Taylor Mead, Viva, Tom Hompertz, and Francis Francine (in drag). In bringing bisexuality and nudity to the Western genre, Warhol demolished the establishment view of the American West and presented it with a raw and often gauche image, closer to the West of our fevered and sex-obsessed minds.

A right-wing, stabilizing force within the factory was Paul Morrissey, the underlooked director of the Andy Warhol films, who went on to direct a very camp 1977 version of *The Hound of the Baskervilles*, in which a urinating dog is out of control. Morrissey's later films are as good or as bad as the Andy Warhol ones, and in that sense, he has remained true to his mentor.

Despite the valiant efforts of Paul Morrissey, camp was virtually extinguished in the United States with the death of Andy Warhol. It had never exactly been over-exposed in American popular entertainment, but with the sexual revolution, and a new gay visibility, it really no longer served a purpose. Much of what the new open society endorsed was in poor or even bad taste, but it was now politically correct to a majority of Americas. Everything could be camp, and, therefore, nothing was camp.

CHAPTER TWO

Apart from That Mrs. Lincoln, How Did You Enjoy the Play?

"Apart from That Mrs. Lincoln, How Did You Enjoy the Play?" or "Apart from That Mrs. Kennedy, What Did You Think of Dallas?" Two classic and tasteless jokes, both associated with political assassination, and both short, to the point and needful of no elaboration. Such jokes seem oddly out of place in a country where any suggestion of killing the president justifies a visit from the Secret Service.

In any discussion of humor, one must be careful not to over-analyze. As E.B. White noted, "Humor can be dissected, as a frog can, but the thing dies in the process." Or as critic Penelope Gilliatt put it, quoting Goethe, "To explain is to destroy."

Women were an early, and easy target, for jokes on the vaudeville stage. The German comedy team of Weber and Fields introduced the classic of the genre around the turn of the 19th century, if not earlier: "Who was that lady I saw you with last night?" "That was no lady, that was my wife!" Henny Youngman (who in 1975 became the first comedian on Dial-a-Joke) had one joke, dating back at least to the 1930s, for which he gained nationwide fame: "Take my wife, Please!" In a similar vein, Youngman would comment, "I miss my wife's cooking—as often as I can." A favorite joke of African American entertainer Bert Williams, dating from around 1910, was "If you have two wives, that's bigamy; if you have many wives, that's polygamy; if you have one wife, that's monotony." An early vaudeville joke had a comedian announcing he had sent his wife to the 1000 Isles on vacation—one week on each island. There was even a song, "I Sent My Wife to the 1000 Isles" by Andrew Sterling, Ed Moran and Harry von Tilzer, which Al Jolson introduced in the 1916 musical *Robinson Crusoe, Jr.,* and similar to the 1909 George Whiting, Irving Berlin and Ted Snyder hit, "My Wife's Gone to the Country (Hooray! Hooray!)."

Mother-in-law jokes were long a favorite on the vaudeville stage and on radio and television, but they disappeared not because of political correctness but because young married couples ceased living with one or another set of parents, and the jokes no longer made sense. There is an extreme dated quality to lines such as "They say every woman has her price; I've got a mother-in-law I can let you have cheap" or "Adam was the luckiest man in the world—no mother-in-law." Of course, one may still make jokes about mothers: "A mother is someone who has something hot waiting for her husband," says the comedian, waiting for audience comprehension.

The burlesque stage might primarily be known for its strippers, but its comedians pandered to an all-male audience with questionable jokes on sex and womanhood. When Cleopatra tries silently to wake Marc Antony, she waves a pickled herring under his nose. "Ye Gods, you need a douche," he responds.

One of the classic comedy routines of burlesque is titled "The Bullfight," in which the straight man explains in order to be a bullfighter, the comic needs a machuka, which the bullfighter pulls out.

COMIC: He does what?
STRAIGHT: He pulls out his machuka.
COMIC: The dirty thing, there are women there.
STRAIGHT: Certainly there are women there. Now you'll have to have one.
COMIC: I've got one.
STRAIGHT: Is it good?
COMIC: You're damn right.
STRAIGHT: Is it a long one?

COMIC: Oh, it's about … What the hell do you want to know for?
STRAIGHT: Well, you see, I must examine your machuka before you go into the arena.
COMIC: I don't know you well enough.
STRAIGHT: Come on, just lay it in my hand. I won't drop it.
COMIC: But if you do, don't drop it in the mud.

American comedians understood the potential of the double entendre but failed adequately to utilize it—unlike their English cousins. One of the most offensive of British female impersonators was Rex Jameson, who appeared in the person of the drunken, well-used and aging Mrs. Shufflewick, proclaiming she was broadminded to the point of obscenity. Mrs. Shufflewick's costume always consisted in part of a fur wrap, which she would advise her audience was known in the trade as "untouched pussy." It is almost as if Americans were unaware of the double meaning of "pussy" until Mollie Sugden as Mrs. Slocombe put them right on the BBC sitcom *Are You Being Served?* One of the most brilliant lines uttered by Mrs. Slocombe occurs as she is being trained to serve in the department store's toy department and examines some wind-up toy dogs. With a totally straight face, she asks, "Do you not have any mechanical pussy?"

The homosexual male was another easy target for burlesque and other comedians. Jokes abounded about "Queer Town," where the elevators only went down. On screen, flower sellers would suggest a pansy as suitable for an effeminate male. In song, Sophie Tucker complained, "I Picked a Pansy in the Garden of Love."

The humor of Lenny Bruce is often difficult to define and never more so than with his routine, "Thank You, Mask Man." The Lone Ranger-type character never stays around long to be thanked. When he is finally persuaded to stay and asked what he would like as a gift, he asks for Tonto and a horse in order that he may perform an unnatural act. The Mask Man tells the outraged crowd that he is no homosexual but would like to try it once, "I like what they do with fags. Throw them in jail with a lot of men. Hmmm. Very clever."

The routine became a 1968 animated film of the same title by John Magnuson and Jeff Hale. Both the film and the original routine have been denounced by the gay community, but they are now accepted as part of gay culture and as an attack on rednecks.

There were few who could escape Lenny Bruce's sickly view—and certainly not his mother. In one memorable 1960 letter to the poor lady, he discusses his financial situation and continues, "I don't know how to ask you this and I guess there is no savoir-faire when you're desperate—but here goes—A friend of mine has this House in Sacramento and most of the tricks are Filipino. It was a $5 house but some of the girls who worked there say that with the tips you can get $7.50 for half and half and $15 for exhibition. There's not many whorehouses that will take an old Jewish woman like you, but I called the Jewish Actors Home and they feel that as long as you've a nice ass on you and can speak a little Filipino, you'll do all right.

"Now you know, I never asked you to work in an out-and-out whorehouse before and I wouldn't now, if it weren't out of dire necessity. I would hate to lose the second car. I've only three payments left."

The disabled are another easy and indefensible target for humor, particularly when such individuals can rise above their disabilities. Helen Keller is the most obvious example. She turned her disability not only into a prime example of fortitude and bravery, but also into a vaudeville act. In 1920, along with her mentor Annie Sullivan, Keller appeared at New York's Palace Theatre, demonstrating lip-reading and answering questions from the audience. She was billed as "Deaf But Not Dumb." A year earlier, Keller had filmed her life story under the title of *Deliverance*, with she and Annie Sullivan playing themselves. Francis Trevelyan Miller and George Alfred Lewis composed a theme song for the film, "Star of Happiness," "dedicated to and suggested by Helen Keller (Blind-Deaf and formerly Dumb)."

As Helen Keller embarked on a journey of self-promotion, jokes about her proliferated:

Why are Helen Keller's legs yellow?
Because her dog is blind, too.

How do Helen Keller's parents punish her?
They rearrange the furniture.
Why does Helen Keller masturbate only with one hand?
Because she needs the other one to moan with.
Thanks to a 1979 NBC made-for-television version of *The Miracle Woman*, new jokes about Helen Keller surfaced, ranging from the mildly offensive ("Do you know about the Helen Keller doll—you wind it up and it walks into walls") to the obscene:
"Why did they cut of Helen Keller's finger while raping her?"
"So she couldn't scream for help."
From 1919 to 1990, the humor of the disabled has remained constant, and if the following is a typical example, it has become a little less offensive:
What has two million legs and can't walk?
Jerry Lewis's kids.
Most politically incorrect ethnic humor involves stereotypes. For example, Jews are dishonest. In the vicinity of a bathhouse, one asks the other, "Have you taken a bath." His fellow Jew responds, "Why is one missing?" Another story, popular with monologists in the 1920s, concerns Goldstein. He calls on Mr. and Mrs. Cohen, and, handing Cohen a dollar, asks him to go and buy a packet of cigarettes. Returning sooner than anticipated, he finds Goldstein and Mrs. Cohen in a passionate embrace. Indignant at Goldstein's conduct, Cohen remarks, "Goldstein, you vas a son of a gun. You hand me a dollar to go out and buy a package of cigarettes and while I am gone you hug and kiss my wife. But I tell you vat I do to get even—I keep the change."
The Jewish humor of Jewish comedians, such as Jackie Mason, tends to be either self-deprecating or self-hating. When President George Bush launched the Gulf War, Jewish comedians reminded their brethren, "The last time we listened to a Bush we wandered in the desert for forty years." Apropos of which, there is the comment from Moses after leaving Mount Sinai with the Ten Commandments: "Now let me get this straight. The Arabs get all of the oil, and we get the tips of our penises cut off?"
Rosie telephones her mother to announce her engagement to an

unemployed African American goy. The mother responds positively to everything her daughter tells her, and when she learns the couple has nowhere to live, she invites them to stay at her home and sleep in the bedroom while papa sleeps on the sofa in the living room. "Yes, but, Mama, where will you sleep?" asks the daughter. "Rosie dear, about me you got nothing to worry," responds the mother. "The minute I'm hanging up I'll drop dead."

Gags relating to Jewish-American princesses constitute a definite sub-genre. For example, a Jewish mother asks that her ashes be scattered over the floor at Bloomingdale's, assuring that her Jewish princess of a daughter will visit her gravesite regularly. There are many others, less quotable:

Why does the Jewish American princess like sexual intercourse doggy-style?

Because she hates to see anyone else having a good time.

What does a Jewish American princess do with her asshole every morning?

She sends him off to work.

With the increased emigration—much of it illegal—from South of the border, the Mexican has replaced the Jew as a dishonest member of society, with the comedian now telling his audience, "I went to Tijuana—to visit my hub caps."

The African American is shiftless and poor. The following appears in a 1928 issue of *Madison's Budget*:

"A little dialogue overheard in the Black Belt.

"Ah hear you-all's left yo' husband, Mandy. Is it true?

"It sure is, Eliza. Dat nigger was so shiftless he couldn't find enough washin' to keep me busy."

Seventy years later, it is now an African American telling the joke, "Your family is so poor, they go to Kentucky Fried Chicken to lick other people's fingers."

Some of the first racist humor, for no apparent reason, was directed at the Polish community:

How did the Polack get 35 holes in his head?

He was trying to learn to eat with a fork.

Within time, anti-Polish humor could be merged with anti-black humor, for a dose of dual racism, as in

What is X/S-ski?

A Polack co-signing for a nigger.

Or with anti-Semitic humor:

What do you call a Polish Jew?

A janitor who owns the apartment building.

The cheapness of the Scottish race was so legendary that each issue of *Madison's Budget* in the 1920s features a section titled "Hoots Mon! A Joyous Assortment of Scotch Jests":

"Ever hear of the two Scotchmen who were invited to a golden wedding? One came with a goldfish and the other brought along a friend named Goldstein."

"At a fire in a tobacco shop in Scotland, the police had great trouble in dispersing the crowd which gathered to inhale the free smoke."

"The Scotch national song is 'Let the Rest of the World Go Buy.'"

"Did you hear of the woman who fasted for 45 days? She got offers of marriage from twenty Scotchmen."

Perhaps because we are jealous of the supposed sexual prowess of the Frenchmen, we ridicule his sexuality as if it were perverse, and question other aspects of his character with a simple verse such as:

The French they are a funny race.

They fight with their feet and fuck with their face.

Or the classic joke,

"How do you know if a Frenchman has been to your house?"

"The trashcan is empty and the dog is pregnant."

Similarly, we demean French courage:

"Why do the French have wide tree-lined boulevards?"

"So the German army can march in the shade."

Or the country's general lack of order:

"We must have rules. Where would you be without rules?"

"France."

At times of national depression, humor is at its strongest. The 1933 election of Franklin Delano Roosevelt as president might be a sign of optimism for some, but for many he was an unpopular politician with an agenda that promised little help and a wife, Eleanor, whose power, both within and without the White House, was disturbing. There were jokes about Roosevelt's middle initial standing for "Deficit," "Double-Crossing" and "Dictator." Fishing alone, Roosevelt escapes drowning thanks to the efforts of a boy scout. The president asks what the boy would like and is told a military funeral. When Roosevelt asks why the child should be thinking of a funeral at such an early age, the boy responds, "When I get home and tell my father that I saved your life, I'll certainly need one." Roosevelt's Work Projects Administration (WPA), providing work for the unemployed, was seen as nothing more than a social program to give money to those unwilling to work:

"Did you hear about the WPA worker who killed himself on the job? His shovel handle broke while he was leaning on it."

Roosevelt's arrogance was the subject of much humor. When he arrived in Heaven, Roosevelt's first project was to write a new constitution. St. Peter looked it over, and commented, "Seems all right, but I wonder how God will like being vice-president."

A new version of the 23rd Psalm was written, titled "The 23rd Spasm":

He [Roosevelt] is my shepherd; I am in want.

He maketh me to lie down on park benches; He leadeth me beside the still factories.

He disturbeth my soul; He leadeth me in paths of destruction for His party's sake.

Yea, though I walk through the valley of the shadow of recession, I anticipate no recovery; for He is with me; His promises and pipe dreams they no longer fool me.

He prepareth a reduction in my salary in the presence of my creditors; He annointeth my small income with taxes; my expense account runneth over.

Surely unemployment and poverty shall follow me all the days of my life; and I will dwell in a mortgaged house forever.

What was surprisingly above humor and attack in regard to Roosevelt was that he was crippled by polio. The media never, under any circumstances, showed photographs or newsreel footage of the president unless he was either seated or standing. The effort and the support that was obviously needed to get Roosevelt into either position were totally unknown to the American public. It is highly possible that a large percentage of the American population was unaware that its president was disabled; a 1934 Oswald the Rabbit animated short, *Confidence*, actually shows a cartoon version of a dancing Roosevelt.

If the president's handicap was not the subject of humor, his wife (whom some at the time considered a handicap and others an asset) quite definitely was. One comic story has Eleanor Roosevelt, Mrs. Benito Mussolini, Mrs. Wallis Simpson, and Mrs. Charles Lindbergh playing bridge. Mrs. Mussolini draws a deuce, Mrs. Simpson a king, Mrs. Lindbergh an ace, and Mrs. Roosevelt a joker. The last calls for a new deal.

An anonymous writer produced a superb parody of Edgar Allan Poe's *The Raven*, titled *The Lady Eleanor*:

> From the White House of the Nation,
> Speaking without hesitation,
> Comes the voice of unchecked knowledge
> From the Lady Eleanor.
> In the limelight, basking daily,
> Speaks the Lady, nightly, daily,
> Like the spring that gushes always
> Ever always—ever more.
>
> Home and office, Love and War,
> Speaks the expert of great problems;
> Race and liquor, sex and more
> Speaks the Lady Eleanor.
>
> And this expert ever flitting,
> Never sitting, never quitting,
> Never tending her own knitting,
> Doles her pills of fancied knowledge,
> Wisdom from her bursting store.

For despite her global milling
Of the voice there is no stilling
With its platitudes galore,
As it gushes on, advising,
Criticizing, and chastising,
Moralizing, patronizing,
Paralyzing ever more
Advertising Eleanor.

The sexual relationship between Eleanor, who was suspected of being a lesbian, and her husband, who was known to have a mistress, also evoked humor, as with Mrs. Roosevelt yelling at her husband, "Franklin, if you can have a mistress, so can I." When Roosevelt said, "I have been in war and I have been in peace," his detractors aped him with, "I have been in war and I have been in Eleanor—and I prefer war."

A first-rate example of later political humor dates from the 1988 presidential campaign, and manages to link everything from the sexual prowess of Gary Hart to the alleged plagiarism of Joseph Biden:

"Jimmy Carter, Richard Nixon, Gary Hart, Joseph Biden, Michael Dukakis, and Ronald Reagan are on a ship that is about to sink. Carter yells, 'Women and children first.' Nixon says, 'Screw them.' Hart asks, 'Is there time?' Biden says, 'Is there time?' Dukakis responds, 'Did you hear what Biden said?' Reagan exclaims, 'Is there something going on I don't know about?'"

One of the most brutal of American crimes occurred in 1957, when a 51-year-old Wisconsin bachelor, Ed Gein, embarked on a series of murders, in which his female victims were skinned, eviscerated and parts of their bodies were eaten. (Gein's "career" was the basis for the 1974 cult movie *The Texas Chain Saw Massacre*.) A vast number of jokes relating to Gein and his crime have survived, recorded in a 1981 book, *Edward Gein: America's Most Bizarre Murderer*:

What did Ed Gein say to the sheriff who arrested him?
Have a heart.
Why were there no mice around Ed Gein's house?
Because there were too many pussies.

What did Ed Gein say when asked how his folks were?
Delicious.

Because it was perceived as a gay health crisis, the AIDS epidemic of the mid-1980s resulted in much homophobic humor:

"What's the difference between herpes and AIDS?"

"One's a love story, and the other's a fairy tale."

"What's the greatest mystery about AIDS?"

"It can turn a fruit into a vegetable."

Or, with a reference to another group with a high proportion of AIDS:

"What is the worst thing about having AIDS?"

"Trying to convince your parents you're Haitian."

Jokes might also be tied to another group at risk and also to the Surgeon General's advice to wear a condom:

"Did you hear the one about the guy who saw a junkie shooting up with the same needle another guy had just used and says to him, 'Hey, don't you know you can get AIDS from doing that?' He says, 'It's OK, man, I'm wearing a condom.'"

Liberace's homosexuality became public entertainment when he was sued by his lover Scott Thorson, and his 1987 death of AIDS resulted in a slew of jokes including,

"How did Liberace live and die?"

"He lived by the piano, but he died by the organ"

or

"How many men can you get into Liberace's car?"

77 — eight in the front and 69 in the rear."

The gay community also found a sick humor in its own tragedy. When it was announced that Rock Hudson had AIDS, gay men would tell each other, in a reference to the favored position for fellatio, that "Rock is feeling better; he's out of bed and on his knees."

Curiously, comic books that might be expected to treat AIDS with humor treated the disease only with respect. In December 1988, Archie Comics began including a public service message on AIDS. DC Comics' *Green Arrow* briefly featured a mobster who blames gays for HIV, with which he is infected in prison. AIDS also can be credited with the publication of two gay-oriented comic books, *Gay Comix* (first published in 1980) and *Safer Sex Comix* (first published in 1988).

Just as AIDS deaths evoked humor, so did the tragedy of the hundreds of thousands of Ethiopians dying of starvation in 1985. The jokes concentrated on the weakness and the skeletal bodies of the victims:

"What's new about the McDonald's restaurant in Ethiopia?"

"It features a crawl-up window."

"How many Ethiopians can you stuff into a phone booth?"

"All of them."

On January 22, 1986, just 73 minutes after takeoff, the spacecraft *Challenger* exploded, killing all seven aboard. The disaster left the country stunned and grief-stricken — President Reagan appeared on television that evening to address the nation — but within days a number of very sick and very tasteless jokes began circulating in reference to the tragedy. At no other time in modern American history had a national catastrophe been greeted with such a display of coarse humor, permeating all levels of society. Jokes such as these were heard in the workplace, in bars and elsewhere from the East to the West coasts:

"How many astronauts can fit in a Volkswagen?"

"Two in the front seats, two in the back, and seven in the ashtray."

"Where did the *Challenger* crew take their vacation?"

"All over Florida."

"What does NASA stand for?"

"Need another seven astronauts."

The most poignant aspect of the *Challenger* disaster was that one of the seven killed had been a schoolteacher, Christa McAuliffe, and her death was witnessed by schoolchildren watching the takeoff on television throughout the country. It was only McAuliffe who was singled out for specific mention in the jokes:

"How do we know that Christa McAuliffe did not have dandruff?"

"They found her head & shoulders on the beach."

"What were Christa McAuliffe's last words to her husband?"
"You feed the dog and I'll feed the fishes."

There is no pat answer as to why so many Americans took refuge from the tragedy in sick humor. That so many of the jokes were directed at McAuliffe perhaps suggests that an inert hatred of schoolteachers as authority figures lurks within the adult psyche. In an Associated Press release, dated May 18, 1986, Dr. Howard Pollio, a psychology professor at the University of Tennessee, suggested that *"Challenger* jokes are a negative way of reasserting that there is some order ....When something goes afoul, something that we expected not to lose control, we get scared. Joking about it brings us back to the world where there is control, where they are limits." *Challenger* jokes might also suggest a fear of an advanced technology that we do not understand, a future over which we, as individuals, have no direct control. Professor Patrick D. Morrow has written, "*Challenger* jokes, using McAuliffe as hostility object, the one astronaut on the mission who was a civilian, thus prone to error like the rest of us mortals, serves as a punching bag, absorbing our deflected vituperation against the technological powers-that-be."

The only other modern tragedy that has given rise to an entire body of humor is the June 12, 1994, killings of Nicole Brown Simpson and Ronald Goldman. The comedy did not begin with football star O. J. Simpson being charged with the murder of his wife and her friend, nor with the sixty-mile chase through Southern California as Simpson threatened to kill himself before a television audience of 100 million. That such a large number of the world's viewers would watch such an escapade is, of itself, either terrifying or hilarious.

The *Challenger* jokes emerged from a need to deal with collective grief. The O.J. Simpson jokes were the result of national frustration at a trial that seemed to have gone hopelessly wrong and in a verdict of not guilty with which few in America could agree. "What's the difference between Christopher Reeve and O.J.?" asked office workers gathered around the coffee maker in the morning. The answer: "O.J. is guaranteed to walk." Unlike the *Challenger* jokes, the comedy concerning O.J. Simpson was presented nightly on American television in monologs from Jay Leno, David Letterman and Bill Maher. The white comedians knew Simpson was guilty and on that they based their humor. The black comedians kept relatively quiet, with Chris Rock and others arguing that Simpson should be given the benefit of the doubt. Once the not-guilty verdict was announced, there was a brief respite, in large part because the majority of Americans were outraged, amazed or (in the black community) elated. But within a very short space of time, the joking returned: "O.J.'s living up to his word and searching for the real killers. But apparently he thinks the real killers are on a golf course in Florida."

Everyone involved with the trial was subjected to jokes. A menu was circulated listing items at Judge Lance Ito's Sidebar & Grill, including:

Kato [Kaelin] Salad—"an empty head of lettuce with very little dressing."

Simpson Alibi Sandwich—"full of baloney and hard to swallow, but lots of stupid people are buying it."

Mark Furhman Chicken Platter—"absolutely no dark meat."

Veal a la Nicole—"well battered and sliced; served without the head."

Dessert—"Sorry, our bakery is temporarily closed; the lawyers have taken all the dough."

It is all here, including contempt for lawyers, the intellectual inadequacy of roommate and witness Kato Kaelin and his taking advantage of a brief moment of fame to pose nude for *Playgirl*, and the alleged racism of detective Mark Furhman.

Much of the humor centered on Simpson's initials being the same as orange juice:

"What was the last thing Nicole Simpson said?"

"I should've had a V-8."

"Why do they call him O.J.?"

"Because he beats the pulp out of women."

"What's the difference between O.J. and tang?"

"Tang won't kill you."

The jokes all have one thing in common: they assume that Simpson is guilty. There are no pro-Simpson gags. Some of the jokes go beyond the immediate suspect, and touch upon other politically incorrect issues. In reference to the police chase, there is the question, "Why did O.J. stay in the Ford Bronco so long?" The answer: "Rodney King called him and told him not to get out of the car." There are penis-related jokes, co-featuring John Wayne Bobbitt and Pee-Wee Herman (who had recently been arrested for masturbating in a theater):

"Did you hear that John Wayne Bobbitt had called O.J. Simpson? He told O.J. he knew what it felt like to be separated from a loved one."

"What do O.J. Simpson and Pee-Wee Herman have in common?"

"They were both arrested for abusing their loved one."

And, finally, there is, arguably, the ultimate in sick humor:

"What did Michael Jackson say to O.J. Simpson?"

"Don't worry I'll take care of the kids."

Jealousy of the rich, the titled and the privileged, is the primary source of bad taste humor. When director Roman Polanski was charged with the rape of a thirteen-year-old girl in 1977, his name became the answer to the question, "What goes into thirteen twice?" With the death of John Lennon in 1980, the question was "What's yellow, ugly and sleeps alone," and the answer was Yoko Ono. Sammy Davis, Jr. provided for a joke involving his skin color, his interracial marriage and his disability:

"What's black and white and has three eyes?"

"Sammy Davis, Jr. and his wife."

Celebrity deaths, particularly the tragic ones, generated humor. Both film star Natalie Wood and newscaster Jessica Savitch died in drowning accidents:

"Why did Jessica Savitch drown so quickly?"

"Because she was an anchor woman."

"What's the only wood that doesn't float?"

"Natalie Wood."

Another joke about the actress links her to the supposed sexual prowess of Grace Kelly:

"What did Grace Kelly have that Natalie Wood could have used?"

"A good stroke."

In 1982, actor Vic Morrow was decapitated by a helicopter blade in a freak accident while shooting *Twilight Zone—The Movie*. The next day, there was a new joke around:

"How do you know that Vic Morrow had dandruff?"

"They found his head & shoulders in the bushes." (Note the same joke four years later in reference to Christa McAuliffe.)

The problem facing the 21st century is that there is no Helen Keller or Sammy Davis, Jr. to be the butt of our politically incorrect humor. All we have is Michael Jackson—and he's been around a while! There is a tragedy in the land, stretching from a divided Middle East to a divided United States of America. A set of playing cards of Iraqi leaders is marketed with great hoopla—but where is the humor? There is not even any originality here. Back in 1916, there were playing cards of movie stars with Chaplin as the Joker. The world, its tragedies and its losers are no laughing matter.

CHAPTER THREE

War

In all American-related wars, the entertainment industry has been used as a propaganda tool. Bad taste has never been of any fundamental concern as the leaders of American popular culture set out to prove their patriotic zeal, although when dealing with post-20th century engagements, the entertainment industry had somewhat of a problem in determining what side it was on.

The North may have been the victor of the Civil War in history, but on film, television, the stage, and the printed page, the South was the winner. Audiences and readers embraced the "magnolia and moonlight" view of the South, a land of aristocratic whites and faithful Negro servants (whom it was almost a misnomer to describe as slaves). D.W. Griffith presented this ideal in a number of one-reel shorts produced in the early years of the 20th century for the American Biograph Company and brought it to full realization in *The Birth of a Nation* (1915), with help from Southern writer and racist Thomas Dixon who provided most of the source material. Halfway through the film, the South has been defeated and enters a bitter period of reconstruction. However, by the film's conclusion, the South is triumphant in defeat, with the Ku Klux Klan having ridden to the rescue of all, and leading a triumphant procession down the streets of the Southern town, at the center of which is Lillian Gish, America's most enduring and beloved screen star. A legend of the motion picture rides beside the legends of Southern mythology.

The score for *The Birth of a Nation* featured a love theme, "The Perfect Song," written by Clarence Lucas and Joseph Carl Breil, which later became the theme for the *Amos 'n' Andy* radio series. The lyrics make no reference to the Ku Klux Klan unlike the many dozens of pieces of sheet music glorifying the organization, the majority of which were published in 1923 and 1924. Prior to the climax of the Klan's notoriety and its August 5, 1925 march down Pennsylvania Avenue in Washington, D.C., its members were not merely content to parade, burn crosses and terrorize majorities, they also wanted to sing in praise of their activities. All the music is basically mediocre, with laughable lyrics and is generally self-published. A typical example is "I'm a Klansman (Hooray!)," written and published by Emory Sutton in 1924 with its chorus:

> I'm a Klansman, I'm a Klansman hoo-ray!
> You can shout it clear so the world can hear
> That I'm a Klansman and the cross lights my way
> That means that I'm a real American I'll say

The music generally espoused one hundred percent Americanism, and the principal villains were Catholics and the Pope. Jews and Negroes were occasionally mentioned, but were definitely in the minority. A typical song is titled "The Ku Klux Klan and the Pope" (1924), whose author is listed simply as "A. Klansman." The songs were not limited in scope and included several blues numbers: "The Ku Klux Blues" (1921), "Those Dog-Gone Ku Klux Klan Blues" (1922), "Those Good Old Ku Klux Klan Blues" (1922), "Ku Klux Klan Blues" (1923), and "Ku Klux Steppin' Blues" (1923).

There is little subtlety to the lyrics—and surprisingly little offense. What is generally more offensive are the sheet music covers, such as that for "Our Mothers of Liberty" by Noah F. Tillery (1924). It features the statue of liberty wrapped in an American flag and with a dagger-holding immigrant representing bigotry, graft and anarchy at her rear. The immigrant is a stereotypical Jewish caricature.

There were some comic songs about the Klan. Popular writers Sam Coslow and Leon Friedman came up with "There's a Bunch of Klucks in the Ku Klux Klan!" (1921) with the chorus,

> There's a bunch of Klucks in the Ku Klux Klan
> And they're all Kookoo that's true,

With their awful hoke, they're an awful joke,
When you watch the things they do.
We ought to pile 'em in some asylum
And never let them out.
'Kause we don't know and they don't know
What the deuce it's all about.
There's the grand high punk with his grand high bunk
And his grand high palace too.
But I've just found out how he got that palace
And I'll tell you
Each little Kluck pays one little buck
But he's out of luck 'Kause he'll get stuck
When he finds they're all Kuckoo
In the Koo-koo Klux Klan.

Equally amusing is "Daddy Swiped Our Last Clean Sheet and Joined the Ku Klux Klan" by Helen Marcell and Peggy Hedges (1924). The only major performer associated with a Klan song is Gertrude Lawrence, who performed the "Ku Klux Klan" fox-trot in the 1923 London revue, *Rats*, warning not to quarrel with the Ku Klux Klan.

The December 6, 1915 Atlanta premiere of *The Birth of a Nation* led to the establishment of the modern Ku Klux Klan, under the leadership of the new Imperial Wizard, William J. Simmons. Simmons, along with many of his colleagues, was present at the Criterion Theatre in Atlanta, George, in August 1922, to view First National's *One Clear Call*, in which the Klan is prevented from lynching a gambler. History does not record what Simmons thought of the film or the abortive lynching. The Klan's last known involvement with the entertainment industry came in August 1937, when it filed suit against Warner Bros., charging infringement of its insignia and defamation in the film *Black Legion*, because of the remark, "Are we in for another reign of terror by a new Ku Klux Klan?" The Klan lost.

No sooner did war break out in Europe in 1914 than some American producers, apparently with covert support from the British Embassy in Washington, D.C., began making films advocating preparedness against a potential German invasion. The most famous of the group are *The Battle Cry of Peace* (1915) and *The Fall of a Nation* (1916), with the latter offering a comic parody of pacifist Henry Ford. Yes, the same Henry Ford whose outspoken anti-Semitism led to his supporting Adolph Hitler.

Once America entered the conflict in 1917, there were scores of films depicting German atrocities. There are outrageous portrayals of German rape in *The Heart of Humanity* (1919), with its realistic attack on Dorothy Phillips by Erich von Stroheim, and in *Hearts of the World* (1918), in which a character named von Strohm threatens Lillian Gish. The sinking of the *Lusitania* was evocatively recreated in a 1918 Winsor McCay animated short of that title, and that same year *Lusitania* survivor Rita Jolivet starred in *Lest We Forget*, which ends with the title, "And They Tell Us Not to Hate the Hun!"

The Kaiser is the subject of comic attack in a number of films. In the short, *Sic 'Em Sam,* Douglas Fairbanks as Democracy defeats and washes down the sewer Bull Montana in Kaiser-like makeup as Prussianism. Harold Lloyd and Bebe Daniels resort to custard pie humor to defeat the Kaiser in *Kicking the Germ out of Germany* (1918). Charlie Chaplin rescues Miss Liberty from the Kaiser by bashing the latter over the head with a sledgehammer marked "Liberty Bonds" in *The Bond* (1918), and the comedian also captures the Kaiser in a dream sequence in *Shoulder Arms* (1918). The melodramatic feature film *The Kaiser, the Beast of Berlin* (1918) was parodied in a two-reel short, *The Geezer of Berlin*, which has the Kaiser roped, the victim of a pie assault and eventually placed in an oven.

Female impersonation also played a role in anti-German film propaganda. Jack Mulhall dons female attire to defend the United States in *Madame Spy* (1918). Female impersonator Bothwell Browne makes his only feature film appearance in Mack Sennett's 1919 comedy *Yankee Doodle in Berlin*, in which he dresses as a sultry female and vamps the Kaiser. This highly vulgar offering finds much humor in the dropping of hand grenades down inside the trousers of two German soldiers.

The music industry produced its share of propagandistic songs, including "We'll Do Our Share (While You're Over There)," "I'm Gonna

Pin My Medal on the Girl I Left Behind" and "We Don't Want the Bacon—What We Want is a Piece of the Rhine," all from 1918. Prior to America's entry into the war, one of the most popular of songs from 1915 was "I Didn't Raise My Boy to Be a Soldier" by Al Bryan and Al Piantadosi. Within two years, Al Bryan, along with Harry Tierney, had produced a rebuttal in "It's Time for Every Boy to Be a Soldier," sung to the original tune.

Being on the right side is always important in a war, not only on the battlefield but also in Hollywood. Even a patriotic film can be subject to misinterpretation, as Robert Goldstein discovered in 1917. The son of a prominent San Francisco costumer, Robert Goldstein had provided the wardrobe for *The Birth of a Nation*, and was so enthused over the film and its success that he determined to produce his own epic, *The Spirit of '76*, which would concern itself with the war of American independence. The film was shot in late 1916 and early 1917, and was set to receive its world premiere at Chicago's Orchestra Hall on May 7, 1917. However, the city's police censorship board banned the production, concerned that it might arouse sectional antagonism toward Britain at a time when she and United States were allies in the war against Germany. Goldstein should have been alerted by the Chicago response, but instead arranged a premiere in Los Angeles at Clune's Auditorium on November 28, 1917.

Within two days on the opening, the film was seized by federal officials and Goldstein arrested for violation of the Espionage Act. On April 29, 1918, he was sentenced to ten years in the federal penitentiary and fined $5,000. While, in retrospect, Goldstein's arrest and imprisonment appears a travesty of justice, it does illustrate the vagaries of patriotism and loyalty. At any other time in history, a film showing the British in a negative light would have been harmless.

The Spirit of '76 was not the only film to run foul of the federal authorities. Because it showed Japanese and Americans fighting in the streets of Yokohama and was calculated to create ill feelings between American and its wartime ally, Japan, *The Girl in the Web* was seized in June 1918. A few months later, *The Caillaux Case* was seized because of its portrayal of atrocities committed by British soldiers.

As of December 7, 1941 for at least the next four years, it was perfectly acceptable to call a Jap a Jap, and the entertainment industry did just that. The collective enemy of the Allied countries was now, as Ronald Frankau sang, "The Jap and the Wop and the Hun." Buck-toothed, slant-eyed and bespectacled, the Japanese stereotype was everywhere. In a double bout of racism, singers assured their listeners, "The Japs Don't Have a Chinaman's Chance," and, filled with patriot zeal, that "We're Gonna Find a Fellow Who is Yellow and Beat Him Red, White and Blue." Don Reid and Sammy Kaye urged "Remember Pearl Harbor." Hollywood produced a large number of propagandistic, anti-Japanese feature films, all with Japanese stereotypes, including *Wake Island* (1942), *Behind the Rising Sun* (1943), *Cry Havoc* (1943), *So Proudly We Hail!* (1943), *Thirty Seconds Over Tokyo* (1944), *First Yank Into Tokyo* (1945), *Back to Bataan* (1945), and *Tokyo Rose* (1946). Cartoons from Warner Bros. were particularly venomous. *Tokio Jokio*, released on May 15, 1943, included a spoof of a Japanese newsreel, *Nippon News*. In *Bugs Bunny Nips the Nips*, released on April 22, 1944, the rabbit took on Japanese soldiers on a Pacific island, selling them ice cream pops with grenades inside.

As academic Robert MacDougall has noted, Pearl Harbor was "America's first significant defeat by a non-white force since the demise of General George Armstrong Custer." The Japanese were compared to rats that had to be exterminated. The enemy was a Jap without personality or individuality. There were good Germans, but there were no-good Japs. America was fighting the entire Japanese nation, but only Hitler and his henchmen in Germany, as the song, "There'll Be No Adolph Hitler Nor Yellow Japs to Fear" by William C. Freeland and George D. Barnard, implies.

The vitriolic propaganda attacks on the Japanese were not matched by the same enthusiastic response to either Italy or Germany. Italy barely existed in the conflict, with *Variety* (May 20, 1942) pointing out, Hollywood "doesn't even bother with Musso." *Sahara* (1943) is typical of Hollywood fare, with Italians depicted as far less villainous than the Nazis. Prior to Pearl Harbor, Hollywood had produced anti-Nazi films, and been the subject of a congressional investigation for so doing, and it continued with similar propaganda throughout the war: *Hitler's Children* (1943), *The Hitler Gang* (1944), *None Shall Escape* (1944), etc. Oliver Wallace wrote the song "Der Fuehrer's Face," recorded by Spike Jones, and featured in the 1943 Walt Disney Oscar-winning cartoon of the same name, in which Donald Duck dreams he is a Nazi worker. Disney also caricatured Hitler in the propaganda short *Education for Death* (1943). Hitler is little more than a gangster figure in American popular entertainment, and Americans at the time really did not care about Germany or the Holocaust. As the Hearst newspapers characterized it, the war in Europe was just a "family fight."

The Office of War Information existed to properly direct hate. The 1942 song by Lewis Allen and Earl Robinson titled "The House I Live In" preaches tolerance, but as performed by Frank Sinatra in a 1945 one-reel short of the same name, it urges a form of limited tolerance. As the singer stops a group of children from fighting, he tells them that Jews, Protestants and Catholics should be free of intolerance and bigotry—in order to unite in the killing of the Japanese. "It's words are right out of democracy's book," commented one trade paper of the short, written by Albert Maltz, one of the Hollywood Ten, jailed for contempt of Congress for demanding the freedom of speech and freedom of choice that the film advocates.

The most subtle of anti-Nazi propaganda was provided by Noel Coward in the song "Don't Let's Be Beastly to the Germans," written for and removed from a 1943 revue *Flying Colours*, and banned by the BBC. With typical Coward sophistication, he wrote, "Let's be free with them and share the BBC with them. They're better than us at honest, manly fun. Let's help the dirty swine again to occupy the Rhine again, but let's not be beastly to the Hun." That one song was worth all the propaganda Hollywood could and did produce.

The Cold War followed World War II with a precision suggestive of more than a little political manipulation. In obvious response to the House Un-American Activities Committee investigation of the film industry which began in earnest in 1947, Hollywood producers were quick to begin production of propagandistic films warning of the dangers of Communism in the Soviet bloc and, to a lesser extent, in China. The insidious activities of Communist spies and sympathizers—often depicted as little more than gangsters—in the United States were the subject matter of such films as *The Red Menace* (1949), *I Was a Communist for the FBI* (1951) and *The Manchurian Candidate* (1962). The work of Communists abroad was documented in *Rogue's Regiment* (1948), *The Big Lift* (1950), *Diplomatic Courier* (1952), *Target Hong Kong* (1953), *Blood Alley* (1955), *China Gate* (1957), *The Beast of Budapest* (1958), *The Quiet American* (1958), and *Satan Never Sleeps* (1962).

The approach was usually heavy-handed, with producers often insisting that it was the patriotic duty of all Americans to see these films (and coincidentally enrich their makers), but there were a handful of comedies with a Cold War theme. Bob Hope starred in *My Favorite Spy* (1951) and *The Iron Petticoat* (1956), while Donald O'Connor and Francis the Talking Mule together did their bit with *Francis Goes to West Point* (1952) and *Francis Joins the WACS* (1954).

My Son John, produced, directed and written by arch-conservative Leo McCarey for release by Paramount in 1952, is often regarded as the most notorious of all Hollywood anti-Communist features. It is the story of a middle-aged American couple, Lucille and Dan Jefferson (played by Helen Hayes and Dean Jagger), who, after sending their two youngest sons off to fight Communism in Korea, discover that their oldest boy, John (played by Robert Walker), is a Communist agent, working at a government job in Washington, D.C. After a confrontation with his mother, John decides to renounce Communism, but on his way to "name names" to the FBI, he is murdered. Luckily, John leaves behind a tape explaining how he went wrong, and this is played to the graduating class at his college as a warning to all college-age Americans.

The film is far more than an attack on Communism. It argues for basic American "values," as represented by the Catholic Jefferson family, and against intellectualism, as symbolized by John's college professor. In that John is a mother's boy and, as played by Robert Walker, somewhat effeminate, there is the strong implication that John is gay, and that somehow the film is suggesting homosexuality is as insidious and counter to American ideals as Communism.

On a lighter note, composer/singer Floyd Tilman took the subject to heart with his 1949 song "This Cold War with You." Radio contributed to the anti-Communist hysteria with *I Was a Communist for the FBI* (Mutual, 1952-1954), starring Dana Andrews as double agent Matt Cvetic. On the musical stage, the Cold War was celebrated in *Silk Stockings*, with music and lyrics by Cole Porter and a book by George S. Kaufman, Leueen Mac-Grath and Abe Burrows, which opened at New York's Imperial Theatre on February 24, 1955. A satire of Soviet Russia, based on the 1939 Greta Garbo film, *Ninotchka*, *Silk Stockings* told of a female commissar (first played by Hildegarde Neff), who is transformed into a romantic woman as a result of a visit to Paris. One of the songs listed the joys of being sent to "Siberia," where one never had to telephone for ice and where there is no unemployment. Two years after its Broadway success, *Silk Stockings* was filmed by MGM, under the direction of Rouben Mamoulian, starring Fred Astaire and Cyd Charisse.

More than ninety feature films have dealt with the Korean War, and a number are concerned specifically with its relationship to the "Red Menace," as in *The Bamboo Prison* (1954), where a captured GI chooses to remain behind the Bamboo Curtain with his "Commie Cutie." *Starlift* (1951) boosted patriotism by showing Hollywood stars such as Doris Day, Virginia Mayo, James Cagney, and Gary Cooper entertaining the troops. In *Battle Hymn* (1957), Rock Hudson is a priest torn between his duty to God to save souls and his duty to his nation to take enemy lives—no reward for guessing what philosophy wins. *Battle Flame* (1959) concerns "female captives of the Chinese reds," rescued by U.S. Marines.

The only classic film generated by the Korean War is *The Manchurian Candidate* (1962), which concerns the brainwashing of a soldier in order to have him shoot a presidential nominee. Producer Frank Sinatra refused to permit the film to be screened for 25 years following the assassination of John F. Kennedy.

While the Vietnam War was analyzed in liberal fashion by the majority of Hollywood productions, there was also *The Green Berets*—an aberration on the nation's screens. *The Green Berets*, produced by Batjac for Warner Bros. release in 1968, directed by John Wayne with uncredited help from another Hollywood right-winger, Mervyn LeRoy, and starring Wayne (as Colonel Mike Kirby), David Janssen (George Beckworth), Jim Hutton (Sergeant Petersen), and Aldo Ray (Sergeant Muldoon), was the first and only major Hollywood film about the Vietnam War, shot while the conflict was in progress. Dealing with the exploits of Special Forces in Vietnam, *The Green Berets* takes a positive view of America's involvement, and looks at the issues only in simplistic terms of black and white. The Viet Cong are the villains, seen raping and injuring children, while the American GIs befriend orphans and small dogs. "Complex issues become so wonderfully simple that the heat of battle often glows as warmly as the bonfire of a boy scout jamboree," commented *Playboy* (September 1968).

With a screenplay by James Lee Barrett, *The Green Berets* is based on the novel by Robin Moore, published in 1965 by Crown. It sold more than three million copies, gave birth to a popular song, "The Ballad of the Green Berets," and a comic strip, *Tales of the Green Berets* (first published April 2, 1965). With the full support of the Pentagon, and the tacit approval of President Lyndon Johnson, the film was shot in large part at Fort Bening, Georgia, with that state doubling for Vietnam. The U.S. army loaned a platoon of Hawaiian soldiers to double for the Viet Cong.

Reaction to the film was definitely mixed. John Wayne justified the production to Associated Press (November 18, 1967) by explaining, "Ever since the revolution of 1917, the Communists haven't compromised once in the family of nations. They're out to destroy us, and logic would tell us that this [the Vietnam War] is the right course."

Wayne was hailed as a hero in Atlanta, and prior to the opening of *The Green Berets* there on July 4, 1968, he and David Janssen served as honorary marshals of the "Salute to America" parade. Some congressman questioned the use of the U.S. military in the film's production, but Senator Strom Thurmond said of Wayne, reported in the *Congressional Record*, June 26, 1968, "He is a true and loyal patriot and a great American. It is men of his caliber and stripe who have built America and made it what it is today—the greatest country in the world."

The critics of the greatest country in the world were less enthusiastic, with the most virulent attack coming from Renate Adler in the *New York Times* (July 7, 1968). She described *The Green Berets* as "a film so unspeakable, so stupid, so rotten and false in every detail that it passes through being funny, through being camp, through everything and becomes an invitation to grieve ... It is vile and insane." As anti-Vietnam War demonstrators picketed the New York opening, police guarded the Warner Theatre on Times Square. Attacks in the left-wing French press forced the seven Paris theaters showing the film to hire uniformed and plainclothes policemen. The film was initially banned in Denmark for fear of violence. In Germany, *The Green Berets* was compared by the Stuttgarter Zeitung to *Kolberg*, the last Nazi propaganda film of Joseph Goebbels. It opened in Frankfurt on August 30, 1968, to a riot outside the theater. Riots also occurred on the streets of Amman, Jordan, after the September 1969 premiere there.

More than 500 feature films have dealt in whole or part with the Vietnam War, with few endorsing the campaign. In recent years, the worst excesses of the Vietnam War are represented by the *Rambo* films of Sylvester Stallone. John Rambo is a half-naked, muscle-bound hero whom one critic has described as holding a machine gun where his penis ought to be. He is the super-American patriot unconcerned with the right or wrong of the Vietnam War, the Rocky of the war effort. Introduced in *First Blood* (1982), recalling in vivid detail his torture by the Viet Cong, the character returned in *Rambo: First Blood Part II* (1985) and *Rambo III* (1988), with each sequel finding less and less audience appeal.

War is hell, but filmmakers, even those as committed to the cause as John Wayne, only proved that whatever else it was, on screen it was far removed from its real-life horror.

CHAPTER FOUR

Religious Ecstasy

In the beginning was the film, and God was probably reasonably pleased with what his community had wrought. The productions might be a little vulgar, but it was not the films themselves in which the problem lay, but rather the individuals involved, who tended to take themselves a little too seriously. America's first depiction of Christ on screen was in the 1912 production of *From the Manger to the Cross*, filmed in Egypt and Palestine by director Sidney Olcott for the Kalem Company. Gene Gauntier wrote the screenplay, with a little help from the *Bible*, and Christ, as a man, was played by a British actor named R. Henderson Bland. There was something distinctly odd about the film in that Gene Gauntier claimed to have conceived the idea in delirium while recovering from sunstroke, and Olcott engaged R. Henderson Bland to play Christ in a silent film over the telephone because he liked the sound of his voice. Bland later wrote of his experiences in the film in a book titled *Actor—Soldier—Poet* (Heath, Cranton, 1939), in which he explained playing Christ had helped him fight the Hun on the battlefields of France. He also attended a screening of the film for Britain's Queen Mary and reported, "The seal was put on the delightful informality of everything by a lady-in-waiting coming over and offering the Queen a cigarette, which she smoked."

Cecil B. DeMille is the American filmmaker most associated with vulgar biblical epics, in which he managed to combine both religious sincerity and sexual titillation. He began in 1923 with *The Ten Commandments*, interpolating both a modern drama and the Biblical story, with the principal characters in the former either being ignorant of or defying the Ten Commandments. *The King of Kings* (1927) is a relatively straightforward telling of the later life, crucifixion and resurrection of Christ, played here by the saintly H.B. Warner, although DeMille did find it necessary to make some "improvements" to the gospels. *The Godless Girl* (1928) is an unintentionally amusing tale of students who are cured of atheism after a spell in a reform school. *The Sign of the Cross* (1932) is pure camp as Christians are executed in the ancient Rome of Nero (played in the most outrageous manner by Charles Laughton). Claudette Colbert refers to her rival Elissa Landi as a "baby-faced Christian," and the film is most remarkable for its leading lady's nudity. As she takes a milk bath, Colbert's breast is quite clearly, if briefly, visible. There is also a young, naked, and very gay, man sitting next to Charles Laughton during the killing of the Christians; only a raised leg obscures his genitals. *The Crusades* (1935) is less Biblical epic than high adventure in the 13th century Holy Land. Victor Mature and Hedy Lamarr are the title characters in *Samson and Delilah* (1949). The 1956 production of *The Ten Commandments* was not a remake of the silent feature, but the story of Moses' birth, exodus from Egypt and presentation of the Ten Commandments to the children of Israel. Charlton Heston is a formidable Moses.

Cecil B. DeMille may be the supreme champion of Biblical epics, but there have been other filmmakers who have gone where they should not. Reginald LeBorg was responsible for *Sins of Jezebel* (1953), with a miscast Paulette Goddard as the title character. Robert Aldrich presented plenty of gore and selected vice in *Sodom and Gomorrah* (1963).

The Last Temptation of Christ (1988) was a serious attempt by director Martin Scorsese, working from the novel by Nikos Kazantzakis, to present Jesus from a modern perspective, and, as a result, was the subject of extreme fundamentalist protest. The same protest might have been better directed, from a strictly fundamentalist viewpoint, at Monty Python's *Life of Brian* (1979), the story of a man whose life parallels that of Christ, and which ends with a musical number from the cross titled "Always Look on the Bright Side of Life." And what about *The Ruling Class* (1971), in which Peter O'Toole at one point believes he is Jesus Christ—and also breaks into song.

The worst of more recent lives of Christ—too boring and long even to be considered as camp—is George Stevens' *The Greatest Story Ever Told* (1965), with Swedish actor Max von Sydow as Christ. At the time he was making this, Stevens had become egotistical and self-absorbed. The legend has it that Max von Sydow came to see Stevens after the film was completed, and after waiting for more than an hour in his office, got up and left, telling Stevens' secretary that if the director asked, "Tell Him, His son was waiting to see Him."

Monks, nuns, and priests have been seen on screen far more frequently than Jesus Christ, but, generally, they have been presented in serious form. The insane Russian monk, Rasputin, has been played by Lionel Barrymore in *Rasputin and the Empress* (1932), Edmund Purdom in *Nights of Rasputin* (1960), Christopher Lee in *Rasputin—the Mad Monk* (1966), and Tom Baker in *Nicholas and Alexandra* (1971).

The most famous monk in fiction, theatre and film is probably Boris Androvsky, a renegade who leaves his monastery in the Sahara, marries Domini Enfilden, and then is persuaded to return to his order by his wife. Androvsky is the central character in the most famous of Robert Hichens novels, *The Garden of Allah*, originally published in 1904 in the U.K. and first published in 1905 by Frederick A. Stokes in the United States, where it was highly praised and sold over 800,000 copies. Hichens loved to shock his readers, and among his other works is *The Green Carnation*, a satire on Oscar Wilde and his followers, published in 1894.

Hichens adapted the novel for the stage, in collaboration with Mme. De Navarro, and it opened at New York's Century Theatre on October 21, 1911, with matinee idol Lewis Wallers in the leading role. The first film version came in 1916, and stars Helen Ware and Thomas Santschi. There was another silent version in 1927, starring Alice Terry and Ivan Petrovich, and then the best-known adaptation, in Technicolor, in 1936, starring Marlene Dietrich and Charles Boyer. The final scene of the last, with Dietrich walking off across the Saharan desert, remains a prime example of camp. A year after its completion, the film was banned in Italy on "moral and spiritual grounds."

Nuns have been known to fly—Sally Field in the television series *The Flying Nun* (1967-1970). They have been possessed—Glenda Jackson in Ken Russell's *The Devils* (1971). They have been portrayed by men—Dudley Moore in *Bedazzled* (1967) and Eric Idle and Robbie Coltrane in *Nuns on the Run* (1990). They have been involved in a parody of the Watergate scandal—Glenda Jackson and company in *Nasty Habits* (1977). And, at their most camp, they have sung and danced—Olive Gilbert, Anna Lee, Peggy Wood, etc. in *The Sound of Music* (1965) and Debbie Reynolds in *The Singing Nun* (1966).

There is something about a habit that brings out the worst in one. In any other disguise would anyone pay attention to the San Francisco group the Sisters of Perpetual Indulgence, led by Jack Fertig as Sister Boom Boom? In 1982, Fertig ran for a seat on the San Francisco board of supervisors as "Nun of the Above," and as a result an ordinance was introduced forbidding candidates from running for office under assumed names. Dan Goggin's musical *Nunsense* was first presented at the Cherry Lane Theatre on December 12, 1985. Based on an original series of greetings cards, it featured Sister Mary Cardelia, who changed her name after the New York opening to Sister Mary Regina. The humor here is more quaint than offensive, and it is no surprise that a goodly number of nuns could be seen in the audience. Far less amusing is rap artist Sister Souljah who, in 1992, asked, "If black people kill black people every day, why not have a week and kill white people?"

On screen, popes and cardinals have always been treated with respect, although Liv Ullmann does disguise herself as a man in order to become pope in *Pope Joan* (1972), and the Chevy Chase comedy *Foul Play* (1978) involves an attempt to assassinate the Pope. *Monty Python's The Meaning of Life* (1983) opens with a magnificent and outrageous number, "Every Sperm is Sacred," taking far-from-subtle but highly pointed issue with the Vatican's stance on birth control, and featuring a line of dancing cardinals.

The motion picture Production Code quite clearly stated that "Ministers of religion in their character as ministers of religion should not be used as comic characters or as villains." Thus, priests and ministers on screen were usually portrayed by the more respectable or at least more beloved Hollywood actors, such as Spencer Tracy in *San Francisco* (1936) and *Boys Town* (1938), Bing Crosby in *Going My Way* (1944) and *The Bells of St. Mary's* (1945), Barry Fitzgerald in *Going My Way*, Gregory Peck in *The Keys of the Kingdom* (1945), and Montgomery Clift, experiencing some emotional distress and a crisis of faith, in *I Confess* (1953). *St. Benny the Dip* (1951) had a group of crooks impersonating priests; Humphrey Bogart pretended to be one in *The Left Hand of God* (1955), as did Rod Steiger in *No Way to Treat a Lady* (1968). Based on a biography of the same title, the 1955 film, *A Man Called Peter*, presented the story of the chaplain of the U.S. Senate, Peter Marshall (played by Richard Todd). The film promoted its hero in advertising as "God's kind of guy."

Outside of the motion picture arena, *Simon Called Peter* remains the most controversial of titles dealing with the priesthood. Originally a 1921 novel by Robert Keable (published by E.P. Dutton), the book was adapted for the stage by Jules Eckert Goodman and Edward Knoblock and opened at the Klaw Theatre, New York, on November 10, 1924. Identified as a "torrid drama" by the *New York Times*, the play and the novel concern an army chaplain who goes to the front and becomes as sinful as the soldiers he is ministering to after succumbing to the real world as represented by a vampish female. The theme is, of course, somewhat similar to W. Somerset Maugham's 1921 short story, *Miss Thompson*, and the 1922 play adaptation, *Rain* (filmed in 1928 as *Sadie Thompson*, 1946 as *Dirty Gertie from Harlem U.S.A.*, 1953 as *Miss Sadie Thompson*, and in 1932 as *Rain*).

Hollywood had its own resident Episcopalian minister, the Rev. Neal Dodd (1878-1966), who came to Los Angeles in 1918 and founded St. Mary of the Angels Episcopal Church, at which the Motion Picture Relief Fund was initially housed. Not only did Dodd marry many Hollywood celebrities, including Jack Pickford and William S. Hart, but he also appeared in some 300 films as a clergyman. As the only minister with a Screen Actors Guild card, he can be seen in *Anna Christie* (1930), *It Happened One Night* (1934), *The Secret Life of Walter Mitty* (1947), and *Sorry, Wrong Number* (1948), among many others. As one director put it, "You could always rely on

Father Dodd never to forget his lines, and he didn't cost as much as an actor because he supplied his own Bible." Dodd refused to marry a divorced character on screen, and once when asked to perform a real marriage while at a studio, he insisted on first removing his makeup. Prior to Dodd's first appearance on screen, a Baptist minister, the Rev. George Le Roi Clarke of Long Beach, starred in a series of two-reel comedies for Paragon Pictures in 1920. These "film oddities," as one contemporary trade paper kindly described them, have not survived for modern evaluation.

In the 'teens and 1920s, Christian Science was the religion of the day in Hollywood, with its celebrants including director King Vidor and actress Jean Harlow (whose death is wrongly attributed to her refusing medical treatment because of her Christian Science). In April 1920, the Church actually announced plans to enter film production, but nothing seems to have come of the idea. Recently, the controversial Church of Scientology has named a number of prominent Hollywood stars among its members, including Tom Cruise and John Travolta. In 1949, Jane Russell formed a Bible reading group whose members, it was claimed, included Marilyn Monroe, Marie Wilson and Terry Moore. Were large breasts a major requirement for membership? Russell was also a member of the quartet that recorded the religious song, "Do Lord" in 1954. Pat Boone, Joel McCrea and Spring Byington were leading members of Moral Re-Armament in the 1950s and 1960s, and, of course, Boone's religious enthusiasm is well known. At least, he has displayed a sense of humor about his faith, appearing at an American Music Awards wearing black leather and fake tattoos—as a result, the Trinity Broadcasting Network lost faith in him and his show, *Gospel America*. In 1953, June Haver announced plans to become a nun, and, ten years later, actress Dolores Hart did take her vows and become a Roman Catholic nun. Hollywood's Jewish community founded the Synagogue for the Performing Arts in 1972 as a show business temple.

Almost as long as there has been radio and television in the United States, there has been religious broadcasting. As early as January 2, 1921, pioneering radio station KDKA-Pittsburgh broadcast a sermon by Dr. E.J. Van Etten of the city's Calvary Episcopal Church, and the good doctor became a regular on the station, promoting the "universality of radio religion." The first major successor to Dr. Van Etten introduced a new and very definite element of camp to religious broadcasting. Her name was Aimee Semple McPherson (1890-1944) and, in 1923, she founded the International Church of the Four Square Gospel. Aimee was a showman and in the same year she founded her church, she also established radio station KFSG-Los Angeles (*Kalling Four Square Gospel*). Because she would arbitrarily change the frequency of her station, President Herbert Hoover tried to take Aimee off the air in 1927, and the evangelist responded with a typical response in the form of a telegram:

> PLEASE ORDER YOUR MINIONS OF SATAN TO LEAVE MY STATION ALONE STOP YOU CANNOT EXPECT THE ALMIGHTY TO ABIDE BY YOUR WAVE LENGTH NONSENSE STOP WHEN I OFFER MY PRAYERS TO HIM I MUST FIT INTO HIS WAVE RECEPTION STOP OPEN THIS STATION AT ONCE.

The stunts which Aimee performed are legendary, most notably her 1926 disappearance when she claimed to have been kidnapped and held for ransom. She was as much a vaudeville performer as a preacher, and in September 1933, she played New York's Capitol Theatre, earning $5,000 a week. Dressed in white and with a large cross dangling in front of her bosom, Aimee thanked God for his kindness in providing her with a steady income. Aimee made a number of screen appearances, including a debate with Walter Huston as one of the *Screen Snapshots* short subjects. Very obviously, Barbara Stanwyck's role in the 1931 Frank Capra film, *The Miracle Woman*, is based on Aimee, as is also, perhaps, the character of Sharon Falconer in Sinclair Lewis' 1927 novel, *Elmer Gantry* (filmed in 1960 with Jean Simmons in the role).

Following in the Aimee Semple McPherson tradition have been Paul Rader, who established WJBT-Chicago (*Where Jesus Blesses Thousands*) in the 1920s, and Kathryn Kuhlman, whose *I Believe in Miracles* (the title of her 1962 bestseller) was a source of great amusement to many television viewers, as well as a parody by Ruth Buzzi, from 1967 until Kuhlman's death in 1976.

The first major television preacher was Catholic Bishop Fulton Sheen, whose program, *Life is Worth Living*, was aired on the DuMont network from 1952 through 1955. It played opposite Milton Berle's *Texaco Star Theater* and *Buick-Berle Show*. *Life is Worth Living* was the only show to survive the competition, and Berle would joke it was because Sheen had such good writers, Matthew, Mark, Luke, and John. In reality, it is probably because Bishop Sheen was so camp and decidedly gay. Sheen continued his broadcasting career into the 1960s, and deserves praise for making a stand against the Vietnam War.

If Bishop Sheen had any competition, it was from the Rev. Norman Vincent Peale with his "power of positive thinking." His 1952 book on the subject was second in sales only to the Bible through 1955 and he was even the subject of a Hollywood feature film, *One Man's Way* (1964), in which he is played by Don Murray.

Far less honorable are some of the successors to Bishop Sheen. The Reverend Ike began radio broadcasting in the 1960s, telling his black audiences, "Lack of money is the root of all evil" and selling them "miracle prayer cloths." In 1983, *Newsweek* described Jimmy Swaggart as "the King of Honky-Tonk Heaven" thanks to his flamboyant tele-evangelism, which continues despite Swaggart's many sexual escapades. In 1987, Oral Roberts warned his viewers that unless they were able to raise $8 million to save his church and university, God would "call him back." They didn't and He didn't.

As vice-president, George Bush, Sr. told one Oral Roberts joke. He noted that the evangelist should have been called Anal rather than Oral, but then continued, if he was, "You couldn't hear jokes like 'What does LORD stand for' 'Let Oral Roberts die.'"

Jim and Tammy Faye Bakker introduced The PTL Club in January 1974 and by 1976, the couple had their own theme park, Heritage Village, in North Carolina. As the government and the Bakkers' church, the Assemblies of God, investigated charges of fraud, drug dependency and sexual misconduct, Jim and Tammy cried effusively on television. The sight of Tammy Faye's mascara running down her face became a source of considerable humor, with one joke asking, "What does Tammy Faye do for Halloween?" to which the response is, "Takes off her makeup." Jim Bakker's predilection for illicit sex, coupled with the worst excess of Oral Roberts, resulted in jokes such as:

"What do you get when you cross Jim Bakker and Oral Roberts?"

"A preacher who will die if he doesn't have sex within two weeks."

The Bakkers, along with Paul Crouch, established the Trinity Broadcasting Network in 1973, but it is not Crouch who epitomizes current religious camp, but his wife Jan. With her incredible wig and garish makeup, viewers routinely turn on to the Trinity Broadcasting Network for a glimpse of Jan in Tammy Faye sobbing mode, with the mascara again flowing profusely.

There is a very thin dividing line between camp and bad taste and bad taste and dangerous, as was very apparent in the rise to fame and popularity of Father Charles Coughlin (1891-1979) in the 1930s. With his own Catholic ministry, the Shrine of the Little Flower, in Royal Oak, Michigan, Coughlin began broadcasting in 1926. However, it was not until the early 1930s that he began preaching against the "Red Menace" and warning of the danger of international Jewry. By 1934, Coughlin was also attacking President Roosevelt, whom he described as "anti-God," and the New Deal. Radio listeners who had once been amused by Father Coughlin began to believe that he might—like Adolph Hitler in Germany—be offering a solution to the Depression. Early in his career, Coughlin had been endorsed by the Ku Klux Klan (which was very obviously anti-Catholic) and, now, Coughlin had the covert support of Nazi Germany, whose anti-Jewish policies he publicly defended. The American Jewish Congress pointed out that there was, for example, a remarkable similarity between a December 5, 1938 article by Coughlin in his magazine, *Social Justice*, and a September 13, 1935 speech by Dr. Joseph Goebbels.

Eventually, the Catholic Church was forced to take a stand and first the Detroit archdiocese in the form of Cardinal George Mundelein and then the Vatican denounced the priest. Father Coughlin was still heard over 63 radio stations as late as 1938, but in 1940, his broadcasts ceased and two years later, the U.S. Postal Service refused to accept *Social Justice*, identifying it as "seditious."

Certainly not camp and certainly dangerous to America's liberal population are the newer breed of cold and tyrannical broadcasters. There is Pat Robertson with what was once the Christian Broadcasting Network and was renamed the Family Channel in 1989. Jerry Falwell has led the Moral Majority since the 1980s. The Rev. Donald Wildmon and his American Family Association, based in Tupelo, Missouri, hates gays, pornography and the National Endowment for the Arts, despite a lack of commentary on any by Jesus Christ. In 1991, he was able to prevent distribution of a British film, *Damned*, in the U.S.A. in which he was interviewed. As the comedian would have it, these television-based evangelists do not favor any particular denomination, but their eyes light up at tens and twenties.

Marjoe Gortner (born 1944) had become a boy evangelist at the age of four, quitting at sixteen and returning to the faith in 1972 with an anti-Vietnam War message. With his name combining those of Mary and Joseph, Gortner came from four generations of preachers, with his grandfather being one of the founders of the Assembly of God Church. With his flamboyant cry of "Thank you, Jeeesus," and his billing as "Marjoe, the Miracle Child," Gortner earned $300,000 a year for his parents. He might have been nothing more than a forgotten name in American religious history had it not been for the 1972 documentary feature, *Marjoe*, which won an Academy Award, and led to Gortner's embarking on an acting career.

Composers of popular music have steered well clear of any controversy regarding religion. About the only suggestive song on the subject is "It Takes a Long Tall Brown-Skin Gal to Make a Preacher Lay His Bible Down," written by Marshall Walker and Will E. Skidmore, and introduced in 1917 by Rae Samuels. A novelty number sung by Singing Sam (Harry Frankel) exposes the hypocrisy of preachers with "(Work and Pray, Live on Hay) You'll Get Pie in the Sky When You Die." The early 1950s saw what might be described as a strong revivalist movement in popular music in large part thanks to America's involvement in the Cold War and a desire for the country to prove its Christianity. Stuart Hamblen wrote and recorded "It Is No Secret What God Can Do" in 1951. The following year, Jane Froman introduced "I Believe" by Erin Drake, Jimmy Shirl, Al Stillman and Irvin Graham; Mario Lanza introduced "I'll Walk with God" as an interpolated song by Paul Francis Webster and Nicholas Brodszky in the film version of *The Student Prince*; Edna McGriff wrote and recorded "Heavenly Father"; and Brucie Weil recorded "God Bless Us All" by Tom Murray and Tony Burello.

Billy Sunday (1862-1935) is referenced in Fred Fisher's song, "Chicago," described as a town he could not shut down, and he can also be found in the poetry of such diverse literary figures as Carl Sandburg and Ogden Nash. Who was Billy Sunday? Born William Ashley Sunday, he was the most famous evangelist of his day, a showman and entrepreneur with a tremendous following in the Midwest. Prior to becoming a preacher in 1891, Billy Sunday was a well-known baseball player, with the Chicago White Stockings in 1883 and the Pittsburgh Alleghanies in 1888. With speeches lacking in Christian compassion, he preached in favor of Prohibition and against the theory of evolution. He despised intellectuals; in 1917, he attacked Isadora Duncan, along with Rousseau and Voltaire, and she responded, "If Mr. Sunday believes there is a hell, I advise him to go there, where he may speak with more authority."

Of all religious groups, probably the Quakers have fared the best in the field of popular culture. There are many, many novels endorsing the simple Quaker lifestyle, written both for children and adults, with the most famous being Jessamyn West's *The Friendly Persuasion* (Harcourt, Brace, 1945). Quakers have been featured on screen since Lubin's 1903 production of *Quaker Dance*, and Clara Bow was surprisingly demure as a good little Quaker girl in the 1922 production of *Down to the Sea in Ships*. The Quakers or Society of Friends were benevolently parodied in Lionel Monckton's musical, *The Quaker Girl*, which opened in London at the Adelphi Theatre on November 8, 1910, with Gertie Millar in the title role, and in New York at the Park Theatre on October 23, 1911, with Ina Claire as its star. The central character,

Prudence, is cast out of her Quaker village for the sin of drinking a glass of champagne. Another character is Jeremiah, a Quaker "only on his mother's side," and in whom "father will pop out."

It is in music that the Quakers have received their most rollicking parody. At least three comic songs take aim at the Society of Friends: "There a Quaker Down in Quaker Town" by David Berg and Alfred Solman (1916), "All the Quakers Are Shoulder Shakers Down in Quaker Town" by Bert Kalmar, Edgar Leslie and Pete Wendling (1916), and, best of all, Lou Klein's "Oh! How That Quaker Knew Her Oats" (1929).

If Quakers have fared best, Mormons have fared the worst on screen. In large part because of a belief that members of the Church of Jesus Christ of Latter Day Saints indulge in polygamy and because it sent its missionaries to European countries, Mormons have been actively attacked in foreign films from the early years of the 20th century. In 1911, the Danish film, *Mormonens Offer/A Victim of the Mormons*, depicting a good Danish girl being hypnotized by Mormon missionaries and shipped off to Utah, was released in the United States. A similar theme was adopted in two 1922 British films, both starring Evelyn Brent, *Trapped by the Mormons* and *Married to a Mormon*. Anti-Mormon feeling in the United States also persuaded producer Jesse L. Lasky to produce the 1917 historical drama, *A Mormon Maid*, starring Mae Murray, and again emphasizing polygamy.

In large part because the film industry was controlled for so many years by Jewish studio heads, Jews figured relatively little on screen. There was a Jewish comedian in silent films named Max Davidson, and there were later stereotypical comedians, including Alexander Carr, Harry Green and George Sidney, but they disappeared in the 1930s. It was almost as if the Jewish studio moguls did not wish to offend viewers in fascist and Nazi countries or even anti-Semitic moviegoers in America. Like African Americans, Jews became invisible in popular culture. The one major exception was Gertrude Berg, who was Mollie Goldberg, in a radio series she wrote from 1929 through 1950, and known in its later years as *The Goldbergs*. In the early years of the 20th century, when the film industry was gentile-controlled,

Jewish stereotypes abounded in one- and two-reel productions. One of the earliest of such stereotypes is Cohen in Edison's *Cohen's Fire Sale* (1907), in which the title character burns down his millinery store in order to collect on the insurance.

This same theme can be found in many Jewish jokes, politically correct only when told by Jewish comedians:

EINSTEIN: Issacs has money to burn.
WEINSTEIN: Vos dot money insured?

Or

"Wasn't there a fire in your store last Vendsay?"
"No, not last Wednesday—next Thursday."

Generally, Jewish performers were persuaded to change their names to less obviously Jewish ones; thus Bernard Schwartz became Tony Curtis and Sophie Kossow became Sylvia Sidney. Often gentile actors would play Jewish roles with, for example, Charles "Buddy" Rogers and Jean Hersholt portraying the male members of the Levy family in the 1928 film version of Anne Nichols' 1922 Broadway hit, *Abie's Irish Rose*.

The biggest offense to the Jewish community came from a British film, David Lean's 1948 production of *Oliver Twist*. Alec Guinness' characterization of the villainous Fagin was described by B'nai B'rith as a caricature of a Jewish stereotype that would have only been approved in Nazi Germany. The Production Code Administration, responsible for the self-censorship of the film industry, agreed with B'nai B'rith and others, and *Oliver Twist* was denied an American release until 1951 when all scenes showing Fagin had been removed by the American distributor, Eagle-Lion.

In other areas of popular entertainment, one can find the occasional gross stereotype as in the 1908 song, "When Mose with His Nose Leads the Band," written by Bert Fitzgibbon, Jack Drislane and Theodore Morse. As the title suggests, Mose has such a large, stereotypical Jewish nose that he uses it in lieu of a baton. Even when the sheet music is Jewish-oriented, as with "Oh, Such a Business" (1899) and "Yonkle, the Cowboy Jew" (1907), the cartoon illustrations on the front cover show grossly stereotypical Jewish figures.

Jewish comedian George Jessel utilized a telephone as part of his act, and one of the classic pieces of Jewish humor, "Cohen on the Telephone," consists of a stereotypical Jew, whose accent makes it difficult for the individual at the other end of the line to understand what he is saying, complaining of a problem at his home. The monolog was introduced in 1912 by Joe Hayman and its best-known delineator is Monroe Silver. In their 1920s vaudeville act, "Between the Acts at the Opera," Willie and Eugene Howard get away with incredible anti-Semitism as they refer to opera star Madame Schumann-Heink as Schumann-Kike. Stand-up comedians such as Lenny Bruce tend to denigrate their own people as much as they offend others:

"The Jews killed Jesus Christ because he refused to become a doctor or a lawyer."

One critic, Maurice Yacower, has suggested that "The stand-up comedian is the eternal outsider, the Wandering Jew."

Angels have been seen on screen in parables, such as *Green Pastures* (1936) and *A Matter of Life and Death/Stairway to Heaven* (1946), in spiritual form, as in *Field of Dreams* (1989), and in the shape of leading players, including Cary Grant in *The Bishop's Wife* (1947) and Clifton Webb in *For Heaven's Sake* (1950). The best known of screen angels is Clarence, an angel trying to earn his wings, played by Henry Travers, who saves James Stewart from suicide in *It's a Wonderful Life* (1946). A brilliant, but politically incorrect, BBC television parody has Stephen Fry as Clarence trying to save Hugh Laurie as Rupert Murdoch from suicide. However, after showing Rupert Murdoch what the world would be like had he not been born, Clarence takes the initiative and drowns him.

The Devil has achieved far more screen time than either God or his angels. He has been played by actors as diverse as Adolphe Menjou (*The Sorrows of Satan*, 1927), Walter Huston (*All That Money Can Buy*, 1941), Vincent Price (*The Story of Mankind*, 1957), Peter Cook (*Bedazzled*, 1967), and soap star diva Susan Lucci in the made-for-television movie, *Invitation to Hell* (1984). While the Devil does not put in a personal appearance, his son has wrought untold suffering to those around him in *The Omen* series, beginning in 1976.

INCORRECT ENTERTAINMENT

The American media has generally steered well clear of anything that the religious right might declare blasphemous. It is highly unlikely, for example, that any radio station here might agree to air a 1994 BBC Radio 1 comedy series, *Eamon, Older Brother of Jesus,* written by and starring Michael Redmond. The premise of the show was that the Holy Family was Irish but had left for Israel, where Mary gave birth to two sons, Jesus and Eamon. The latter is constantly overshadowed by his younger brother and bitterly complains to his father Joseph, "When was the last time you saw Jesus in the carpenter's shop? He's hardly set foot in here since he became Mr. Big Boy Messiah." Two years after its initial airing, the BBC announced an expanded version, and it quickly raised the ire of the British *Sunday Times,* owned by Catholic Rupert Murdoch, who is not noted for the quality of his American television programming. After publishing a sample joke—Roman centurion pointing to the Virgin Mary and sneering: "Who's that? I wouldn't give her one"; Eamon: "Nobody ever has, in fact"—the *Sunday Times* was able to persuade the BBC to drop the series. One can always rely on the good taste of American media moguls like Rupert Murdoch.

It was not until the end of the 20th century that the religious right struck back with a vengeance that even the most hateful of Gods would have applauded. As already noted, television was the obvious medium for such vengeance—after all, few religious right-wingers, many of whom might better be described as poor white trash, have little literary taste beyond the more unpleasant chapters of the Old Testament—but the written word did have one right-wing champion. Frank E. Peretti is the leading novelist of the New Christian Right, whose books have been described by Jared Lobdell in *National Review* (August 20, 1990) as "celebrations of the power of prayer and 'watchcare' that support the Host of Heaven and protect the people of God." While Fundamentalism is the guideline of Peretti's novels, evil is represented by the New Age Movement with its concern for animal rights and the environment.

In *Piercing the Darkness* (Crossway, 1989), Peretti depicts a leading American university, here called Bentmore and presumably Harvard, promoting a New Age/Satanic curriculum for American children.

The child welfare system is operated as a police state that seizes the offspring of Christian parents, while the American Citizens Freedom Association (i.e., the American Civil Liberties Union) is described as "that infamous association—one could say conspiracy—of professional, idealistic, legal technicians, whitewashed, virtuous and all-for-freedom on the exterior, but viciously liberal and anti-Christian in its motives and agenda."

Born in Lethbridge, Alberta, Canada, on January 13, 1951, Frank E. Peretti is the son of a minister and himself an ordained minister. He served as associate pastor of a community church from 1978-1984 before spending three years working in a ski-making factory. Since 1988, Peretti has been a professional writer and public speaker. In his first novel, *This Present Darkness* (Crossway, 1986), the principal character is a professor of psychology, who teaches students "sixty-four dollar words which impress people with your academic prowess but can't get you a paying job." The professor is part of an anti-Christian conspiracy, funded by Arab oil interests, the Common Market and the World Bank. Since publication of *This Present Darkness*, Peretti has published more than half-a-dozen novels that have sold in excess of five million copies.

As the religious right marched into the 21st century, Frank Peretti was the one intellectual member of a group that included Pat Robertson, who manages to be both a media mogul and an evangelist, Jerry Falwell, whose Moral Majority is neither, and Ralph Reed, who was described by *Time* magazine in 1995 as the "Right Hand of God."

Rightwing or left, at least Catholics could point with pride at an entertainment industry that had been accorded its own saints in the 20th century. Because he was a Roman actor, St. Genesius was named the patron saint of the motion picture. Because she saw a vision, St. Clare became the patron saint of television. And, befitting an industry dominated by publicity and promotion, because of his writings, St. Frances de Sales was named patron saint of publicists.

CHAPTER FIVE

"This Race Business"

There was nothing new about racism in 20th century entertainment. It was as obvious and as prevalent as it had been in the previous century. What is perhaps remarkable is that the newest of entertainment media, the motion picture, was forced to defend its racist portrayals remarkably early in its existence. On October 15, 1910, the leading film trade paper, *The Moving Picture World*, editorialized in outrage at the "hyper-sensitiveness about this race business," continuing,

"There are funny looking people belonging to every race. Among a whole race of people there is bound to be some similarity, as we know. Therefore, among a whole race of people the funny ones taken together are perhaps so similar that they may be easily embodied into a distinct type. We do not believe a sensible man of any race would deny that there are funny specimens of that race. We do not believe he would deny that there are also characteristic proclivities or instincts that are peculiar to his race. For instance, the Jewish people are noted for their business instinct, while the colored man is noted for his fondness for chicken or watermelon. There is nothing disgraceful about either of these things, so why not admit it, especially if it is true?"

Aside from some early offensive images, Jews have suffered relatively little from motion picture stereotyping. The same is not true of African Americans, who have perhaps been the most hurt in all aspects of 20th century popular entertainment. The physical slavery of the 19th century continued into the 20th century as a form of mental and emotional slavery. The entertainment industry never regarded the African American as anything more than a second-class citizen and depicted him or her accordingly.

In the late 1900s and early 20th century, "coon" songs were popular on the vaudeville stage. Female performers of such numbers were identified as "coon shouters," and they would often be supported by two or three young black children, identified as "picks" (short for pickaninnies). Paul Dresser was a leading writer of such songs, including "I'se Your Nigger If You Wants Me, Liza Jane" (1898), "You'se Just a Little Nigger, Still You're Mine, All Mine" (1898) and "Niggah Loves His Possum or Dee He Do, Do, Do" (1904). Other "coon" songs include "The Whistling Coon" (1888), "Little Alabama Coon" (1893), "Mammy's Little Pumpkin Colored Coons" (1897), "That Nigger Treated Me Allright" (1899), "Every Race Has a Flag But the Coon" (1900), "Coon! Coon! Coon!" (1901), and "If the Man in the Moon Were a Coon"(1905).

The most prominent of "coon" songwriters was African American Ernest Hogan, responsible for "All Coons Look Alike to Me" (1896) and "The Phrenologist Coon" (1901). While his and other songs stereotyped black Americans and encouraged usage of the words "coon" and "nigger," neither Hogan nor "coon" songs in general elicited much criticism from the African American press in the early years of the 20th century. It was not until 1909 that a leading black newspaper, the *Indianapolis Freeman*, editorialized that, "coon" songs must go. It was not until the mid-'teens that such songs did finally disappear from the vaudeville stage.

The first comic strip with a central black character was "Por Lil' Mose" by Richard Fenton Outcault, which initially appeared in the *New York Herald* in January 1901. While the character was sympathetically depicted, he was a stereotype, living in "Coon Town," Georgia.

Compared to other areas of American society, vaudeville was remarkably integrated. White and black entertainers worked together on stage and shared dressing room accommodation backstage while the audiences before which they appeared were often segregated. Ernest Hogan was popular with white vaudeville audiences from the 1890s through the early 1900s, although he was attacked during a New York race riot in September 1900. Bert Williams was arguably the greatest of African American performers, who would wear blackface on stage to heighten his colored image. He was a brilliant pantomimist and comedian who, like all great comedy performers, embodied a hint of pathos. The pain of the racism he faced in society is never more evident than in Williams' theme song, "Nobody":

> When life seems full of clouds and rain
> And I am full of nothin' but pain,
> Who soothes my thumpin', bumpin' brain?
> Nobody!

In the 1917 edition of the *Ziegfeld Follies*, Eddie Cantor, one of his greatest admirers, appeared alongside him in blackface playing Williams' son.

Cantor's 1929 book, *Caught Short! A Saga of Wailing Wall Street*, features a cartoon of the comedian in blackface knocking on industrialist J.P. Morgan's door and announcing, "I'm the Kuhn of Kuhn, Loeb and Company."

Like many other of the greatest Jewish entertainers, most notably Al Jolson, Eddie Cantor appeared throughout his career in blackface. On stage, blackface entertainment dates back to the minstrel days of the mid-1800s. On screen, it was present through the 1930s and 1940s. As late as September 1939, the Hollywood Bowl hosted a blackface minstrel show. On radio, from 1926 through 1960, white comedians Freeman Gosden and Charles Correll wrote and starred in *Amos 'n' Andy*. The pair donned blackface for a 1930 screen adaptation, *Check and Double Check*, but for the television series on CBS from 1951-1953, they were replaced by African American performers, Alvin Childress and Spencer Williams, Jr.

Aside from all-black productions, produced (usually by white Americans) exclusively for black audiences, very few American films, until at least the 1950s, display any positive images of African Americans. Lazy and subservient characterizations were the norm, with the leading exponent being Stepin Fetchit (born Lincoln Perry). His screen name says it all, and the only positive thing that can be written of him is that audiences from the late 1920s through the 1950s were familiar with his work and enjoyed his performances. Equally distasteful are performances by Willie Best, who often played as Sleep 'n Eat, Mantan Moreland and Clarence Muse.

Racism was not limited to the films themselves, but also their presentation. In Southern states, African Americans were required to sit in the theater balconies, often referred to as "nigger heaven." When African American movie patrons in Pennsylvania sued a Harrisburg theater owner for denying them the right to sit wherever they wanted in 1915, the state Superior Court ruled that management could seat Negroes apart from white patrons.

A book could be written about racist black caricatures in Hollywood cartoons—and one has, *That's Enough Folks!* by Henry T. Sampson. The number of offensive animated shorts produced in Hollywood over five decades runs into the many hundreds. Typical, and perhaps the best known, is Bob Clampett's *Coal Black and De Sebben Dwarfs*, a Warner Bros. cartoon from 1943, featuring prevailing stereotypes in a parody of the story of Cinderella. Quite rightly, the NAACP protested the ridiculing of African American soldiers at a time when blacks were actively involved in the military. The 1946 Walt Disney feature film *Song of the South* combines both animation and live action. While the animated segments were of little concern, the live action sequences were considered offensive by the NAACP and the National Negro Congress in that they featured the stereotypical Uncle Remus, played by James Baskett. As created in 1881 by Joel Chandler Harris in *Uncle Remus: His Songs and Sayings, the Folk-Lore of the Old Plantation*, the Uncle Remus character was an ex-slave who had never been reconstructed and remained subordinate to his white employers. The Walt Disney Company has yet to release the film on DVD.

Because *Song of the South* received its premiere in segregated Atlanta, James Baskett was not invited. However, he was awarded an Honorary Oscar, the first black American male to win an Academy Award. Back in 1939, Hattie McDaniel was the first Negro woman to be honored by the Academy of Motion Picture Arts and Sciences—for her work in *Gone with the Wind*. In reality, McDaniel's characterization is demeaning. She deserves more credit for the fun she has with the role of Malena, the maid, in *Alice Adams* (1935).

That is one of the very, very few positive characters played by African Americans during Hollywood so-called "golden age." The other major example of a positive depiction of an African American maid is that of Theresa Harris, as Chico, not merely playing opposite but supporting Barbara Stanwyck in *Baby Face* (1933). Also worthy of mention are Louise Beavers, as the mother whose daughter wants to pass for white, in *Imitation of Life* (1934); Dooley Wilson as pianist Sam in *Casablanca* (1942); and Ethel Waters recreating her 1950 stage role as housekeeper Berenice Sadie Brown in *Member of the Wedding* (1952). Hal Roach's *Our Gang* comedies are praiseworthy for their use of black kids — "Sunshine Sammy" Morrison, Allen Clayton "Farina" Hoskins, Jr., Matthew "Stymie" Beard, and William "Buckwheat" Thomas, Jr. — in non-stereotypical roles. It might be argued that dancer Bill "Bojangles" Robinson belongs in this group but, in reality, he is nothing more than a subservient black stereotype, cheerfully performing alongside Shirley Temple in four films from the 1930s.

The caste system within early 20th century black society was responsible for a racial separation between those who were brown or black and those who were "white" or "yellow." The "white" Negro could pass for white. The "yellow" Negro could pass for, and find a better lifestyle as, a Native American or Hawaiian. In an era before black was beautiful, the whiter the skin, the more appealing the African American. This caste system resulted in at least two popular songs. The first from the 'teens concerns an African American woman who recognizes her boyfriend playing in a Hawaiian orchestra on Broadway and sings, "They May Call You Hawaiian on Broadway, But You're Just a Plain Nigger to Me." In the 1920s, two white entertainers, Al Bernard and Russell Robinson, recorded "It Takes a Cincinnati Yellow to Satisfy a Georgia Brown," composer(s) unidentified. Here, a white male American impersonates a black female American, singing of his/her preference for a light-skinned Negro. The producers of the 1930 docudrama *The Silent Enemy* believed they were filming an authentic story of Native American life, played by Native Americans, but at least one African American insinuated himself into the cast.

The city of Los Angeles might have welcomed the film industry, but it was most intolerant toward non-white participants. Hispanic actor Antonio Moreno developed parts of the Silver Lake neighborhood of the city in the early 1940s, and included a racial covenant in the title deeds to his properties, forbidding the conveying, leasing, renting or occupation "by any person of either the Negro, African or Asiatic race, or any person not of the Caucasian race." Al Jolson, whose entire career is built on blackface performing and in one 1930 film, *Big Boy*, plays a Negro stable boy in blackface throughout, was active in the late 1930s advocating a physical wall be built around portions of the San Fernando Valley in order to keep African Americans out.

Luckily, South Central Los Angeles was accessible to African Americans, and from there, black servants went out to work in Beverly Hills, Bel Air and other affluent white communities. In July 1935, *Daily Variety* reported that director King Vidor had trouble locating 500 Negro extras for *So Red the Rose* until he remembered that Thursday was the maid's day off, and shot the scene that day.

It would be impossible to list the number of films denigrating the Native American. Just about every Western from Hollywood's golden age is at fault. Even the 1939 Warner Bros. cartoon *Sioux Me* parodies "Indians" with a medicine man working to end a drought. On stage, as late as 1946, Irving Berlin's *Annie Get Your Gun* (filmed in 1950) features "Indian" stereotypes. Irving Berlin is far from being the only composer at fault. Back in 1921, Lew Brown and Albert von Tilzer were responsible for "Big Chief Wally Ho Woo (He'd Wriggle His Way to Her Wigwam)."

As with most ethnic types, the half-breed has been more acceptable to American taste than the pure-bred Native American. The best-known novel featuring a half-breed is Helen Hunt Jackson's 1884 romance of *Ramona*, which has been filmed in 1910, 1916, 1928, and 1936. The last features a dreadful portrayal of Ramona's husband, Alessandro, by Don Ameche, who is definitely not suited for "Indian" characterizations.

Two major silent films depict the North American Indian in a sympathetic light, but both are marred by having a white man, actor

Richard Dix, play the central character. In *The Vanishing American* (1925), based on a Zane Grey novel, Dix is a young Navajo in love with a white woman. At the film's conclusion, he dies in her arms after warning the white man of his tribe's planned attack on them. In *Redskin* (1929), he is a college-educated "Indian," who outwits white prospectors, and helps bring prosperity to his tribe through the oil on their reservation. The film even boasts a patronizing theme song, "Redskin, Redskin, Boy of My Dreams." Whenever Hollywood depicted an "Indian" in a sympathetic light, he or she was played by an actor or actress with another ethnic background. Even in the original 1924 version of *Peter Pan*, the "Indian" maid Tiger Lily is played by Chinese-American actress Anna May Wong. There might be references to the "noble savage," but Hollywood's presentation was always ignoble.

Curiously, Hollywood's finest example of the noble Native American savage was nothing of the kind. Iron Eyes Cody (1907-1999) symbolized Native American pride and was associated with a number of popular causes, as well as starring on screen and television from the 1920s through the 1980s. In reality, he was a child of Italian emigrants, a fact well known to Native Americans with whom he worked.

"When does a Mexican become a Hispanic?"

"When he marries your daughter."

Hispanics have fared reasonably well on screen with few negative representations, and stereotypes generally limited to happy, smiling mariachi-playing Mexicans rather than greasy Mexican villains (although there have certainly been a few of those dating back at least to the second decade of the 20th century). Typifying America's view of Mexican life and culture is *Rio Rita*, the 1927 Broadway musical by Guy Bolton and Fred Thompson. On stage and in 1929 and 1942 screen adaptations, Mexico is depicted as a colorful land of banditos and senoritas, with the Texas Rangers just close enough across the Rio Grande to provide a sense of safety and civilization.

Mexican revolutionary Pancho Villa was played by non-Hispanic Wallace Beery in *Viva Villa!* (1934). Another Mexican hero, Emiliano Zapata, was portrayed by Marlon Brando in *Viva Zapata!* (1952).

Zorro, the hero of old California created in 1919 by Johnson McCulley, was played on screen by Americans Douglas Fairbanks, Sr., Tyrone Power and George Hamilton, together with Welshman Anthony Hopkins, and others from 1920 through 2005.

Mexico provided Hollywood with three major stars of the 1920s and 1930s, Dolores Del Rio, Lupe Velez and Ramon Novarro. The last was representative of the "Latin Lover," sensual and attractive to American women, some of whom were actually Latin (Gilbert Roland and Antonio Moreno), but most of whom were not (John Gilbert, Ricardo Cortez, etc.). The Mexican bandit, the Cisco Kid, created by O. Henry, was a romantic figure, initially played in the sound era by non-Hispanic (Oscar-winning) Warner Baxter in *In Old Arizona* (1928) and in the 1950-1956 television series by Spanish-born Duncan Renaldo.

Aside from the present, the strongest period of anti-Mexican feeling was during World War II, when American anger was directed against those who were visually different, primarily the Japanese. The Zoot Suit riots of June 3-10, 1943, in Los Angeles, resulting in the savage beatings of many Hispanics, exemplify this racist attitude.

Realistically, both the Chinese and Japanese suffered equally from stereotyping in pre-World War II Hollywood. Japanese figured significantly less on screen, but there were two major Japanese stars of silent film, Sessue Hayakawa and his wife Tsuro Aoki. The latter was on screen from 1914 through 1924 and is generally forgotten. Her husband also began his film career in 1914, but is remembered today not for his vivid silent portrayals but as one of the stars of *The Bridge on the River Kwai* (1957). Famous and wealthy as the couple might be, the law forbade their owning a palatial Los Angeles mansion.

Sessue Hayakawa's most important American film is Cecil B. DeMille's 1914 production of *The Cheat*, in which he plays a Japanese businessman living on Long Island who brands his mistress. When the film was reissued in 1918, and in response to complaints from the Japanese embassy, the Sessue Hayakawa character became Burmese. Hayakawa repeated his performance in a 1937 French film titled *Forfaiture*. For the 1923 American remake, the character became Indian and was played by an American actor, and in the 1931 version, the character becomes an American with a fascination for Oriental art.

It seemed remarkably easy for Hollywood producers to switch nationalities, and, in their eyes, Sessue Hayakawa was versatile enough, or more likely Oriental enough, to play a Chinese detective in *Daughter of the Dragon* (1931). There was no discernible difference between the Japanese and the Chinese in Hollywood movies, except that in *Daughter of the Dragon*, the Chinese players, led by Anna May Wong, had good diction and the Japanese represented by Hayakawa did not.

Daughter of the Dragon stars Anna May Wong in the title role. She was the only Chinese-American to become a star not only in Hollywood but also in Europe, and one of the few considered popular enough to carry a film. Generally, if the central character in a film was Chinese, he or she was played by a Caucasian star. The inscrutable Chinese warlord in *The Bitter Tea of General Yen* (1933) is portrayed by Swedish actor Nils Asther. Lon Chaney adopted Chinese makeup for *Shadows* (1922) and *Mr. Wu* (1927), with the former film inspiring the song, "Ching, Ching, Chinaman" by Eve Unsell and Louis F. Gottschalk. Ruby Keeler was "Shanghai Lil" in a musical number from *Footlight Parade* (1933). Edward G. Robinson was a Chinese trying to Americanize himself in *The Hatchet Man* (1932). Sylvia Sidney was the unlikely title character in a 1932 non-operatic version of *Madame Butterfly*. Helen Hayes and Mexican-born Ramon Novarro were inhabitants of San Francisco's Chinatown in *The Son-Daughter* (1932). Pearl Buck's novels might be considered sympathetic to the Chinese by some, but their Hollywood adaptations were heavily Westernized, with Luise Rainer and Paul Muni starring in *The Good Earth* (1937) and Katharine Hepburn starring in *Dragon Seed* (1944). Not exactly Chinese, but close enough by Hollywood standards, is Mongol warrior Genghis Khan, played by John Wayne in *The Conqueror* (1956).

Early 20th century writers of Chinese-based novels and short stories presented their characters as innately evil. Englishman Arthur Sarsfield Ward is best known as Sax Rohmer, creator of Dr. Fu Manchu, and in his short story, "The Black Mandarin," published in *Collier's* (November 4, 1922), he wrote,

"The Chinese still believe that the yellow race can dominate the world, and the Oriental mind spells out the means in a manner altogether opposite to Western ideas."

Fu Manchu is the most evil of Chinese characters to appear on screen, although it must be acknowledged that he has a reason for a hatred of the West in that the English killed his wife and child during the Boxer Rebellion. The Sax Rohmer character first appeared on screen in a series of 1923 British shorts starring Harry Agar Lyons. His best-known screen impersonator is Swedish actor Warner Oland, the star of *The Mysterious Dr. Fu Manchu* (1929), *The Return of Dr. Fu Manchu* (1930) and *Daughter of the Dragon* (1931), in which he is killed and instills his hatred of the English into his daughter, Anna May Wong. Strange how a Swedish actor can have a genuinely Chinese daughter! Myrna Loy became Fu Manchu's daughter in *The Mask of Fu Manchu* (1932) and Boris Karloff played the title character. The film is still much admired for its torture scenes, including a brutal whipping of leading man Charles Starrett, which appears to bring Myrna Loy to orgasm. There was also a radio serial from 1932-1934 and 1939-1940, a later fifteen-episode serial, *Drums of Fu Manchu*, in 1940, a television series, *The Adventures of Fu Manchu*, in 1956, and a handful of British feature films in the 1960s, starring Christopher Lee. As late as 1980, Peter Sellers starred in a parody, *The Fiendish Plot of Dr. Fu Manchu*.

Warner Oland became typecast as a Chinese in feature films such as *Shanghai Express* (1932) and in the series of *Charlie Chan* productions. As created by Earl Derr Biggers in 1925, Charlie Chan was a soft-spoken, kindly Chinese-American detective, based in Hawaii, and famed for his aphorisms. Warner Oland first brought him to the screen in *Charlie Chan Carries On* (1931), and following Oland's 1937 death, Charlie Chan continued on screen in 1938 with Sidney Toler in *Charlie Chan in Honolulu*. Charlie Chan was an enduring and endearing figure, with a number one son played by Keye Luke and a number two son played by Sen Yung. In no way can he be considered a racial stereotype in that he is far more intelligent than the Caucasian villains he encounters and the Caucasian police with whom he works. The only problem with the films—and it is, of course, an over-riding one—is that he is always played by a non-Chinese. The same problem applies to the other two popular detective series generated by the success of Charlie Chan. The *Mr. Moto* series, based on a character created by John P. Marquand in 1936, is played by Austrian actor Peter Lorre, beginning with *Think Fast, Mr. Moto* (1937), revived as a radio series in 1951, and last heard of with *The Return of Mr. Moto* (1965), which was an incredibly mediocre work starring Henry Silva, who neither sounds nor looks Oriental. Hugh Wiley created Mr. Wong, and British actor Boris Karloff played him in five films between 1938 and 1940. For one last film, *Phantom of Chinatown* (1940), Keye Luke replaced Karloff, but playing Wong's son, Jimmy Lee.

The attitude toward the Chinese is more patronizing than derogatory. This approach is apparent in songs such as "In Blinky Winky Chinky Chinatown," written in 1925 by William Jerome and Jean Schwartz, who were also responsible for "Chinatown, My Chinatown." The stereotype of the kindly "Chink" was established in 1919 by D.W. Griffith with *Broken Blossoms*, based on a 1916 Thomas Burke story, "The Chink and the Child." Here, the saintly Chinaman (and Buddhist) in London's Limehouse district, played by Richard Barthelmess in yellowface, is compared to the viciousness and intolerance of the English. At the same time, the film creates another stereotype, in showing the Chinese predilection for opium and opium dens. It has also been suggested in recent years that as the girl, played by Lillian Gish, for whom the Barthelmess character shows affection, is underage, the saintly Chinese is in fact a pedophile. Such critics perhaps do not understand the difference between passion and compassion. (In a 1936 British remake, the Barthelmess character was played by Welsh actor Emlyn Williams.)

While Chinese stereotypes abound in Hollywood films of the 1920s and 1930s, the Japanese are barely acknowledged. That invisibility changed with Pearl Harbor. The villainous Japanese, as represented by Sessue Hayakawa, were suddenly resurrected, while the Chinese sank into oblivion. This change in attitude is never more obvious than with a couple of songs popularized by British comedian George Formby, some of whose films were released in the United States. In the 1930s, one of his better-known songs, "Mr. Wu," was about a stereotypical Chinese laundryman who changed occupation and became a window cleaner; with the outbreak of World War II, Formby began singing "Mr. Wu's an Air Raid Warden Now." Not that the racism ceased; in reference to the blackout, the song noted, "If you have a chink [of light] at your window, you'll have another one at your door."

"Until the war," wrote Jules Feiffer in *The Comic Book Heroes* (1965), "we always assumed [the Oriental villain] was Chinese. But now we know what he was! A Jap; a Yellow-Belly Jap; a Jap-a-Nazi Rat."

Europeans have been accepted on America's movie screens as have European immigrants been integrated into American society. Swedes were ridiculed in a relatively kindly fashion with the dumb characterization of El Brendel (1891-1964) in vaudeville and in films as he mispronounced "j" as "y" and introduced the phrase, "yumpin' yimminy." The Betty White character of Rose on the television series *The Golden Girls* (NBC, 1985-1992) continued the El Brendel tradition with her Norwegian-American rather than Swedish-American stupidity and reference to a "Fjord Fiesta" automobile. There was minor comedic racism in the 1930 song by Alfred Bryan and Harry Moll, "Twenty Swedes Ran through the Weeds," in which the Minnesota football team takes on Notre Dame and its Norwegian Knute Rockne.

In that he was not Italian but of Scottish-Irish descent, one might criticize the Italian theatre and film characterizations of George Beban, but his tear-jerking recitation of "Mia Rosa" did nothing to hurt Italian-Americans, and nor did his 1915 film, *The Italian*. Far more offensive are novelty songs such as "Wop, Wop, Wop!," written and performed by James Brockman in 1908, and "Wop Blues," written in 1924 by Sam M. Lewis, Joe Young and Jules Buffano. The only major, and continuing, racist attitude toward Italian-Americans is embodied in the notion that all have some connection to the Mafia. Both criminality and a lack of linguistic ability are evidenced in that familiar bumper sticker, "Mafia Staff Car—You Toucha My Car—I Breaka Your Face."

Ireland is a land which must be heaven because your mother comes from there. It has produced kindly priests, as represented by Bing Crosby and Barry Fitzgerald, and heroic leading men who sometimes play policeman, such as Pat O'Brien. So much of the immigrant audience for Hollywood films consisted of Irish men and women that Hollywood stars in the late 'teens and 1920s overwhelmingly pretended to be of Irish ancestry. In 1918, *Photoplay* published a piece on performers of Irish ancestry, claiming the Irish "propel the production side of the photoplay business even as Wilsonian democracy propels the civilized world." Among those claiming to be "Irish" were Mary Pickford, Anthony Quinn, Lillian Gish, and even Adolphe Menjou. In 1923, Rudolph Valentino demonstrated his solidarity with the Irish people in an excruciatingly poor piece of verse titled "Erin":

> The green sod is red now—
> Rebellion.
> The green sod is white now –
> Purity.
> The green sod is blue now,
> With truth.
> And the green sod is ever green.
> It is growth—none can stop natural growth.
> Erin—land of dreams—Awaken.

If there was racism in regard to the Irish on screen, it was the racism of patronage, the insulting depiction of the stage Irish as invented by directors such as John Ford. The American film industry saw Ireland in terms of art and history. Producer Samuel Goldwyn was somewhat taken aback when George Bernard Shaw said to him, "The trouble with you, Mr. Goldwyn, is that you're interested only in art; while I'm interested only in money."

There were some racist jokes directed against the Irish, all focused on a lack of intelligence. A favorite vaudeville joke had the comedian commenting, "Just because I'm stupid, don't think I'm Irish." Much later in the century, a favorite joke on St. Patrick's Day was,

"What is three miles long and has an I.Q. of zero?"

"A St. Patrick's Day parade."

Just as after December 7, 1941, it became acceptable to depict the Japanese in derogatory fashion, so, since September 11, 2001, have many Americans considered it OK to offend Arab sensibilities. In fact, American popular culture has been denigrating the Arab world throughout most of the 20th century. Attacks on Arabs are never subtle, and they are often so insidious as to slip by without notice because Americans are very much attached to the negative concept of Arabs and Islam. Comic books never depict an Arab in a favorable light; the Arab is dirty, backward and anti-West, and the prevalent theme in American popular culture is the Arabs (Them) versus the West (the United States or Us).

In literature, it was Edith M. Hull who established the Arab antihero with her 1921 novel, *The Sheik*. It tells of a young Englishwoman, Diana Mayo, who is captured by an Arab chieftain, with no standards of morality, while touring the desert, unchaperoned, and who eventually falls in love with her captor. "The central idea of it stands out, poisonously salacious in conception," wrote the *Literary Review* (March 5, 1921). "It is not prudery to stamp it as vicious." With its acknowledgement of rape fantasy, the novel proved tremendously popular with women, and was filmed the following year with Rudolph Valentino in the title role. A sequel, *The Son of the Sheik*, was released in 1926, again with Valentino in, as it happened, his last film appearance. The film made an important change in the storyline, with the Sheik revealed at the close as a Westerner whom Diana Mayo might safely marry. The far-from-subtle change is emblematic of how the film industry would always view an Arab—as an outsider, a foreigner, no better than a Negro with whom there could be no intermarriage.

The Sheik is not the only novel with an Arabian theme. Clare Sheridan's *Substitute Bride* (1931) described harem life in Algeria. In similar fashion, Christina Nicholson's 1978 novel, *The Savage Sands*, concerns sixteen-year-old Catherine Scott, who is abducted from Paris in 1828

and becomes a concubine to the Bey of Algiers. Far more politically motivated is Richard Chesnoff's *If Israel Lost the War* (1969), in which the 1967 Six Day War is won by the Arabs; Thomas Harris' *Black Sunday* (1975, filmed in 1977), in which Arab terrorists plot to blow up the Super Bowl; Paul Erikson's *The Dynast* (1979), with a Saudi Arabian attempt to bribe a bank chairman; and Howard E. Hunt's *The Gaza Intercept* (1981), in which Arab terrorists steal a neutron bomb and plan to drop it on Tel Aviv.

In *Network* (1976), Arabs are attempting the takeover of a U.S. television network. (And when Vanessa Redgrave made reference to "Zionist hoodlums" attacking Palestinians, it was *Network* screenwriter Paddy Chayefsky who denounced her at the Academy Awards presentation.) Adding to everything that is wrong with the 1987 film *Ishtar* is the song "I Look to Mecca." Disney's *Aladdin* (1992) begins with a song that describes Arabia as "barbaric." As the *New York Times* (July 14, 1993) editorialized, it is this "tongue-in-cheek bigotry" that Americans have come to expect from the Hollywood film industry. Disney has continued its negative depiction of Arabs on screen with *The Return of Jafar* (1994), in which Arabs are described as "desert skunks"; *Father of the Bride Part II* (1995), with the Arab-American couple, the Habibs; and *Kazaam* (1996), featuring black marketer Mustached Malik and his henchmen Hassem and El-Baz,

It has been estimated that there are more than 900 American films in which the Arab image is distorted. Arabs wrapped in bed sheets all look alike. Jack G. Shaheen, who has written prolifically on the subject, argues in that Arabs are Semites portrayed as hook-nosed villains, there is a distinct parallel between the Hollywood message and the Jewish image in Nazi films. Arabs can be comic figures as in the Bing Crosby-Bob Hope vehicle *Road to Morocco* (1942) or the Abbott and Costello feature, *Lost in a Harem* (1944). In *Oh, God! You Devil* (1984), when Yasir Arafat is seen on television, the Devil boasts, "I've had this guy for years."

Arabs are seen as anti-Christian as in *East of Sudan* (1964) or as vicious terrorists with whom only an American superhero such as Chuck Norris can deal as in *The Delta Force* (1986), produced by the

Israeli filmmakers Golan and Globus. Arabs are also depicted as terrorists in many other films, including *The Little Drummer Girl* (1984), *Into the Night* (1985) and *Iron Eagle* (1986). Arabs have threatened Brooke Shields in *Sahara* (1984), Goldie Hawn in *Protocol* (1984) and Kathleen Turner in *The Jewel of the Nile* (1985). Ted Whitehead's 1977 play, *Mecca*, concerns the rape of an English girl on vacation in Morocco by two Arabs.

On stage and screen, Arabs have been presented as folk heroes, such as Ali Baba, Sinbad and Aladdin, but as never very clean or wholesome ones. There is never anything totally positive about the Arab on stage in musicals like *Chu Chin Chow* (1916) and *The Desert Song* (1926), both of which have been multi-filmed. They are the subject of comic songs such as "Ahab the Arab" written and recorded in 1962 by Ray Stevens.

If, as there is no question, it is the African American who was most subjected to racism in popular entertainment as the 20th century began, then, it is equally sure, that as it ended, it is the Arab and Arab Americans who have replaced him.

CHAPTER SIX

Bad Taste and the Motion Picture

"It was the night before Christmas and all through the ward, not a creature was stirring. It wasn't a house, you see. It was a hospital ward, and all the creatures were paraplegics.

"Then in walked Hope. Two kinds of Hope. Both very real. The kind that's defined in dictionaries. And a guy named Bob."

So begins a Paramount press release, dated December 27, 1954, and issued to promote the Bob Hope vehicle *The Seven Little Foys*. For a comedian who made a career out of exploiting audiences that had no choice but to welcome him, be they under military orders or incapacitated, it is typical. And it is equally redolent of the type of publicity released by a motion picture industry unrestrained by the bonds of good taste. Unfortunately, as poet Carl Sandburg once remarked, in comparing Hollywood to Harvard, the former "is not as clean as Harvard, but nevertheless far reaching."

Publicists did have a sense of humor, as evidenced by the following release put out by an unknown author promoting the 1928 Dolores Del Rio vehicle *Ramona*: "An illuminating angle on Fornication in the Wide Open Spaces was revealed to Hollywood sex experts during the filming of sheep-breeding sequences of *Ramona* in Southern Utah.

"One buck sheep, it was disclosed by old-timers in the sheep-humping art, performs an average of 75 to 80 sexual acts per night. Seventy-five percent of the breeding, on the average is productive, the buck requiring less than 60 seconds to re-charge his battery for effective intercourse.

"Sheep-herders in Utah, on the other hand, claim that their average, as compared with the bucks, is approximately three mounts per night, with a net result of productivity. Incidentally, the sheep-herders disclosed, the art of breeding sheep for pleasure has undergone a revolutionary change in the last quarter-century. Whereas the sheep-herders in the past placed the animals' hind legs in their boots, they now merely fasten the sheeps' tails onto their pants-buttons.

"Members of the *Ramona* Company, fresh from Hollywood, were startled by the rapid-fire action of the buck-sheep. Comments among the troupers varied as to the desirability of possessing the fast-trigger mechanism of the bucks.

"'I would rather be an elephant,' said Warner Baxter, the Indian lover in *Ramona*. 'It takes an elephant 48 hours to perform once, while a buck-sheep reels off 200 times, but the elephant has a perpetual pleasure, whereas the buck is getting just a spasmodic series of thrills.'

"'I envy the bucks,' declared Roland Drew, the Spanish lover in *Ramona*. 'They get variety, all in one night, and that is what I crave.'"

The industry supports its own senior citizen facility, the Motion Picture Country House and Hospital, and while its benevolence is unquestioned, not everything associated with the charity is beyond reproach. Every year from 1969 through almost to the end of the century, the residents of the Motion Picture Country House and Hospital were paraded in wheelchairs for the entertainment of visitors under the collective name of the "Ding a Lings" chorus. One year, two residents, silent star Viola Dana and Mae Clarke, who was the recipient of a grapefruit in the face from James Cagney in *The Public Enemy*, appeared as the vaudeville act, "Topsy and Eva," with Mae Clarke in blackface. The dressing in outrageous costume of the aged and infirm by volunteers was supposedly therapeutic, but for whom it is not clear. The annual Golden Boot awards, honoring Western achievement on behalf of the MPCH, bring out the worst in the industry's conservative minority. At the seventh annual dinner in August 1989, Johnny Cash was honored and proclaimed, "I thank God for the freedoms that we have in this country—including the freedom, the right to burn the flag. I also thank God for the right to bear arms. And if you burn my flag, I'll shoot you." Presumably, that is what the Motion Picture Country Hospital exists for—to aid the victims of the gun-swinging, easy shooting fraternity.

In its defense, the film industry has never shied away from the truth of its existence—at least during its so-called "golden age." Few pretended that what they created was art, and nobody within defended the industry's lack of integrity. Despite what today's film and television executive might voice at awards presentations, there is no bravery involved in producing entertainment, particularly for profit. This is not a life and death situation, and it is the ultimate in bad taste to suggest that it is. The studio moguls—Harry Cohn, Jack L. Warner, Louis B. Mayer and company—knew how to make films on time and under budget. They expected the same of their contract staff, and the only acceptable answer to a question was "Yes." As early as February 1929, the fan magazine *Photoplay* published a photograph of Cecil B. DeMille going to work for Louis B. Mayer. It was captioned:

"Yes, Mr. DeMille."

"Yes, Mr. Mayer."

Despite a curious dedication, "To the ultimate sanity of the white races," a highly obscure volume from 1932 by R.G. Burnett and E.D. Martell, titled *The Devil's Camera: Menace of a Film-ridden World*, provides a remarkably intelligent discussion of the lack of morality and good taste in the motion picture. It quotes Aldous Huxley:

"The white man's world as revealed in the films: a world of crooks and half-wits, morons and sharpers ... A world where men and women have instincts, desires and emotions, but no thoughts. A world, in brief, from which all that gives the modern West its power ... has been left out."

From the thoughts of Aldous Huxley, the book moves on to examine the American and British films screened at a theater in Bombay and Poona, and quotes a native filmgoer:

"I am an Indian. I suppose you white people would call me a nigger. I am unacquainted with other sides of Western civilization, but what I have seen to-night, and on numerous other occasions in these places, convinces me that the ordinary middle-classes in England and

America are the most debased and immoral cretins any race or nation have ever produced."

The authors of the book describe the exploitative descriptive phrases used in posters promoting the latest films from the West, and then ask, "Is it any wonder that Mahatma Gandhi wants to draw a sanitary cordon round his beloved India?" Individuals as diverse as Aldous Huxley and an Indian moviegoer were questioning what was wrong with Hollywood. In response, in 1933, Hollywood re-launched the Motion Picture Production Code, designed to self-censor its products and make them palatable not just for American but for world consumption.

As a whole, the Production Code does not make entertaining reading. It is in the specifics that the document becomes fascinating. Here, dated November 8, 1939, are a list of words that must be omitted from all motion pictures: alley-cat (applied to a woman), bat (applied to a woman), broad (applied to a woman), "Bronx cheer" (the sound), chippie, cocotte, God, Lord, Jesus, Christ (unless used reverentially), cripes, "fanny," fairy (in a vulgar sense), the finger, "fire" (cries of), goose (in a vulgar sense), "hold your hat," "in your hat," Jees, damn, hell (excepting when their use shall be essential and required for portrayal in proper historical context), louse, lousy, madam (relating to prostitution), nance, nerts, nuts (except when meaning crazy), pansy, razzberry (the sound), slut (applied to a woman), son-of-a, tart, tom-cat (applied to a man), "traveling salesman" and "farmer's daughter" jokes, whore, and jerk.

It continues with a list of words "obviously offensive to many patrons in the United States and, more particularly, to patrons in foreign countries," that must also be omitted. One can only ponder why such words are offensive to "many" and not all U.S. moviegoers: chink, dago, frog, greaser, hun, hunkie, kike, nigger, spig, wop, and yid.

The first, and most detailed, section of the Production Code deals with Crime, which must never be presented in such a way as to show sympathy with crime or to inspire others with a desire for imitation. The Production Code notwithstanding, the film industry has always been obsessed with crime, one of the most popular of genres, and has glorified real-life criminals from Al Capone to Bonnie and Clyde. These most famous of "modern" criminals did not actually appear on screen, but the same is not true of some of the classic gangsters of American history. Between 1914 and 1930, Al Jennings starred in some ten feature films. He also appeared as a headliner in vaudeville in 1921, preaching in dull and deadly fashion against outlawry. Emmett Dalton of the Dalton Gang went to so far as to attack "fake" motion pictures representing the lives of him and his brothers in 1914, and in 1918, he starred in *Beyond the Law*, playing himself and his two siblings.

W.B. "Bat" Masterson never appeared in films, but he was a great admirer of cowboy legend William S. Hart. While the actor was appearing on stage in *The Squaw Man* in 1905, the outlaw wrote him that Hart's photograph served "as a reminder of those days on our western border that have passed into history and made way, as I view it, for a more unstable and effete civilization." What would Masterson, who had become a real estate agent, make of the effete cowboys of Mel Brooks' *Blazing Saddles* and Andy Warhol's *Lonesome Cowboys*?

Much has been made of paid product placement in recent motion pictures and the insinuation of communist propaganda in Hollywood films of the 1930s and 1940s. The manipulation of the motion picture is, in reality, even more subtle. In the 1950s, the Sloane Foundation, founded by Alfred P. Sloane of General Motors, funded a number of Warner Bros. cartoons with capitalistic messages, including *By Word of Mouse* (1955) and *Yankee Dood It* (1956).

Despite its reputation for sleaze, bad taste and other sundry vices, Hollywood is very protective of its name. The Hollywood Walk of Fame, the name by which the line of stars embedded on Hollywood Boulevard is known, and the Hollywood Sign above the city are strictly the copyright and trademark of the Hollywood Chamber of Commerce, and woe betide anyone attempting to use such emblems without payment of an appropriate fee. A fee of $25,000 is also required of any celebrity wanting his or her name on the Walk of Fame; stardom is a secondary requirement. The star ceremony is generally linked to a commercial and often tasteless venture. For example, when comedian

Buddy Hackett received his star in April 1998, it was tied in with the re-release of *The Little Mermaid* in digital sound, "something worthy," as Hackett explained to the small crowd of onlookers.

Neither is the honoring of Hollywood celebrities limited to the sidewalk. Edward Everett Horton has a lane named after him in the San Fernando Valley, at the point where the 101 freeway appears to make a curve in order to avoid going through what was once his home. George Burns and Gracie Allen are honored with streets crisscrossing at Cedars-Sinai Medical Center. Bob Hope has a drive in his honor in adjacent Burbank, close to the NBC studio with which he was long associated and to his home in Toluca Lake. The Los Angeles City Council is fond of naming intersections in honor of political figures such as Raoul Wallenberg and Andrei Sakharov. A less unlikely figure for such an honor is Carmen Miranda, but there it is, at the junction of Hollywood Boulevard and Orange Drive, adjacent to Grauman's Chinese Theatre — Carmen Miranda Square. Chica Boom Chick — and Chica Boom Chic.

A comic opera of sorts broke out in the Los Angeles area in the summer of 1937, when the Culver City Chamber of Commerce declared its anger that despite being the home of three major studios — Metro-Goldwyn-Mayer, Hal Roach Productions and David O. Selznick Productions — the theatergoing public at large assumed that all films were made in Hollywood. In desperation, Culver City decided to change its name to Hollywood. Blaine Walker, president of the Chamber of Commerce, explained, "Our board of directors was unanimous in voting to change the name of Culver City to Hollywood. We believe the registered voters of the town will be almost 100 per cent back of the suggestion. Sixty per cent of the motion pictures made in California are made in our city, but we don't get the credit for it."

The Hollywood Chamber of Commerce fought back, and, in protest, actors John Boles and Richard Dix formed "Hollywood-for-the-Hollywoodians," declaring, "It would be a crime to sit idly by and permit Culver City to usurp the name of Hollywood."

Of course, Culver City never did change its name to Hollywood, and now the only safe way to visit the drug- and crime-infested community is to look in on the mock-up of Hollywood Boulevard at Walt Disney World in Florida or make a trip to the City Walk complex at Universal City in the San Fernando Valley.

CHAPTER SEVEN

Bodily Functions and Dysfunctions

Stuffing one's mouth is not in the best taste. Celebrities at public events, such as charity lunches or dinners, are cautioned by their managers or "minders" simply to pick at the food. Never give your public the opportunity to watch you eating and, later, to comment upon your bad habits. At the end of the 19th and beginning of the 20th century, eating on film was basically limited to stereotypical black children eating stereotypical water melons. Obviously, the black races knew no better than to share their eating habits with the world.

Food was initially associated on screen with humor in the form of pie throwing and falling on banana skins. In *By the Sea* (1915), Charlie Chaplin falls on a banana peel, which he has just thrown away, and in *The Pilgrim* (1923), both Chaplin and Mack Swain slip on a banana peel dropped by a young boy. All the gags in *The Battle of the Century* (1927) originate because of Laurel and Hardy's slipping on a banana peel; in *From Soup to Nuts* (1928), Oliver Hardy slips on a banana peel while carrying a large cake, and in *The Hollywood Revue of 1929*, he slips on a banana peel and somersaults into another, even larger cake. Harold Lloyd slips on a banana peel in *Feet First* (1930), and Woody Allen revived the gag routine in 1973 with *Sleeper*, in which he deals with a giant banana peel.

By the making of *Sleeper*, the banana had also taken on a sexual—phallic—significance. Josephine Baker's nightclub routine in Paris in the 1920s included her performing in a skirt of synthetic bananas, and in *His Captive Woman* (1929), Dorothy Mackaill—a white actress—appears in a nightclub sequences wearing a dress made of bananas.

No one has yet identified the origin of the custard pie in the face gag. Pies are thrown at Mabel Normand in Keystone's *The Ragtime Band* (1913), and she throws one at Roscoe "Fatty" Arbuckle in Keystone's *A Noise from the Deep* (also released in 1913). The largest custard pie fight ever staged is in the 1927 Laurel and Hardy short, *The Battle of the Century*, in which more than 3,000 pies from the Los Angeles Pie Company are thrown. The "golden age" of pie throwing was recreated for the 1935 Warner Bros. short *Keystone Hotel*. From the 1930s through the 1950s, the Three Stooges resorted to pie throwing in countless comedy shorts, and in December 1998, some of that footage was used in television commercials for the Carl's Jr. hamburger chain, with its slogan, "If it doesn't get all over the place, it doesn't belong in your face." There are pie throwing fights in *Jiggs and Maggie in Court* (1948) and *Joe Palooka in Humphrey Takes a Chance* (1950), both based on popular comic strips. Director Blake Edwards staged a Technicolor custard pie fight for *The Great Race* in 1965, and throughout the 1960s, Soupy Sales had been at the receiving end of hundreds of custard pies—actually made with shaving cream—on television.

The Marx Brothers are impoverished hotel guests, desperately seeking food, in *Room Service* (1938), and in *Love Happy* (1949), Harpo Marx pilfers food from a gourmet grocery store. The title of the 1979 film *Who Is Killing the Great Chefs of Europe?*, based on the mystery novel by Nan and Ivan Lyons, is self-explanatory. Roald Dahl's novel, *Charlie and the Chocolate Factory*, became a 1971 screen hit as *Willy Wonka and the Chocolate Factory* and in the new century was the basis for a Johnny Depp feature, most noteworthy for the actor's adopting the body language and mannerisms of Michael Jackson.

Food has widely been celebrated in popular song, with emphasis on specific fruits and vegetables. "Yes! We Have No Bananas" sang Eddie Cantor in 1923 to words and music by Frank Silver and Irving Cohn. A year later, songwriters Jack Meskill, Willie Raskin, Dave Ringle, and Sammy Fain responded "Here Comes the Banana Man, We've

Got Bananas Now." By 1926, William Tracey, Hugh Aitkin and Dinty Moore were questioning, "What! No Spinach?," while Al Frazzini, Paul De Frank and Irving Mills were telling us, "When Banana Skins Are Falling, I'll Come Sliding Back to You." In 1927, Ted Waite announced, "I've Never Seen a Straight Banana." "Please No Squeeza Da Banana," written in 1944 by Jack Zero and Ben Jaffee, was a hit the following year for Louis Prima and His Orchestra. A 1946 radio commercial warning against the storage of bananas in refrigerators—a warning that subsequently proved to be a myth—was adapted by Leonard MacKenzie, Garth Montgomery and William Wirges into the popular song "Chiquita Banana," introduced by Xavier Cugat and His Orchestra in the 1947 film *This Time for Keeps*. At one point in the 1920s, it seemed there were so many songs about bananas that one composer was lamenting, "I've Got the Yes! We Have No Banana Blues."

Eddie Cantor had another comedy hit in 1930 with "Now's the Time to Fall in Love (Potatoes are Cheaper, Tomatoes are Cheaper)," written by Al Sherman and Al Lewis. Merv Griffin, along with Freddy Martin and His Orchestra, had a big hit in 1949 with "I've Got a Lovely Bunch of Cocoanuts," written in 1944 by British composer Fred Heatherton.

In 1910, Alfred Bryan and Charles E. Johnson had introduced the "Dill Pickles Rag." In 1913, Gene Buck and Dave Stamper were telling that "Chic-Chic-Chic-Chic-Chicken" to lay a little egg for them. The sentimental 1925 ballad by Billy Rose, Al Dubin and Joseph Meyer, "A Cup of Coffee, a Sandwich and You," was parodied by Richard Connell as "An Oyster, a Cloister and You." In 1927, the vaudeville comedy team of Van and Schenck were telling of the joys of "Pastafazoola," which they co-wrote along with Frank Sabini and Edward Clark. A year later, Billy Jones and Ernest Hare, better known on radio as the Happiness Boys, were singing Clarence Gaskill's "I Love to Dunk a Hunk of Sponge Cake." In 1929, Edith Johnson wrote and recorded "Nickel's Worth of Liver." In the 1930 film *Be Yourself!*, Fanny Brice sang of "Cooking Breakfast for the One I Love," written by husband Billy Rose and Henry H. Tobias.

Some strange eating habits have been captured on film. In *The Gold Rush* (1925), a hungry and desperate Charlie Chaplin boils and eats one of his boots. Bette Davis serves up a rat as a gourmet treat for sister Joan Crawford in *What Ever Happened to Baby Jane?* (1962). On a Southern prison farm in *Cool Hand Luke* (1967), Paul Newman participates in a grossed-out egg swallowing contest. In an over-the-top performance in *Vampire's Kiss* (1989), Nicolas Cage eats a cockroach. With its highly original focus on anal sex, *Last Tango in Paris* (1973) features Marlon Brando and a non-traditional use of butter.

Too much eating is not necessarily the cause of obesity, but obesity has been the cause for much politically incorrect laughter. One joke concerns actor Raymond Burr's having an out-of-body experience and a homeless family moving in. In 1946, Kay Kyser had a hit with "Huggin' and Chalkin'," written by Clancy Hayes and Kermit Goell, which tells of a woman who is so large that when her boyfriend drew a chalk mark around her, he met someone coming the other way. Even more offensive is "The Too Fat Polka," written by Ross Maclean and Arthur Richardson, and which was a hit for Arthur Godfrey in 1947. Here, we are told of the lady in question that "I don't want her, you can have her, she's too fat for me." In its way, "The Too Fat Polka" is far more derogatory of the overweight than Al Jolson's 1923 hit, "That Big Blonde Momma," written by Billy Rose and James Monaco, wherein the girlfriend has "a little of this and mountains of that." At least Al Jolson loves his "momma."

In the early years of the silent cinema, John Cumpson and John Bunny were two overweight comedians whose humor is totally lost (if it was ever there) on modern audiences. Roscoe "Fatty" Arbuckle has the sad propensity to make us laugh and shudder; the gags in his films are still amusing but less so is the accusation (presumed false) that he raped and murdered a young actress in San Francisco in 1921. The comedian's weight of 320 pounds obviously was an issue in the district attorney's filing charges against him. Had he been young and handsome, there would probably have been no trial.

There have been other fat comedians since. Roseanne (born 1952) announced, "I'm fat and I'm proud of it," but later went on a diet as her popularity plummeted. She failed to understand it was lack of originality not a preponderance of fat that had anything to do with her failing career. John Belushi (1949-1982) specialized in fat slob characterizations, including a parody of Marlon Brando on television's *Saturday Night Life*. Louie Anderson (born 1953) is too nice to be a comedian and is better suited to hosting antiquated game shows on television. Sam Kinison (1953-1992) was a foul-mouthed comedian who specialized in deliberate bad taste along with too much primal screaming. He is noted for having claimed that the AIDS epidemic was caused by "a few bored fags." Just as the slightly stupid comic sidekick to the screen hero would often be fat and often played by Bert Roach in early talkies, so generally was the stupid one in comedy teams fat, as, for example, Lou Costello of Abbott and Costello.

Vaudeville comedienne and songstress Trixie Friganza (1870-1955) glorified in her oversize form, explaining that the only way in which a fat woman could do the "shimmy" dance was to walk fast and stop short. In later years, another comedienne/songstress who emphasized her weight was Britisher Tessie O'Shea, billed as "Two Ton Tessie" and notably featured in the 1966 film *The Russians Are Coming The Russians Are Coming*.

There were some curious "freak" acts on the vaudeville stage with decidedly peculiar bodily attributes. Billed as "The Man Who Grows," Willard (real name Clarence E. Willard) starred in vaudeville between 1913 and 1914. His act consisted solely of adding seven-and-a-half inches to his height of five-feet, nine-and-a-three-quarter inches, extending his arms from anywhere between eight and fifteen inches, and making one leg four inches longer than the other. *Variety* noted that he had to be seen to be appreciated. There should have been little enthusiasm for watching Doss, a 1916 vaudeville performer, who could move his hunchback from the rear to the front.

Fat suddenly took on a new cultural aspect on October 9, 1996, when the BBC broadcast the first episode of *Two Fat Ladies*. The cooking show featured two very large and very aristocratically British ladies, Jennifer Patterson and Clarissa Dickson Wright. American audiences took to the show in a big way—no pun intended—when it was brought over here by the Food Network. Jennifer drove her motorbike around the British countryside, with Jennifer in the sidecar, and both were advocates of everything that it was claimed unhealthy to eat, including red meat, butter and lard. Neither lady had any interest in slimming nor cooking food that was low in calories. Both were happy to admit they were camp, and eagerly courted a gay audience. The double act ended with the death of Jennifer Patterson, but Clarissa Dickson Wright has continued on British television as a single and outraged the animal rights community by lovingly rearing a baby lamb and then slaughtering it for food.

The obese can, arguably, decrease their weight. There is nothing that little people can do to restore their physical stature. General Tom Thumb was the most famous of 19th century midgets, and he and his wife were also featured in early 20th century vaudeville. Consisting of between fifteen and twenty performers, Singer's Midgets was the best-known act of its type in American vaudeville from the mid-teens through the 1930s. Under the direction of Leo Singer, the troupe presented a revue with music, performing animals and even a playlet. The company was not without its critics, and Robert Benchley wrote in *Life* (November 20, 1924), "If the Ku Klux Klan will include thespian midgets in their list of undesirables we will promise to take out a two-weeks' guest card in the order." On screen, Billy Barty, at three feet, nine inches, was the most prominent of little people, never speaking but always risqué in *Gold Diggers of 1933* and *Footlight Parade* (both 1933), along with other films of the 1930s, until finding his tongue later, and also becoming a voice for his people with the 1957 establishment of Little People of America. In 1938, the little people of Hollywood made their own musical Western with *The Terror of Tiny Town*, and a year later, the little people terrorized much of Culver City as they descended on the community to play Munchkins in *The Wizard of Oz*.

If little people are too small and fat people are too big, what does one make of the two-headed individuals thrust upon an unsuspecting cinema audience in *The Incredible 2-Headed Transplant* (1971) and *The Thing with Two Heads* (1972)? Ray Milland and Rosie Grier are the unlikely combination in the latter, and just to watch Milland humiliate himself thus at the end of a fairly respectable career is, for some, worth the cost of admission.

That most extreme form of eating—cannibalism—was glorified in a 1902 song by Charles H. Taylor and Jerome Kern; "My Otaheite Lady" is the nostalgic ballad sung by a sailor mourning his cannibal love. In 1938, Raymond Scott was responsible for the lyric-less "Dinner Music for a Pack of Hungry Cannibals." Cannibals did appear in person in a handful of films. *Among the Cannibal Isles of the South Pacific* (1918) has explorers Martin and Osa Johnson being captured by cannibals—unfortunately for filmgoers, who had to sit through the patronizing adventure dramas of these two, they escape. Always anxious to prove their bravery, the Johnsons returned to the same location for a sequel, *Head Hunters of the South Seas*, in 1922. The producers responsible for *King Kong*, Merian C. Cooper and Ernest B. Schoedsack, shot footage of *Gow, the Head Hunter*, a silent feature reissued with sound in 1934.

King Kong's star Fay Wray screams to great effect in the 1932 Technicolor production of *Doctor X*, in which a series of murders is linked to cannibalism. The film is further enhanced by the title doctor's search for "synthetic flesh."

The Naked Prey (1966) has a hapless colleague of director/star Cornel Wilde being coated in mud and baked alive. (Wilde finishes up nude, although he manages to direct himself in such a way that absolutely nothing is visible front or rear.) The 1971 Brazilian film, *Comoera Gostos o Meu Frances*, released in the United States as *How Tasty Was My Little Frenchman*, is notable for a leading man, Arduino Colasanti, who appears in much of the film not only nude but with all his body hair shaved off. The film, which manages to be both a political treatise and a black comedy, concludes with Colasanti's being eaten by his native wife and her family. Another Brazilian production from the "Cinema Novo" period, *Macunaíma* (1969), released in the United States as *Jungle Freaks*, also deals with cannibalism. In director Peter Greenaway's typically outrageous *The Cook, The Thief, His Wife & Her Lover* (1989), the leading man, Alan Howard, is baked and eaten at a plush restaurant owned by the crooked husband of his lover,

Helen Mirren. And there can be nobody unfamiliar with Anthony Hopkins' Oscar-winning performance as "Hannibal the Cannibal" Lecter in *The Silence of the Lambs* (1991), based on the best-selling Thomas Harris novel of the same title.

In *Road to Zanzibar* (1941), Bing Crosby and Bob Hope were close to being boiled alive for dinner in the cannibals' cooking pot, and Bob Hope escaped a similar fate in *Call Me Bwana* (1963). Jimmy Durante was captured by cannibals in *On an Island with You* (1948), and Bud Abbott and Lou Costello went the same route in *Africa Screams* (1949). Far less sophisticated, and far more offensive, was the 1992 American film of *Auntie Lee's Meat Pies*.

The comedic aspects of cannibalism became both sick and camp in later films such as *Cannibal Man* (1971), *Cannibal Women in the Avocado Jungle of Death* (1989) and *Cannibal, The Musical* (1996). As well as providing the usual amount of nudity associated with his films, with *Porcile/Pigsty* (1969), Pier Paolo Pasolini offered a portrait of a medieval soldier who is also a cannibal.

On stage, the best-known exponents of cannibalism are Sweeney Todd and Mrs. Lovett. As portrayed by Len Cariou and Angela Lansbury in the Hugh Wheeler and Stephen Sondheim musical that opened at New York's Uris Theatre on March 1, 1979, Todd is the barber who "finishes off" his clients with a razor slash across the throat and Mrs. Lovett disposes of the bodies in her meat pies. As a melodrama, *Sweeney Todd* was written by George Dibden Pitt and first produced in 1842 with Robert Vivian in the title role. When it was revived on Broadway at the Frazee Theatre in 1924, the *New York Times* (July 19, 1924) described the production as "flavorsome." The best-known exponent of Sweeney Todd is British character actor Tod Slaughter, who toured for years in this and other classic melodramas and captured his performance on screen in a 1936 film, *Sweeney Todd, The Demon Barber of Fleet Street* (released in the U.S. in 1939).

The artificiality—and sheer camp—of cannibalism on screen and stage pales in comparison to the real-life brutality of a Paris slaughterhouse was captured on film by Georges Franju in his 1949 documentary short, *Le Sang des Betes/Blood of the Animals*.

Eating on screen truly came of age in New York in 1992 with the first film festival devoted to the subject of food, *Meals on Reels*.

The 1988 release of *A Fish Called Wanda* provoked the National Stuttering Project into action, as it denounced "the cruel and demeaning" portrayal of a stutterer by Michael Palin, and the character's ridicule by Kevin Kline. The reality is that stuttering is nothing new on screen, and dates back to the early years of the talkies. Western heroes often had stuttering buddies, as did Ken Maynard in *Alias: The Bad Man* (1931), Jack Hoxie in *Gold* (1932), and Johnny Mack Brown in *Branded a Coward* (1935) and *Little Joe, the Wrangler* (1942). In *Deep Valley* (1947), Ida Lupino has a stuttering problem until she finds true love. Some character players, such as Roscoe Ates, specialized in stuttering roles. At least one song, "You Tell Her—I Stutter," written in 1922 by Billy Rose and Cliff Friend, ridicules a young man who has problems expressing his love to his girlfriend. When he tries to tell her father, he gives him a shower bath.

As a result of the protests from the National Stuttering Project, along with additional protests from the National Committee for Adoption, which objected to a negative comment on an adopted child not being "a real kid," *A Fish Called Wanda* was quite heavily cut for its first television airing on ABC on September 15, 1991. Its creators protested, but to no avail—the age of political correctness had well and truly arrived.

The disposal of what we eat and drink was generally avoided in films of Hollywood's "golden era." Toilet gags were forbidden under the Production Code, and toilets themselves were not seen on screen except for the outer "lounge" area of a ladies room, which was generally a convenient location for gossip aiding in plot development.

There might be the occasional dry heave in "older" films and the element of surprise leading to the spitting out of water or similar liquid from the mouth, but vomiting did not become fashionable on screen until the 1990s. There had been a few earlier examples, most notably induced by the Devil in *The Exorcist* (1973), the result of John Belushi's overeating in *National Lampoon's Animal House* (1978) and Jill Clayburgh's throwing up into a Manhattan trash bin after her husband has left her in *An Unmarried Woman* (1978). In 1986, a group of school kids have a communal vomit in *Stand by Me*, and both Winona Ryder and Shannen Doherty throw up in *Heathers* (1989). After discovering that the woman administering a blow job in *The Crying Game* (1992) is a man, Stephen Rea throws up — an unusual successive act to ejaculation.

There was at least one regurgitation act popular on the vaudeville stage, and that was Hadji Ali (1892-1937), billed as "The Egyptian Enigma." He would swallow and spit out various objects, including nuts and live goldfish, and the culmination of the act was his swallowing of water and kerosene. He would spit out the latter, setting fire to a model house and then regurgitate the water to put out the fire. Hadji Ali toured America in the 1920s and 1930s, and can be seen in two films, the 1930 short subject *Strange as It Seems* and *Politiquerias*, the Spanish-language version of the Laurel and Hardy vehicle *Chickens Come Home* (1931).

"Vomiting. It's everywhere in cinema these days, from the big studio pictures to the scrappy independents," noted the *Los Angeles Times* (May 12, 1998). Among actors and actresses throwing up on screen that year were Denzel Washington in *He Got Game*, Meg Ryan in *City of Angels*, Elliott Gould in *The Big Hit*, and Benicio Del Toro in *Fear and Loathing Las Vegas*. As the average age of theatergoers dropped to between fifteen and twenty-five so did filmmakers acknowledge the need for at least one barfing scene to satisfy that audience.

Terry Gilliam, director of *Fear and Loathing in Las Vegas*, is also co-responsible for the supreme classic of all vomiting scenes in *Monty Python's The Meaning of Life* (1983). Mr. Creosote, the world's most obese man, played by Terry Jones, eats his way through a restaurant menu, using an array of vomit buckets, before self-exploding over his fellow diners.

Defecation has only a minor role in popular culture, but the same is certainly not true of urination. On September 17, 1980, viewers of the NBC *Monday Night at the Movies* were shocked to see Richard Chamberlain, as a Westerner shipwrecked in 17th century Japan, being humiliated and urinated upon in *Shogun*. In 1994, *USA Today* suggested that Hollywood films have been "Flush with scenes of urination," mentioning toilet scenes featuring Demi Moore in *Indecent Proposal*, Burt Reynolds in *Cop & ½*, Huey Lewis in *Short Cuts*, Richard Harris and Robert Duvall in *Wrestling Ernest Hemingway*, Ralph Fiennes in *Schindler's List*, Tom Hanks in *A League of Their Own*, and Danny Glover in *Lethal Weapon 2*. As far as can be ascertained, the first film to make reference to a chamber pot is the 1930 "B" picture, *The Dude Wrangler*, in which a city couple camp out in a tent and the wife is heard to ask, "Oh, what a large cup. What is that for?" The first mainstream film actually to show a penis with urine flowing, rather than a simulated incident, is probably the 1996 French costume film, *Ridicule*, which received an "R" rating for such graphic nudity.

The best-known incident in Hollywood's past concerning urination involved Lee Tracy, a Broadway actor who had caught Hollywood's attention after playing Hildy Johnson in the original, 1928 production of *The Front Page*, and who had been featured in two prominent MGM productions of 1933, *Dinner at Eight* and *Bombshell*. In November 1933, the studio sent Tracy to Mexico City to play reporter Johnny in *Viva Villa!* Tracy had long had a drinking problem, and he did not take kindly to being awakened on the morning of November 19 by Mexican soldiers marching outside his hotel window. What happened next is subject to speculation. "The wildest exaggerations were circulated and published," said Tracy some years later. "When I came back to Hollywood, I heard that I had stood on a hotel balcony, and deliberately insulted the Mexican flag." What is known is that Tracy did stand on the hotel balcony, and, clothed or unclothed, urinated on the troops below.

The Mexican government reacted angrily to the incident, making Tracy a scapegoat in its opposition to the filming of the life story of Pancho Villa, and taking the opportunity to excoriate the film industry for its continued portrayal of Mexicans as villains. "It seems fantastic that a professional career, built after years of endeavor, should summarily be tossed on the ash heap for so trivial an offense," editorialized the fan magazine *Photoplay* (February 1934).

"If the Tracy incident had occurred in the United States, the whole matter would have blown over in a week. Undoubtedly Mexican newspaper enterprise was largely, if not altogether, responsible for the attitude taken by the Mexican government. The parading cadets, whom Tracy is alleged to have insulted, appeared to have taken the matter lightly but when the press of the capital found good copy in the incident, the hue and cry for the Americano's scalp arose."

Lee Tracy was summarily discharged by MGM on November 23, 1933, and his part reassigned to Stuart Erwin. Tracy never worked again for the studio, but did continue to appear on screen through *The Best Man* in 1964.

There is something about location shooting that brings out the worst in Hollywood actors. Less known than the Lee Tracy affair is the time when Victor McLaglen was shooting *South of Pago Pago* in 1940. While telling a joke to producer Edward Small's brother, he took the opportunity to pee — on the man's leg.

"Golden showers" are nothing new in pornographic films. In her pre-1972 and *Deep Throat* productions, Linda Lovelace was pissed on frequently. In Radley Metzger's *The Punishment of Anne* (1979), the title character is required to urinate in front of a man as a form of humiliation.

The most famous example of urine in a work of art is the photograph by Andres Serrano titled "Piss Christ." The 1987 work shows a crucifix submerged in a twelve-by-eighteen-inch Plexiglas tank of blood-flecked urine, and is, perhaps, intended to juxtapose fundamental Christianity and the AIDS crisis created by the exchange of bodily fluids. "Piss Christ" is responsible for the right-wing attacks on various aspects of American culture and the demands for the dismantling of the National Endowments for the Arts and for the Humanities. In March 1989, the Reverend Donald Wildmon first saw a photograph of "Piss Christ" in a museum catalog, and a month later it was revealed that the photograph was on display at the Southeastern Center for Contemporary Art in Winston-Salem, North Carolina, in an exhibit partially funded by the NEA. The right-wing subsequently demanded an end to subsidized spending on "perverted, deviant art."

There is one story as entertaining as the Lee Tracy pissing incident, and that concerns John Wayne. In his autobiography, *Just Tell Me When to Cry*, director Richard Fleischer is on the RKO studio lot in 1945. Production is at a standstill, and when the producer asks why, the assistant director explains, "John Wayne hasn't shit yet." The actor was unable to begin the day's shooting until he had a bowel movement. "Who else could halt production for hours, at great cost to the studio, by peristalsis alone? It was too awesome to think about," writes Fleischer.

Excrement has seldom been featured on screen, and when it has, it is generally of the animal variety. In John Waters' *Pink Flamingos* (1972), Divine eats dog shit, and Peter Greenaway's *The Cook, The Thief, His Wife & Her Lover* (1989) opens with a restaurant customer, who has apparently failed to pay his bill, being stripped naked, covered in and forced to eat dog shit. The 1996 British feature *Trainspotting* (which is either a glorification or condemnation of drug culture) has actor Ewen Bremner accidentally soiling his bed while staying at his girlfriend's house and the excrement flying all over the living room while the family "enjoy" breakfast. The film also features what must be the most offensive (and obviously overused) toilet ever to be seen on screen. (It is not the first toilet to be so featured; in his 1984 debut feature film, *Top Secret!*, Val Kilmer also pops out of the bowl.)

Bodily functions are the primary source of humor on *South Park*, the animated series created by Trey Parker and Matt Stone, and first broadcast on the Comedy Central cable network on August 13, 1997. The four featured children, Eric Cartman, Kyle, Kenny and Stanley, are the personification of everything pure and unspoilt. They find childish humor in farting and other natural bodily functions, and it is only we, the audience, who are offended, outraged or bemused by their behavior and their commentary. Just as Mary Pickford was America's Sweetheart in the first quarter of the 19th century, so have the children of *South Park* become the new American sweethearts for the century's end and the start of a new one.

The glorification of a piece of shit with the name "Mr. Hanky" might imply comedy at its most subversive and most leftwing, but, in reality, there is much that is conservative in the editorial commentary on *South Park*. The series raises serious issues on everything from pedophilia to the war in Afghanistan. A 1999 feature film, *South Park: Bigger, Longer & Uncut*, whose subtitle apparently was not understood by the Hollywood hierarchy that released the production, raises major issues as to the rating system of the Motion Picture Association of America (which, of course, rated the film "R").

Watching *South Park* one is reminded of a classic and anonymous piece of doggerel:

> Said a printer pretending to wit:
> "There are certain bad words we omit.
> "It would sully our art
> "To print the word F ...,
> "And we never, oh, never, say Sh ..."

CHAPTER EIGHT

Sex

Sex was never out of sight or out of mind in 20th century America, and I am sure that here is the chapter that most readers have been eagerly awaiting. Was it worth trawling through piss and shit to get this far? In 1907, Arthur J. Lamb and Alfred Solman were responsible for the highly suggestive song, "All She Gets from the Iceman Is Ice." In 1913, Sophie Tucker was singing "I Wonder Where My Easy Rider's Gone," written by Shelton Brooks, a song that was later to closely associated with Mae West—and one whose meaning was completely clear as voiced by either entertainer.

The 1920s saw no pause in the sexual revolution. In 1922, Marian Harris sang to her "Brother-in-Law Dan," in a number written by Joe Jordan, "You can love much better than brother Joe can." In 1926, Gus Kahn, Raymond B. Egan and Walter Donaldson assured us "There Ain't No Maybe in My Baby's Eyes." Irving Kahal and Harry Carroll wrote "If My Baby Cooks as Good as She Looks" in 1926, which asked, "I wonder if she's as good at the oven as she is in the parlor at lovin'?" The liberated mother made an appearance on screen in the 1926 film *Dancing Mothers*, as Alice Joyce escapes the tedium of home life, and in the 1929 song, "Mama's Gone Young—Papa's Gone Wild."

Screen nudity is nothing new. As early as 1914, pioneering female filmmaker Lois Weber presented "The Naked Truth" in her allegorical feature, *The Hypocrites*, in the nude form of Margaret Edwards, who is glimpsed in more than one shot full-length and facing the camera. Audrey Munson (1891-1996) was one of the leading female models of her day, posing for sculptors and photographers in the nude.

Her sculpted form adorns many prominent Manhattan landmarks. She starred in four films—*Inspiration* (1915), *Purity* (1916), *Girl o' Dreams* (1917), and *Heedless Moths* (1921)—and was nude in them all. *Purity* resembles one of those "naturist" films of the 1950s, whose audience comprised mainly frustrated, aged and unattractive men.

Aficionados of ladies underwear need look no further to enhance their hobby than Hollywood's early talkies in which just about every actress from Mary Astor and Clara Bow to Joan Crawford and Ann Harding sport their teddies. Now virtually an unknown term, a teddy was a one-piece female undergarment from the 1920s that combined both a chemise and panties. The 1931 Paramount film *The Smiling Lieutenant* features Claudette Colbert and a bevy of scantily-clad chorus ladies singing "Jazz Up Your Lingerie." Claire Trevor's panties are the *raison d'etre* for the 1934 Fox Film *Hold That Girl*, just as lingerie plays an important role in the plot of the 1926 Christie comedy, *Up in Mabel's Room* (based on a 1919 farce of the same title). Lovers of men in y-fronts should look no further than *Risky Business* (1983), starring Tom Cruise.

As it has done for more than half-a-century, Frederick's of Hollywood continues to distribute scanty and saucy underwear—primarily female but also male—to the civilized world from an address on Hollywood Boulevard. In a community where sleaze is the operative word, the lingerie museum of Frederick's of Hollywood seemed oddly archaic with displays of undergarments from the likes of Madonna, Cher, Lana Turner, Zsa Zsa Gabor, Mae West, Natalie Wood, and even Ethel Merman and Doris Day.

Two women are primarily responsible for introducing sex to popular literature. The one is totally forgotten today. The other is remembered with affectionate ridicule for her posturing and breathless pronouncements. Mary MacLane (1881-1929) was the first American female to bring raw sex to the printed page with her 1902 book, *The Story of Mary MacLane, by Herself*. Female readers were tantalized by the author's detailed account of her sexual escapades, which one contemporary reviewer described as "ridiculous rot." In 1903, MacLane published two books, *The Devil's Letters to Mary MacLane,* by Himself and *My Friend, Annabel Lee*. *The New York Times* reviewer doubted the existence of the author. A final volume, *I, Mary MacLane, A Diary of Human Days*, appeared in 1917.

The theme of all the books was the same. As a 1917 critic described it, "She was careless toward men in their crude sex-rapacity in a way no 'regular' woman would dare or care to be. No man could wring one tear from her, nor cause a quickening of her foolish heart, nor any emotion in her save mirth."

In 1918, the Essanay Company brought Mary MacLane's story to the screen with *"I, Mary MacLane (Herself)" in Men Who Have Made Love to Me (By Herself)*. Staring into the lens of the camera between puffs of her cigarette, Mary MacLane (Herself) announces, "So that you may know me, I, Mary MacLane, will tell you of six piquant love episodes in my life—all of them damnably real."

In her search for true love, the cynical Mary MacLane becomes enamored of the Callow Youth, the Literary Man, the Baronet's Younger Son, the Prize Fighter, the Bank Clerk, and the Husband of Another. In the end, she can only wonder if true love really exists, but is assured by her newly-married maid that it does.

The film was not successful, and Mary MacLane slipped quickly into obscurity. She was found dead and alone in a cheap Chicago hotel room, and it was several days before anyone realized who she was. Fifty people attended the funeral of a woman who wrote of having a thousand lovers.

Providing a far more sophisticated approach to sex was British novelist Elinor Glyn (1864-1943), who was as much a personality during most of her life and every bit as outrageous as was Barbara Cartland in later decades. Glyn had more influence on the world than Cartland but failed to produce any number approaching the more than 700 novels of the latter. Glyn's most famous novel on the subject of sex was *Three Weeks*, first published in 1907 and filmed in 1916 and 1924. Its notoriety gave birth to an anonymous verse:

> Would you like to sin
> With Elinor Glyn
> On a tiger-skin?

Or would you prefer
To err
With her
On some other fur?

The novelist came to Hollywood in 1920, remaining there through 1929, and being feted by all of Hollywood's most famous residents from Charlie Chaplin to Marion Davies. She wrote a number of films, but most importantly she rewrote the meaning of the word "It" to symbolize sex appeal. Clara Bow was the personification of "It" and she was starred in Elinor Glyn's 1927 film of the same name. It has taken more than a generation of homosexual men to change the meaning of "gay," while Elinor Glyn rewrote the meaning of one word in a matter of months.

As much a personality at one time as Elinor Glyn was her sister, Lady Duff Gordon, who designed clothes under the name of Lucile. Lady Duff Gordon actually presented a fashion show at New York's Palace Theatre in December 1917, and she proved so popular that she was held over for a second week.

Sex on stage was once represented by the saucy farces of Avery Hopwood, including *Ladies Night* (1920), in which a young man blunders into a Turkish bath on ladies night, and *The Demi-Virgin* (1921), set in Hollywood and with a last act featuring a great deal of undressing by the female members of the cast. The latter was denounced by Rabbi Stephen A. Wise in the *New York Times* (March 12, 1922) as "just theatrical filth, gutter garbage of the foulest, rankest kind … I would not have the author and producer tarred and feathered, because even pitch may be defiled." More explicit depictions of sexual themes on stage in the 1920s include *The Rubicon*, adapted from the French of Edouard Bourdet by Henry Baron, which opened at New York's Hudson Theatre on February 21, 1922, and involved a young bride's determination to keep her virginity.

Michael Arlen's novel *The Green Hat: A Romance for a Few People* (Doran, 1924) was a major bestseller and adapted into a hit play that opened at the Broadhurst Theatre on September 15, 1925. It starred

Katharine Cornell as Iris March, the sexually active heroine who eventually kills herself as did her husband, Boy Fenwick, at the play's opening (rather than acknowledge he has syphilis). Greta Garbo starred in the first, 1928, screen adaptation, *A Woman of Affairs,* and Constance Bennett in the 1934 version, *Outcast Lady.*

The first popular foray into sexual promiscuity in the 20th century was *Sapho*, adapted by Clyde Fitch from the French (of course) novel by Alphonse Daudet. Despite its title, the play has no connection to the lesbian world but concerns a young woman, first played by Olga Nethersole, who takes a young man as her lover and holds him against his will. The Hearst press described the production, which opened at Wallack's Theatre on February 5, 1900, as "an insult to decent women and girls." Its success was thus assured.

It was not only women who were subjected to sexual scrutiny on stage. On January 18, 1927, *The Virgin Man*, adapted by William Francis Dugan from the British play, *Three Birds*, by H.F. Maltby, opened at New York's Princess Theatre. It concerned three predatory females attempting to seduce a Yale student and contained lines such as "It's women like you wreck men's homes." *The New York Times* (January 19, 1927) opined that *The Virgin Man* "strove to be one of the town's minor sex-circuses, but, in reality, it succeeded only in being the worst play of the season."

Les Avariés by Eugene Brieux concerns a man infected with syphilis who marries and bears an infected child. The initial French opening in 1901 was prohibited by the censor, but the play was performed in Belgium the following year, and eventually received a Paris opening in 1905. (Brieux was also responsible for a 1903 play *Maternitie*, which dealt with abortion and was taken up by George Bernard Shaw.) Translated as *Damaged Goods*, the play opened at New York's Fulton Theatre on March 14, 1913, starring Richard Bennett (the father of actresses Joan and Constance). It was sponsored by the Medical Review of Reviews and its Sociological Fund, and prior to the presentation, the Reverend John Haynes Holmes of the Church of the Messiah addressed the audience. The play was subsequently revived, to little interest, in May 1937. It was also filmed in 1914 by the American

Film Mfg. Co., again with Richard Bennett as the central character, and with some scenes shot at a Los Angeles hospital, showing syphilis sufferers. A 1937 exploitation film *Marriage Forbidden* is also based on *Damaged Goods*.

Hereditary syphilis had already been introduced to theatergoers by Henrik Ibsen with *Ghosts*. When the play was first presented in an afternoon performance in 1894, the *New York Times* (January 5, 1894) described it as "awful," but within five years the newspaper was hailing it (on May 30, 1899) as "shocking but wonderfully clever." Ibsen may have made hereditary syphilis respectable, but it and other forms of venereal disease were still treated in exploitative fashion on screen. The first major interest in venereal disease came in 1919 with five feature films on the subject, produced, one suspects, in response to the imminent return from Europe and World War I of American soldiers who might have picked up the disease as well as other undesirable and un-American social habits.

The first film, *The Scarlet Trail*, written and directed by John S. Lawrence, was endorsed by the American Defense Society, Social Hygiene Division. A young lady discovers that her fiancé has syphilis, transmitted by his father who had led an unclean life. The woman refuses to renounce the proposed marriage, but the husband-to-be chooses the honorable solution and ends his life with a bullet. Public Health Films was responsible for *Fit to Win*, which the trade paper *The Moving Picture World* (April 12, 1919) warned "does not belong in a family theatre to be shown to a mixed audience of men and women ... A spade is called a spade." The story concerns five young enlisted men in France, four of whom spend their leave with immoral women. Now physically unfit to serve, they are branded slackers. In *The Solitary Sin*, only one of three young men is told the facts of life by his parents; as a result, of the remaining two, one contracts syphilis and the other goes insane from self-abuse. The latter film was reissued in 1924 as *T.N.T. (The Naked Truth)*.

Social Hygiene Films of America released *Wild Oats*, in which a wealthy young man, who has contracted syphilis, helps a country boy escape the same fate. Jack Warner, one of the founders of Warner

Bros., produced *Open Your Eyes*, which showed "not only the effect of sexual disease on those who live vicious lives, but upon the innocent victims related to the men and women who break the moral law." Twenty-one years later, Warner was to produce *Dr. Ehrlich's Magic Bullet*, with Edward G. Robinson starring as the German doctor who found a cure for syphilis.

By the fall of 1919, the cycle of venereal disease films seemed out of control, and one of the trade papers, *Exhibitor's Trade Review* (September 6, 1919) announced, "This publication will hereafter accept neither advertising nor publicity concerning any picture dealing with venereal disease or sex hygiene, which is intended for commercial exploitation in the theatres of the United States before mixed audience in the manner of dramatic productions. We believe that such pictures may well be exhibited for the good of the community at certain times, in certain places and under certain auspices. But the place for them is not the motion picture theatre, the time is not the accepted hours of theatrical entertainment, and the auspices should not be those of the exhibitor or the industry. The responsibility for showing such pictures in a beneficial manner belongs exclusively to medical or public authorities."

Exploitation films dealing with venereal disease, and other sexual matters, were relatively commonplace in the 1930s and 1940s. Among such titles are *The Seventh Commandment* (1932), *The Road to Ruin* (1934), *Sex Madness* (1938), *No Greater Sin* (1941), *Mom and Dad* (1945), *Bob and Sally* (1948), and *The Story of Life* (1948). The last four were screened before sexually segregated audiences. The films were not exclusively devoted to the dangers of venereal disease; for example, *Sex Madness* features a burlesque show that leads two female members of the audience to contemplate lesbianism. There is something here for everyone!

The presentation of prostitution on stage in the 20th century can be traced back to George Bernard Shaw and *Mrs. Warren's Profession*. Written in 1898, the play concerns itself with the daughter of a prostitute, her quest for marriage and her coming to terms with her mother's profession. *Mrs. Warren's Profession* was suppressed after one

New York performance in 1905. The closing and later relative failure of the play did little to discourage others from tackling the theme of prostitution. The 1920s saw Broadway productions of *The God of Vengeance* (1922) by Sholem Asch, *A Good Bad Woman* (1925) by William J. McNally, *The Shanghai Gesture* (1926) by John Colton, *Lulu Belle* (1926) by Edward Sheldon and Charles MacArthur, and *Maya* (1928), adapted by Ernest Boyd from the French of Simon Grantillon. A prostitute, played by Estelle Winwood, is the central character in British author Frederick Lonsdale's *Spring Cleaning*, which opened at New York's Eltinge Theatre on November 9, 1923. The character is used by the husband to bring an errant wife to her senses.

Despite more than 350 films in which they appear, prostitutes seldom gave the impression that they did too much business on screen, despite being played by such glamorous stars as Clara Bow (*Ladies of the Mob*, 1928), Greta Garbo (*Anna Christie*, 1930), Mae Clarke (*Waterloo Bridge*, 1931), Marlene Dietrich (*Blonde Venus*, 1932), Joan Crawford (*Rain*, 1932), and Bette Davis (*Of Human Bondage*, 1934). There were plenty of novels and plays dealing with the subject, and Hollywood took full advantage despite often blurring the job description. A whore is seldom just a whore, and motion pictures generally take up their subjects' lives after the worst is over. As Marlene Dietrich says in *Shanghai Express*, "It took more than one man to change my name to Shanghai Lil," but the men involved are not present at this time. In fact, prostitutes didn't really exist on screen from the mid-1930s through into the 1960s and films such as *Irma la Douce* (1963), *The Happy Hooker* (1975) and *The Best Little Whorehouse in Texas* (1982). Gay male prostitutes are represented by Jon Voight in *Midnight Cowboy* (1969) and straight ones by Richard Gere in *American Gigolo* (1980).

The haunting Richard Rodgers/Lorenz Hart number "Ten Cents a Dance" might seem to relate to a dance hall girl, but from the lyrics, it is very obvious she is little more than a prostitute. Far more explicit, but still surprisingly unidentified by radio censors of the day, is "Flat Foot Floosie," written in 1938 by Slim Gaillard, Slam Stewart and

Bud Green, and introduced by the first two under their recording name of Slim and Slam.

Condoms were first advertised on television in the 1980s, but it was not until 1991 that a major television network, Fox, aired its first condom commercial. By this time, both the straight and the gay porno industries insisted that their performers use condoms while shooting (in every sense of the word). In *Trainspotting* (1996), Ewan McGregor became the first actor in a mainstream film to be photographed wearing a condom—on his penis. On the *Tonight Show* in March 1999, actor Ben Affleck openly discussed condoms, complaining that manufacturer Trojan had sent him a box, but they were not the "Magnum" variety for larger men. As a result, Durex sent Affleck a box of its "Ultra-Comfort" range, described as "baggy" and "bigger."

The earliest reference on screen to condoms is in the 1933 Warner Bros. production of *Convention City*, directed by Archie Stout, written by Peter Milne and Robert Lord, and starring Joan Blondell, Adolphe Menjou, Dick Powell, and Mary Astor. Contemporary reviewers must have been in a state of denial, because they all ignored the reality of the leading characters in the film working for a company manufacturing condoms. State censorship boards were less approbatory.

In particular, they took exception to risqué dialogue such as that between a group of women at the convention. One lady comments, "I'm so tired from the Ever-Ready Bandage Company," to which her colleague responds, "Listen, sister, if they tire you, you better leave town before the Hercules Tool Company gets here." When it became apparent that the film could not be released because of its dialogue and subject matter, studio head Jack L. Warner ordered that the negative and every print of the film be destroyed. No copies of *Convention City* are known to be extant today, although happily the script survives.

While their celebrity clients might remain anonymous, Hollywood's madams are all well known. In the 1920s and early 1930s, Lee Francis would pay off the Los Angeles vice squad with champagne and caviar. In the 1930s, Francis was replaced by Ann Forrester, known by the police as the "Black Widow." After she was eventually arrested and charged with pandering, one of her protégés, Brenda Allen, took over in the 1940s, working in partnership with Hollywood vice squad sergeant Elmer V. Jackson. The couple had more than 100 "party girls" working for them out of a house above the Sunset Strip. From a similar location, Barrie Benson operated her brothel in the 1950s. In the 1970s and 1980s, Elizabeth Adams became known as the "Beverly Hills Madam," and when she retired in 1988, her operation was taken over by Heidi Fleiss, whose career came to an end with her arrest in 1997.

There are any number of headings under which homosexuality might appear in this book. Religion has certainly played an active role in intolerance toward the gay man and woman. Mystery writers such as Ngaio Marsh and other commentators have somehow linked homosexuality with substance abuse. And, of course, how often does the gay character end up dead on the printed page or on the small and large screen?

It is the supposed effeminacy of the homosexual that forms the basis for entertainment, not the sexual aspects of his life. As early as 1907, Arthur Conan Doyle wrote a short story for *The Strand* magazine in which the central criminal character was a young American who dressed in female attire and is described as a "Mary Jane." John Buchan's 1916 novel *Greenmantle* has as its villain a German officer named Colonel Stumm, who enjoys feminine things but at least is a real man.

A vast number of female impersonators played the vaudeville circuit in the first thirty years of the 20th century, and while it is obvious that most, if not all, were homosexual, the majority hid their sexuality and often maintained a married status. The most "camp" were Francis Renault and Karyl Norman. The latter billed himself as "The Creole Fashion Plate," and was identified by his fellow vaudevillians, according to Milton Berle, as "The Queer Old Fashion Plate." Texas-born Barbette (real name Vander Clyde) was an aerial acrobat, who removed his wig at the conclusion of the performance, and was taken up in Paris in the 1920s by Jean Cocteau, Man Ray and other intellectuals.

The film industry was most associated in the public eye with homosexuality, and a number of its leading men — J. Warren Kerrigan, William Haines, Ramon Novarro, etc. — were homosexual. As early as 1917, the fan magazine, *Motion Picture,* published a piece entitled "He, She, Or It," in which it noted the difficulty in determining "who's who and what's what" in view of the number of actors donning female attire for their roles and vice versa. This same theme was echoed in a 1925 song by Edgar Leslie and James V. Monaco, "Masculine Women! Feminine Men!," introduced on the vaudeville stage by Belle Baker.

There was a lot of suggestive commentary around about Hollywood's leading men. In the 1928 musical comedy, *Whoopee!,* the song, "Ever Since the Movies Learned to Talk," noted, "though the hero's big, everyone knows he makes every stitch of his clothes." Many novels from the early 1930s dealing with Hollywood themes are heavy with commentary on the industry's leading men. *Queer People* (the title has no reference to homosexuality) by Carroll and Garret Graham, published in 1930, talks of "women of all sexes and men of none." In Jack Preston's *Screen Star* (1930), a Hollywood actress finds her actor boyfriend in bed with his boyfriend. In Haynes Lubou's *Reckless Hollywood* (1932), there are references to a "nance" and a "fairy," and an extra says of the stars, "They're Mr. and Mrs. God according to the sex, and you can't even be sure of that in this town." Both the gay and straight communities knew all about Hollywood and the theatre apparently. British actor Ian McKellen once commented that he wanted to become an actor because "I'd heard everyone in the theatre was queer."

In the 1940s, it was claimed that communists in Hollywood were able to insinuate propaganda into Hollywood films. Well, a decade earlier, it would seem that there were those in the studios able to place a number of gay references into films. A red necktie was a fashion accessory popular with gay men for identification purposes. In a 1932 Betty Boop cartoon, *Any Rags,* Koko the clown is clearly depicted as a gay character, and after his bid is accepted at an auction, the auctioneer says, "Sold to the man in the red necktie." When a hefty Martian male fondles comedy leading man El Brendel in *Just*

Imagine (1930), the latter remarks, "She's not the queen. He is." When an effeminate male secretary loses at chess, the leading man in *Daughter of the Dragon* (1931) makes reference to the queen being indecently exposed.

By the early 1930s, it was apparent that the entire entertainment industry was going to crack down on homosexuality. In 1930, *Variety* reported that Hollywood producers would no longer accept "too pretty, dainty or over-marcelled" chorus boys in film musicals; "It has been discovered the average American film fans resent effeminate men." In 1931, the RKO vaudeville circuit announced that none of its performers could make reference to a "fairy" or a "pansy."

Yes, there were still a few gay references on screen and obvious gay performances from the likes of Franklin Pangborn, but, by the mid-1930s, gays were as hard to spot on screen as were Jewish entertainers. A 1936 handbook for motion pictures producers, writers and reviewers pointed out, "No hint of sexual perversion may be introduced into a screen story. The characterization of a man as effeminate, or a woman as grossly masculine would be absolutely forbidden for screen portrayal. This means, too, that no comedy character may be introduced into a screen play pantomiming a pervert."

There were still gossip items suggesting homosexuality activity in Hollywood, but it was not until the 1950s and publication of *Confidential* that the rumors became explicit. In July 1957, *Confidential* suggested that Liberace's theme song should be "Mad about the Boy" and in November 1969, it questioned Chuck Connors if "Those early sailor movies could blow your career."

In both the straight and the gay world, the ballet and homosexuality are linked as closely as any gay couple. Some ballet dancers, notably Rudolf Nureyev, have flaunted their homosexuality, while others remain vaguely closeted. On the ballet stage, there have been a number of male duets as well as more elaborate couplings smacking of homoeroticism, including Martha Graham's "Phaedra's Dream" (1983), Boris Eifman's "Tchaikovsky: The Mystery of Life and Death" (1993) and Matthew Bourne's all-male version of "Swan Lake" (1995). The British DV8 Physical Theatre, founded in the mid-1990s, has toured the world with its all-male ensemble, as has Matthew Bourne.

The best-known transsexual is Christine Jorgensen, who told the story of her life in a biography titled simply *Christine Jorgensen* (Eriksson, 1967), which formed the basis for the 1970 film, *The Christine Jorgensen Story*. Mike Sarne's screen adaptation of Gore Vidal's *Myra Breckinridge* (1970) is far better than critics initially thought, although there is something decidedly distasteful about Rex Reed becoming Raquel Welch. The Robert Louis Stevenson story was given a new, transsexual lease on life with *Dr. Jekyll and Sister Hyde* (1972), with Ralph Bates becoming Martine Beswick, and *Dr. Jekyll and Ms. Hyde* (1995), with Tim Daly becoming Sean Young.

Bestiality has been hinted at in at least two Hollywood films. One is an obscure 1932 feature, *She Wanted a Millionaire*, produced by Fox and directed by John Blystone. Beauty contest winner Joan Bennett is married to jealous millionaire James Kirkwood. When she announces she wants a divorce, Kirkwood says that he plans to give her to his large wolfhound, Baskerville, and when she faints, Kirkwood carries her down to the kennels in order that the dog may sniff her. The film was based on the true story of Frederick G. Nixon-Nirdlinger, "a connoisseur of women," who tried to create the perfect wife. Insanely jealous, Nixon-Nirdlinger constantly accused his wife of infidelity, and when in 1931, he tried to strangle her, after accusing her of having an Italian lover, she shot and killed him. Cecil B. DeMille's *The Sign of the Cross* (1932) features a virtually nude Christian girl tied to a stake, screaming as a large ape approaches — and the implication is quite clearly that the animal has sexual designs on her.

S&M or sadomasochism, named for the French Marquis de Sade and the Austrian Leopold von Sacher-Masoch, has existed on the outer edge of the sexual experience probably as long as there has been sex. However, it was not until the 1990s that it became semi-respectable with designer Gianni Versace introducing a collection of costumes featuring the dominatrix look. Madonna brought the image to music videos with "Express Yourself" and "Justify My Love," and British import Anne Robinson brought it to television at the end of the 20th century with the game show, *The Weakest Link*. The Anne Robinson dominatrix look is, of course, influenced by the body-hugging leather attire, complete with kinky boots, preferred by Honor Blackman as Cathy Gale in *The Avengers* television series (first seen on Britain's commercial television from 1961-1969). The manner in which Honor Blackman used judo throws on the male villains must have provided many a wet dream for the male viewers of the series. When Blackman went on to play Pussy Galore in the James Bond feature, *Goldfinger* (1964), she was replaced by Diana Rigg as Emma Peel, who emphasized a more rubber-like, but equally S&M look.

Anne Rice's novel of sadomasochism, *Exit to Eden*, was transformed into a 1994 film comedy about a dominatrix (Dana Delaney) and a submissive (Paul Mercurio). Director Garry Marshall handled it all very conservatively with the emphasis on the supposed humor provided by Rosie O'Donnell as an undercover cop. The film was banned in Saskatchewan. Tony Guzman's *Philosophy in the Bedroom* was not banned anywhere in large part because it was not screened very much. Based on the works of the Marquis de Sade, the film offers no visual imagery of sadomasochistic acts but concentrates only on dialogue about what is planned and what has transpired. The emphasis was obviously on the degradation of women, but as *Variety* (April 17, 1995) complained, it was "all talk and no play."

S&M was definitely not mainstream in the 21st century, and when the British department store Harvey Nichols—so beloved of *Absolutely Fabulous*' Patsy and Edina—introduced an ad campaign featuring the head of a woman wearing a dog collar and leash, feminists were outraged.

Incest has yet to be featured in popular mainstream American entertainment, although *My Sister, My Love* (1978) has Lee Grant and Carol Kane as two siblings whose interest in each other is more that sisterly, and *Spanking the Monkey* (1994) has a son caring for all of his bedridden mother's needs. Incest has made it to British Television—on Channel 4's soap opera, *Brookside*. A love affair, including scenes in bed, between two very attractive young performers, John Sandford and Helen Grace, playing brother and sister, were severely criticized when first broadcast in October 1996. The main complaint was the glamorization of incest; not only was the couple appealing but also there was a total lack in their conversation of any suggestion that they saw anything wrong in what they were doing.

All of the above categories of sexual activity are well presented by the adult film industry in what is often described as pornography and is outside of the scope of this study. Suffice it to say that, like bad taste and political incorrectness, pornography is nothing new to the entertainment industry, and the Library of Congress holds a collection of pornographic films dating back to the early years of the 20th century. The depiction of the sexual act is often crude, and never more so than in a 1928 piece of animated pornography titled *Eveready Harton in Buried Treasure*.

Sex was first brought to mainstream American television by Ruth Westheimer. Petite and well past her prime, Dr. Ruth, as she is known, has the accent and some of the mannerisms of, and is the little people's answer to, Arnold Schwarzenegger. Radio audiences heard her as early as May 1980, and she first came to television with *Good Sex with Dr. Ruth Westheimer* on the Lifetime cable network on August 27, 1984. An alternative lifestyle and print substitute for Dr. Ruth is Dan Savage, whose syndicated column, "Savage Love," has been published since 1991. Outrageous and highly explicit, Savage describes heterosexuals as "breeders" and encourages his readers to address him with the salutation, "Hey, faggot." He has also been heard on selected radio stations since September 1994.

Sexual confusion reached its peak, if not its climax, in 1981 with the off-Broadway production of Caryl Churchill's *Cloud 9*. Described by Frank Rich in the *New York Times* (May 20, 1981) as "one daft writer," Churchill conceived a comedy of which Evelyn Waugh might have been proud, wherein a British explorer in 1880s Africa seduces his friend's wife (played by a man), the schoolboy son (played by a woman), and the black servant (played by a Caucasian) before marrying the lesbian governess. All that in Act One. In Act Two, the schoolboy is now middle-aged and in love with his sister and a younger male and considers himself lesbian. His sister is torn between her husband and a woman she meets in the park. The transsexual casting is both confusing and liberating—and that is really what sex in the 20th century was all about.

CHAPTER NINE

"Ain't It Grand to Be Blooming Well Dead"

Most Americans were first introduced to the concept of death as an aspect of popular culture with the 1973 publication by Pantheon Books of Michael Lesy's *Wisconsin Death Trip*. The book gathered together newspaper accounts and related photographs by Charles Van Schaick, chronicling the deaths of ordinary citizens in the state of Wisconsin in the 1880s and 1890s. The ages of the subjects vary from babyhood to old age, and the manner of their living and passing is presented in a prosaic, almost lifeless format. It is as if the compiler, Michael Lesy, is as dead to the individuals he is documenting as the individuals themselves.

As Michael Lesy writes in his introduction, "The pictures you're about to see are of people who were once actually alive." In life, we are always living with death, but never before did the public's attitude toward the passing of celebrities change more than in the 20th century. Death was never sensationalized by early filmmakers. When leading man Robert Harron died in 1920s, and there were rumors of suicide, his last film, *Coincidence*, was about to be released. Rather than rush the film into distribution on the basis of the publicity surrounding the death of the star, producer Metro held the film's release up for more than six months and then quietly distributed it without fanfare and with no publicity as to its star and his demise.

Within a matter of a year, the attitude toward celebrity deaths dramatically changed. The passing of the century's first great personalities was celebrated in maudlin fashion by the songwriters. In 1921, George A. Little and Jack Stanley were responsible for "They Needed a Song Bird in Heaven (So God Took Caruso Away)," and in 1926, following the death of Rudolph Valentino, J. Keirn Brennan, Jimmy McHugh and Irving Mills opined "There's a New Star in Heaven Tonight."

The fixation with celebrity deaths began in the 1920s, influenced in part by the tragedy of the (still unsolved) murder of director William Desmond Taylor in 1922 and the drug-induced passing of matinee idol Wallace Reid the following year. In that he was so much a part of American popular culture—the country's foremost entertainer and philosopher—the death of Will Rogers in a plane crash in Alaska on August 15, 1935 shocked the nation more than any other celebrity death up to that time. There was a massive memorial service at the Hollywood Bowl, a two-minute silence was observed in 12,000 movie theaters across America, and President Franklin D. Roosevelt declared, simply, "He loved and was loved by the American people."

Since Will Rogers' death, it has been neither heroics nor affection that has fed the celebrity death cult. The fascination with television comedian Bob Crane is a result of his unsolved murder in Scottsdale, Arizona, on June 29, 1978, and as a 2002 bio-film, *Auto Focus*, graphically demonstrated, it is sleaze that fuels the continuing interest. The Hollywood death cult is best exemplified by James Dean, who died in an automobile crash in Paso Robles, California, on September 30, 1955, and Marilyn Monroe, who died of a drug overdose on August 5, 1962. Both were young, both icons, and both linked to "scandal," be it only homosexuality in Dean's case and much more, including the Kennedy connection, in Monroe's.

The life and death of James Dean was celebrated in the *roman à clef*, *Farewell, My Slightly Tarnished Hero* (1971) by Edwin Corley. In *The Inner Circle* (1979), Jonathan Fast wrote of a mysterious cult that worships a Mexican panther god and each ten years must provide fresh human meat to appease the deity. The human meat is selected from within the film industry, and includes Jean Harlow, James Dean, Marilyn Monroe, and Freddie Prinz. The death of Marilyn Monroe also resulted in a slew of novels, including Alvah Bessie's *The Symbol* (1966, and the basis for a 1973 made-for-television movie), John Rechy's *Marilyn's Daughter* (1988) and Sam Toperoff's *Queen of Desire* (1992). In 1963, Pete Seeger wrote, with Norman Rosten, and recorded "Who Killed Norma Jean?"

A death cult does not necessarily flourish around the famous. There are still buffs and others who talk of the suicide of Peg Entwhistle, who, in September 1932, jumped off the Hollywoodland (later Hollywood) sign. She was only 24 years old, and, coincidentally, had just appeared in the film, *Thirteen Women*, ironically playing a trapeze artiste.

As the century progressed, film fans began seeking out the final resting places of their loved ones. One of the earliest "reference" works published was *Michael's Memory Map* in 1976, produced by an unemployed actor named Michael Chellel. In 1989, Everett Grant Jarvis self-published *Final Curtain*, providing not only death dates, but causes of death and interment locations. Since then, a publishing industry has grown up documenting the final resting places of Hollywood's dead. It is a growing market, with, for example, Natalie Wood's grave at Westwood Memorial Cemetery receiving more than 100 visitors a day. In 1988, Grave Line Tours was established, driving its tourists around in a converted hearse. One enterprising individual sells photocopies of celebrity wills. Thomas T. Noguchi, the Los Angeles County coroner, became known as "the coroner to the stars," and in 1993, he published *Coroner*, revealing autopsy gossip about Natalie Wood, Marilyn Monroe, Sharon Tate, William Holden, and many others.

The most impressive of Hollywood graves is that of Al Jolson at Hillside Memorial Cemetery. Built at a cost of $84,000, it includes a half life-size bronze figure of the entertainer on his knees in classic pose, and features a waterfall cascading down the hillside. Floodlit at night, it is a familiar site to drivers on the San Diego Freeway heading to and from LAX, but many probably are unfamiliar with the site's purpose. One of the most popular cemeteries is Home of Peace Memorial Park and Mausoleum in East Los Angeles, established in 1902, not because it is the final resting place of movie moguls Carl Laemmle, Louis B. Mayer and Jack Warner, but because here lie Curly and Moe of the Three Stooges.

The best known of Los Angeles cemeteries is Hollywood Forever, a sixty-acre site adjacent to the studio of Paramount Pictures, which opened in 1899 as Hollywood Memorial Park. Here lie such luminaries as Marion Davies, Cecil B. DeMille, Douglas Fairbanks, Sr. and Jr., along with the victim of Roscoe "Fatty" Arbuckle's alleged attack and rape, Virginia Rappe. On August 23 each year, hundreds of fans and the fascinated gather together to honor the anniversary of the death of the cemetery's biggest star, Rudolph Valentino. Here is what can only be described as the classic Hollywood version of Mexico's Day of the Dead, but celebrated on a year-long basis.

When Hollywood Memorial Park filed for bankruptcy in 1997, it was taken over by entrepreneur Tyler Cassidy, who not only renamed it, but also opened a gift shop, and organized a series of events there, including picnics and film screenings. The dead of Hollywood have finally become an integral part of Hollywood bad taste, with life (or rather death) deservedly imitating art.

In the 1930s, British comedy songwriter and performer Lesley Sarony introduced "Ain't It Grand to Be Blooming Well Dead," in which the performer sings of his funeral with "the earth worms blooming well wriggling" and "the mourners blooming well laughing." "We all come from earth and we all go back, they say," he warns, "so don't throw that brick; it might be your Auntie May." The American equivalent of "Ain't It Grand to Be Blooming Well Dead" is the far from comedic "Gloomy Sunday," which was first performed in 1936. Written by László Jávor with music by Rezső Seress, the song was first heard in Hungary in 1933, and given English-language lyrics by Sam M. Lewis. Paul Robeson introduced the song, which became a best-selling recording by Billie Holiday in 1941.

Incredibly depressing and dirge-like, particularly as performed by Paul Robeson, the song tells of a lover who is carried to church one Sunday, and can never again see his or her lover again because "the earth and the flowers are forever above me." The implication is that the singer has committed suicide. "Gloomy Sunday" quickly gained fame as *the* suicide song, not only because of lyrics advocating self-killing but also because several listeners took the song too literally. One such individual was the composer, who committed suicide in 1968. President Roosevelt asked that "Gloomy Sunday" not be played on radio during the war because of its negative impact on American soldiers separated from their loved ones.

"Gloomy Sunday" lacks the bite and cynicism of what are the greatest comments on death in popular song, "Is That All There Is?," as recorded in 1969 by Peggy Lee. The song was written by Jerry Leiber and Mike Stoller and was inspired by Thomas Mann's *Disorder and Early Sorrow*. In its source and its resonance, "Is That All There?" is more reminiscent of Kurt Weill and Berthold Brecht than any other American composition.

One of the greatest sentimental ballads of the 19th century is "In the Baggage Coach Behind," written in 1896 by African American composer Gussie Davis. It tells of a young man trying to care for his baby on a train ride while the body of his dead wife lies "in the baggage coach behind." Eugene O'Neill has his hero refer to the song as "a lousy tear-jerker" in *A Moon for the Misbegotten*. The first 20th century equivalent of "In the Baggage Coach Behind" is "Two Congregations," written in 1901 by Jeffrey T. Branen and Leo Friedman. Here, a woman refuses to marry her fiancé in one church upon learning that the funeral of the girl he abandoned for her is taking place in another.

As early as 1901, Charles K. Harris had celebrated the advent of the telephone exchange with the sad lament, "Hello Central, Give Me Heaven." That same year, Harry Heister mourned the assassination of President McKinley with "The Royal Will." Three days before his death in 1906, Paul Dresser composed his own requiem, "The Judgment Is at Hand." So overwhelmed was he by the sinking of the *Titanic* that Thomas Hardy wrote the poem, "The Convergence of the Twain: Lines on the Loss of the Titanic," and that same year, 1912, Mark Beam and Harold Jones composed "The Band Played 'Nearer My God to Thee' as the Ship Went Down." In 1925, Vernon Dalhart introduced "The Death of Floyd Collins," in which the Rev. Andrew Jenkins and Irene Spain told the story of a young spelunker trapped in a Kentucky cave.

The blues was at one time synonymous with death, with numbers from 1924 including "Bloody Razor Blues," "Dying Gambler's Blues," "Bullet Wound Blues," and "Graveyard Bound Blues." In 1926, Anita Gonzales and "Jelly Roll" Morton composed "Dead Man Blues," in 1927 Victoria Spivey wrote and recorded "TB Blues" and the following year, "Blind" Lemon Jefferson wrote and recorded "See That My Grave Is Kept Clean." In comic vein, Cecil Mack and Cecil Smith wrote of a Western shoot-out in 1912 in "The Last Shot Got Him," and the following year, Bert Williams asked in a song he wrote with Thomas J. Gray, "If I Should Die Before I Wake, How Will You Know I'm Dead?" The best known of such comic songs is Sam Theard's "I'll Be Glad When You're Dead, You Rascal You," recorded in 1931 by Louis Armstrong.

A comedian of the 1950s with a small but loyal following was Brother Theodore, the only member of his family to survive Dachau. In his stand-up routine, he would philosophize on life and death in intimate and soul-searching fashion.

The first major concept of death in a theatrical format came with the American adaptation by Benjamin F. Glazer of Hungarian Ferenc Molnar's allegorical romance *Liliom*, presented by the Theatre Guild on April 20, 1921. Joseph Schildkraut starred as the title character who badly treats his wife and spends most of the play in limbo. There was a 1921 film version, *A Trip to Paradise*, with Bert Lytell as the principal character, now renamed Curley, and a later 1930 screen adaptation, *Liliom* with Charles Farrell far from believable in the title role. Playing opposite Farrell in the 1930 film is Rose Hobart, who played Grazia in the original American stage production of *Death Takes a Holiday*. Adapted by Walter Ferris from the Italian of Alberto Casella, *Death Takes a Holiday* opened at New York's Ethel Barrymore Theatre on December 26, 1929. Philip Merivale starred as death, who, adopting the title of Prince Sirki, is curious about life and visits the castle of Duke Lambert and falls in love with one of his guests, Grazia. Ultimately, death leaves without destroying life. A 1934 film version stars Fredric March as Prince Sirki.

A 1948 Twentieth Century-Fox film, *Jungle Patrol*, based on an unproduced play by William Bowers, has a group of American pilots in New Guinea during World War II recall the film of *Death Takes a Holiday*. They ponder, in relationship to their current situation, if death is taking a holiday from claiming their lives.

Generally, the theatrical approach to death was allegorical. Sutton Vane's play *Outward Bound*, which opened at New York's Ritz Theatre on January 7, 1924, starring Leslie Howard, Alfred Lunt and Margalo Gillmore, is set on a ship en route to a port that is either heaven or hell. Initially, the passengers do not know they are dead, but gradually realize the truth. Paul Osborn's *On Borrowed Time*, based on the novel by Lawrence Edward Watkin, opened at New York's Longacre Theatre on February 3, 1938, and has a small boy holding death captive in an apple tree in order to prevent his taking the boy's grandparents. The play and the novel perhaps both have their origins in "The Pardoner's Tale" from Chaucer's *The Canterbury Tales*.

The most famous of plays with a death theme is Thornton Wilder's *Our Town*. Set at the beginning of the 20th century in the small town of Grovers Corners, the first part of the play deals with George's courtship of Emily. In the second half, Emily is on the verge of death and meets with all those residents of the town who have passed on before returning to the living to give birth to her second child. *Our Town* opened at Henry Miller's Theatre on February 4, 1938, with Martha Scott as Emily. A 1940 screen adaptation gave the actress her first screen role, and also helped make a star of William Holden as George Gibbs. The play was also adapted as a 1955 television musical in which Frank Sinatra introduced the song, "Love and Marriage." *Outward Bound* was filmed in 1930 with Leslie Howard reprising his stage role as Tom Prior, and *On Borrowed Time* was filmed in 1939, starring Lionel Barrymore and Beulah Bondi as the grandparents and Cedric Hardwicke as death.

Joseph Kesselring's *Arsenic and Old Lace* opened on Broadway on January 10, 1941. This comedy of two maiden aunts who murder twelve elderly men by serving them elderberry wine laced with arsenic was a tremendous hit in no small part thanks to having Boris Karloff play the criminally insane nephew Jonathan, whose face has accidentally been altered by a Dr. Einstein to resemble that of Boris Karloff.

Arsenic and Old Lace was filmed in 1941 by Warner Bros. starring Cary Grant, Raymond Massey as Jonathan, and Josephine Hall and Jean Adair as the two aunts, but could not be released until 1944 after the Broadway production had closed. Boris Karloff was featured in a 1946 radio version, and in the 1945, 1955 and 1962 television productions.

The most harrowing reference to death on screen is, of course, not in a live-action drama but in the 1942 Walt Disney animated feature, *Bambi*. As Bambi's mother shows him the first new grass of spring, she senses danger and tells him to run and not look back. If he had looked back, he would have seen his mother being shot and killed by hunters. *Bambi* probably gave more children nightmares than any other 20th century entertainment, and certainly did more for animal rights and the anti-hunting lobby than PETA or any other similar organization. In a brilliant parody, Marv Newland created *Bambi Meets Godzilla* (1962), in which the baby deer is seen grazing until a gigantic foot comes down and squashes him into oblivion.

Death has made an appearance in Ingmar Bergman's *The Seventh Seal* (1956) and Roger Corman's *Masque of the Red Death* (1964). Jessica Lange portrayed death in *All That Jazz* (1979), and Robert Redford was Mr. Death in a 1962 episode of *The Twilight Zone*, "Nothing in the Dark."

Many of Hollywood's morality tales have dealt with death, including, from the "golden age," *Camille* (1937), with Garbo proclaiming, "I always look well when I'm near death," and *Dark Victory* (1939), with Bette Davis dying with exquisite taste from a brain tumor. The latter has much the same audience impact as the made-for-television movie, *Brian's Song* (1971), with Chicago Bears football player Brian Piccolo (played by James Caan) dying of cancer. But both *Dark Victory* and *Brian's Song* have less of the schmaltz of *Love Story*, based on the novel by Erich Segal, with its fast-moving illness and death of Ali MacGraw. The comedy-fantasy *Here Comes Mr. Jordan* (1941) has prizefighter Robert Montgomery sent to heaven before his time. So popular was the concept here that the same characters reappeared in *Down to Earth* (1947), and

INCORRECT ENTERTAINMENT

Here Comes Mr. Jordan was remade as *Heaven Can Wait* in 1978 and *Down to Earth* in 2001.

There were a number of silly films featuring death rays in the 1930s, including *Chandu the Magician* (1932) and *The Invisible Ray* (1933), as well as the serials, *Flash Gordon* (1936) and *Flash Gordon's Trip to Mars* (1938).

Death Row histrionics were shown at their best by Susan Hayward in *I Want to Live!* (1958) and at their worst by Terry Moore in *Why Must I Die?* (1958). Death Row was also featured in *The Player* (1992), *Dead Man Walking* (1995) and *Last Dance* (1996), among late 20th century releases. In the late 1920s, Fletcher Henderson composed "Send Me to the 'lectric Chair," introduced in 1927 by Bessie Smith, and the following year, "Blind" Lemon Jefferson wrote and recorded " 'lectric Chair Blues."

Death was not always taken seriously on screen. In the Laurel and Hardy vehicle *Way Out West* (1937), when Laurel is asked by Lola if her dear daddy is really dead, he responds, "Well, we hope he is, they buried him." Charlie Chaplin has his tramp character dream of death and paradise in *The Kid* (1921). In *Monsieur Verdoux* (1947), Chaplin is the title character dispassionately killing and incinerating the bodies of his female victims. Before his execution, he points out that his killings are small scale compared to the legalized mass murders in the world—but Verdoux, and by extension Chaplin, is so amoral that he fails to recognize that all killing is a crime against humanity. The Grim Reaper is given a hard time in *Monty Python's The Meaning of Life* (1983).

Thorne Smith's best-known work, from 1933, is *Topper*, which concerns the exuberant George and Marion Kerby, who are killed in an automobile crash but denied immediate access to heaven. In ghostly form, the two make life a comic hell for meek banker Cosmo Topper. The Kerbys were played by Cary Grant and Constance Bennett, and Topper by Roland Young in the 1937 film version, which led to a 1939 sequel, *Topper Takes a Trip*, and a final 1941 production, *Topper Returns* (in which Grant and Bennett did not). So popular was the character of Topper that he returned for a 1953-1956 television series, starring Robert Sterling, Anne Jeffreys and Leo G. Carroll, and a 1979 made-for-television movie.

The other classic comedic novel on the subject of death is British writer Evelyn Waugh's *The Loved One: An Anglo-American Tragedy* (Little, Brown, 1948), which forms the basis for the 1965 film, directed by another Britisher, Tony Richardson. Terry Sothern and yet another Englishman, Christopher Isherwood, serve Evelyn Waugh well in their adaptation of his wicked and cynical look at the funeral business in Southern California.

The concept of ghosts is a popular one for the film industry, ranging from the serious such as *The Scoundrel* (1935) with a dead Noel Coward, *The Uninvited* (1944) and *The Innocents* (1961) to the many comical incarnations, including *Ghost Catchers* (1944), with Olsen and Johnson, and, of course, *Ghostbusters* (1984).

Ghosts and reincarnation are interlinked, and the film industry has approached the latter with equal zeal and a generally more serious attitude. Morey Bernstein's best-selling book, *The Search for Bridey Murphy*, about a housewife who had lived a previous existence, became a highly successful film in 1956. Far less popular was Barbra Streisand's curious musical comedy of reincarnation, *On a Clear Day You Can See Forever* (1970). Actress Shirley MacLaine's belief in reincarnation was brought to the small screen in *Out on a Limb* (1987). There have been some strange examples of reincarnation: Oliver Hardy comes back as a horse in *The Flying Deuces* (1939) and a dog comes back as Dick Powell in *You Never Can Tell* (1951). Terry Moore believes her uncle is reincarnated as a horse in *The Return of October* (1948). Heroine Charlotte Austin was a gorilla in a previous life in *The Bride and the Beast* (1958). Chevy Chase returns as Benji the dog to find his murderer in *Oh, Heavenly Dog!* (1980) — No prize for guessing who wins the acting honors. *The Mummy* (1932) has been the subject of many sequels and more reincarnations than faced by Zita Johann in the title role. The film has its origins in H. Rider Haggard's 1887 novel, *She*, with its concept not only of eternal life but also sexual potency. The latter is generally missing from film versions beginning in 1908 with a one-reeler from the Edison Mfg. Company and including a 1935 version starring liberal politician-to-be Helen Gahagan Douglas and a 1965 version with Ursula Andress. The dead have been reanimated in a large number of very forgettable films, ranging from *The Man They Could Not Hang* (1939) and *The Man with Two Lives* (1942) through *The Horrible Dr. Hitchcock* (1962), *The Frozen Dead* (1966) and H.P. Lovecraft's *Re-Animator* (1985).

Actual and would-be suicide victims on screen include Richard Basehart in *Fourteen Hours* (1951—and he lives) and Sissy Spacek in *'Night, Mother* (1986—and she dies). Mae Clarke commits a powerful suicide leap in the 1931 screen adaptation of Ben Hecht and Charles MacArthur's *The Front Page*. In 1948, Moira Shearer chose suicide in *The Red Shoes*. Comic and fake suicides have included Bud Cort in *Harold and Maude* (1971) and Tom Conti in *Reuben, Reuben* (1983).

The film industry's fixation with violent death is generally considered to have its beginnings in slasher films, sometimes described as splatter films, a genre most associated with the 1960s and 1970s. The films always feature deranged villains with knives, razors, machetes, or chain saws, isolated settings and plotlines that will appeal most readily to adolescent audiences. Because of nausea such films can induce, they have become labeled by some as *cinéma vomitif*, giving them an almost classic categorization that they most certainly do not deserve.

Director Herschell Gordon Lewis was a pioneer of the genre with such productions as *Blood Feast* (1963), *Two Thousand Maniacs* (1965), *Color Me Blood Red* (1965), and *The Gore Gore Girls* (1973). The slasher film reached its zenith with Tobe Hooper's *The Texas Chain Saw Massacre* (1974), in which a family of chain saw and razor-wielding maniacs prey on foolish teenagers, and which is loosely based on the career of Wisconsin serial killer and cannibal Ed Gein. The cannibalistic theme of many of the slasher films is evident in *Night of the Living Dead* (1968) and its sequel, *Dawn of the Dead* (1978).

The slasher films on American screens were often imported, but there were many homemade efforts, including *Carnival of Blood* (1970), *The Corpse Grinders* (1971), *Scream Bloody Murder* (1972), *Three on a Meathook* (1972), *Hollywood Meat Cleaver Massacre* (1976), and *The Incredible Torture Show* (1976). The slasher film went mainstream with John Carpenter's *Halloween* (1978), Sean S. Cunningham's *Friday the 13th* (1980) and Wes Craven's *A Nightmare on Elm Street* (1984). The genre's influence on music videos is evidenced by Michael Jackson's *Thriller* (1983).

While slasher films might generally be considered to be a 1960s through 1980s genre, they can be traced back much further. The 1918 production of *Behind the Door* has a sea captain and former taxidermist taking revenge for the rape-murder of his wife by skinning alive the German submarine lieutenant responsible. After being taken "behind the door," the German dies as his ordeal commences, prompting the taxidermist hero to declaim, "I swore I would skin him alive, but he died on me—damn him!" In 1934, Edgar G. Ulmer directed *The Black Cat*, in which a villainous Boris Karloff is tied up, stripped to the waist, and skinned alive by Bela Lugosi.

Mutilation is a theme in at least three major Hollywood films. Lon Chaney stars in Tod Browning's *The Unknown* (1927) as Alonzo, who performs as an armless knife thrower but really has two useable limbs. The beautiful Estrelita, played by Joan Crawford, falls in love with him because she hates the touch of a man's hand and feels secure in his presence. Poor Alonzo arranges to have his arms amputated only to discover the fickleness of women as Estrelita has now fallen in love with strongman Malabar, who does have two arms and two hands. In revenge, Alonzo plans to have Malabar's arms torn from their sockets by stampeding horses. While the film is not as entertainingly outrageous as its storyline might suggest, there is a delightful sadomasochistic quality to the relationships on screen. Tod Browning's favorite illustrator was, apparently, Aubrey Beardsley, and one suspects that both men shared a similarly sexually depraved view of the world. Paul Leni's 1928 production of *The Man Who Laughs*, based on a lesser-known Victor Hugo novel, concerns a young man, played by Conrad Veidt, whose mouth has been carved into a hideous grin by gypsies. He makes his living as a sideshow attraction as do the title characters in Tod Browning's *Freaks* (1932). When aerialist Cleopatra seduces one of their number for financial gain, she is transformed into a freak, a duck woman, "one of us."

Rumors of the existence of "snuff films," in which an individual, usually female, is killed and mutilated on camera, have routinely circulated since the 1960s, despite a report in the September 1984 issue of *Playboy* that the New York Police Department is "not aware of any authentic snuff films seized in the U.S....at any time." Such rumors reached their peak in October 1975, when it was reported that private screenings of snuff films were taking place in New York, with admission tickets selling for $200 apiece. The object of this gossip proved to be an 82-minute feature film titled *Snuff*.

The film, featuring a Charles Manson-like character and obviously influenced by contemporary "slasher" productions, opens with two women on motorbikes capturing a third. It concludes with the script girl on the set telling the director how much she admires his work; she is invited to have sex with him on camera, and is then cut apart. "This scene is well presented and alone justifies all the shouting," reported the trade paper *Boxoffice* (April 19, 1976). When *Snuff* opened at New York's National Theatre on February 17, 1976, there was such a public outcry that the New York District Attorney was forced to investigate. That investigation revealed the film was, in the words of *Playboy* critic Bruce Williamson (June 1976), a "dreary trifling hoax." *Snuff* was, in reality, a 1970 film, *The Slaughter*, shot in South America, at a cost of $33,000 by Roberta and Michael Findlay. The final four-minute killing segment was filmed in New York by Allan Shackleton. The Findlays claimed to know nothing of what had happened to their film until the release of *Snuff*, and worked out a financial settlement with Shackleton.

Snuff was distributed by Shackleton's Monarch Releasing Corporation, which advertised in *Boxoffice* (November 10, 1975), "The film that could only be made in South America ... Where life is cheap." To which *Hustler* (July 1976) responded, "Not only is life cheap in South America, but apparently so is talent." *Snuff* received its world premiere at the Uptown Theatre, Indianapolis, on January 16, 1976, before an audience of less than two dozen and primarily consisting of the media and police officers. The Los Angeles premiere took place at Mann's Hollywood Theatre on March 17, 1976.

Snuff films have figured prominently in at least two mystery novels, Joseph Wambaugh's *The Glitter Dome* (William Morrow, 1981, filmed by HBO in 1983) and Richard Nehrbass's *A Perfect Death* (HarperCollins, 1991). The subject is also central to Gregory McDonald's novel, *The Brave* (Barricade Books, 1991), which chronicles the last days of Rafael Brown, an impoverished slum dweller with a wife and two children, after he has agreed to "star" in a snuff film. Rafael wastes the "advance" he is paid on toys his children cannot play with and on food his wife cannot cook, and, at the book's conclusion, it is revealed the contract the illiterate Rafael has signed for his wife to receive $30,000 after the film is made is worthless. The third chapter of the novel contains a graphic and gruesome description of Rafael's death, as the producer tells him what will take place, from the pulling of the first fingernail to the disemboweling.

The screen adaptation of *The Brave* was initially as bloody as the novel itself. While the film was in the planning stages, the original director, Aziz Ghazal, bludgeoned to death his ex-wife and daughter before killing himself with a gun on December 1, 1993. The project languished until it was taken up by actor Johnny Depp, who co-wrote and directed the film version in 1997. Depp stars as the central character, with Marlon Brando playing his would-be murderer. With Brando's mumbling of his lines, it is virtually impossible to comprehend what his character has in mind for Depp, and the focus is on the poverty of his life rather than his impending death. The 123-minute film was jeered at the Cannes Film Festival, and has never been released in the United States.

The fascination with the notion, if not the actuality, of snuff films gave rise in the early 1980s to the birth of "Death Films." The first of these is probably *The Killing of America* (1981), featuring footage of the shooting of Lee Harvey Oswald, the Kennedy assassination, U.S. soldiers killing civilians in Vietnam, the Jamestown Massacre, etc., and ending with the message, "While you watched this movie, five more of us were murdered. One was the random killing of a stranger."

From film, these highly offensive documentaries moved to video. The best-known series is *Faces of Death* (1978), with sequel volumes in 1981 and 1985, consisting of what is basically newsreel footage of autopsies, suicides, executions and, often, animal slaughter. *Death Scenes* (1989) is introduced by Dr. Anton Szandor LaVey, leader of the Church of Satan, and features gruesome police photographs of death scenes in the 1930s and 1940s. By the end of the century, there were internet sites, such as *Death Becomes You*, offering one-stop shopping for customers boasting "The Morbid Mind," with an unhealthy interest in death on film and video. The same mentality that guarantees an audience for "Death Videos" is also responsible for the continuing interest in the Abraham Zapruder film of the Kennedy Assassination.

As of the end of the 20th century, the culture of Death was alive and well in the United States. Artist Joe Coleman has based his career on portraits of killers, including Charles Manson and Carl Panzram. Derek Humphrey, founder of the right-to-die Hemlock Society, authored a best-selling 1991 volume on suicide titled *Final Exit*. Black Death vodka, imported into America from Belgium in 1991, proved popular among young drinkers, in large part thanks to its logo of a grinning skull wearing a black top hat and its endorsement by guitarist Slash of the group Guns 'N Roses. Also in 1991, Death cigarettes, featuring a skull and crossbones as its logo, were introduced, with the company arguing that the name "disseminates an anti-smoking message directly to smokers."

In 1992, Marion "Suge" Knight and Dr. Dre founded the rap music label Death Row Records, whose logo depicts a hooded convict strapped into an electric chair. With its first release of Dre's "The Chronic" in 1992, the company became a major player in the recording field, but in a vicious example of life imitating art, Death Row Records, which had glamorized gang violence, itself became a victim, and since 1997, eight individuals associated in some way with the company or Marion "Suge" Knight have been murdered.

Other "modern" death-related groups include Florida Death Metal from the 1980s and the Swedish group, Dismember, from the 1990s. While these heavy metal bands endorsed everything from sadism and fascism to Satanism and violence, they did not actually go as far as to advocate killing.

CHAPTER TEN

Bimbos in History

Throughout the 20th century, bimbo was the most commonly used term in reference to an unintelligent woman. To feminists, and later to most members of either sex, it is the epitome of bad taste, evidence of both a derogatory and arrogant attitude in its user. While its basic meaning—stupid—has not changed, its usage has. Bimbo is a condensed form of the Italian bambino, and was first used by American soldiers serving in Italy during World War I. It may first have appeared in print in *American Magazine* as early as November 1919, and here, as elsewhere, it referred to a man. Novelist P.G. Wodehouse has a fondness for describing some of his male characters as bimbos—for example, in *Bill the Conqueror* (1936) and *Full Moon* (1947)—and as late as 1990, Vice President Dan Quayle was described on the television talk show, [Phil] *Donahue*, as "the stereotypical bimbo." That, of course, is the same Dan Quayle who in 1992 denounced the *Murphy Brown* television series and labeled unwed, single mothers as unfit parents.

The Historical Dictionary of American Slang dates the feminine use of bimbo from 1920, and notes that it was originally used to refer to a whore or that delightfully descriptive word, a floozy. The first reference in song is "My Little Bimbo Down on the Bamboo Isle" by Grant Clarke and Walter Donaldson, which was introduced by Aileen Stanley in the 1920 revue, *Silks and Satins*. Within a relatively short number of years, bimbo was in general use to describe an uneducated American female. *Literary Digest* (March 14, 1925) noted that college students call a woman "in humorous disrespect, a 'bimbo.'" It remained popular, as a derogatory term, through into the 1980s, and on *Cheers* in 1986, one of the characters made reference to "the bimbo du jour."

The classic bimbo developed into the classic dumb blonde, represented by Jayne Mansfield and by Marilyn Monroe not so much of herself but in reference to the roles she played. "What do you do if a blonde throws a pin at you?" is the question The politically incorrect response: "Run like hell, because she's got a grenade in her mouth." The basic idea is that a blonde suggests both sexuality and stupidity, neither of which she is particularly aware of. The stereotype does not always apply, as with Grace Kelly, and the stereotype can also be exposed as a stereotype, as with Judy Holliday in *Born Yesterday* (1950).

Arguably, America's first dumb blonde was Hope Hampton (1897-1982), who actually started out life as a brunette. She was primarily famous for being famous and incredibly well off as a result of a 1923 marriage to financier Jules Brulatour. He sponsored her film appearances and a disastrous engagement with the Philadelphia Grand Opera. She could very well have been, but probably wasn't, the basis for the would-be opera star wife of Orson Welles' *Citizen Kane*. Often billed as "The Duchess of Park Avenue," Hampton was a perennial favorite at New York first-nights, explaining, "I'm a supporter of everything, especially myself." In the 1960s, she could be seen at the Peppermint Lounge nightclub, performing the twist, and was named Miss Twist of 1962.

In response to the passive image of American womanhood, the film industry invented the vamp, or at least stole the idea from a Victorian painting, "The Vampire," by Sir Edward Burne-Jones and an 1897 verse by Rudyard Kipling of the same title. Kipling's verse began with the words, "A Fool There Was," and this was the title of the first American feature film — there had been a couple of earlier shorts — warning of the danger to both men and pure (and slightly naïve) women of the vamp. The 1915 film, *A Fool There Was*, was based on a 1909 play by Porter Emerson Browne, and starred Theda Bara, a Cincinnati native whose real name was Theodosia Goodman. Theda Bara is an anagram of "Arab Death." When Theda Bara uttered those immortal words, "Kiss me, my fool," audiences laughed — and audiences continued to laugh at these weird vampish incarnations. It did not help that the vamps never really won. They might enjoy a few nights of unbridled sex with a husband who should have known better, but, ultimately, the husband returned to his forgiving wife and the vamp finished up alone and aging. During World War I, a critic joked that the vamp was making the world safe for sin. The reality was that the vamp was nothing more than another woman held up to public ridicule.

Following in the tradition of Theda Bara came such vamps as Kitty Gordon, Louise Glaum, Nita Naldi, and Valeska Suratt. The last, who also appeared on the vaudeville stage as well as in eleven films between 1915 and 1917, was positively loony. After once describing herself as the ward of Satan, she later decided she was the Virgin Mary. It was probably in the latter casting that she sued Cecil B. DeMille in 1928, claiming that he had stolen the script for *King of Kings* from her.

The vamp was also celebrated in music. In 1917, Lee Johnson dedicated "When That Vampire Rolled Her Vampy Eyes at Me" to Theda Bara. In the 1914 edition of the *Ziegfeld Follies*, Bert Williams starred in a parody of *A Fool There Was*, singing "The Vampire," for which he provided the music, with words by Earle C. Jones and Gene Buck. In a later revue, *Oh, Look!*, from 1919, the Dolly Sisters sang of "The Vamp," written by Byron Gay.

As late as 1955, the vamp was very much a part of American culture, satirized in a musical of the same name by John Latouche, Sam Locke and James Mundy. Carol Channing starred as a composite of Theda Bara and Pola Negri, but the show is of most interest for its featuring Steve Reeves in the role of Muscle Man.

The bimbo and the dumb blonde label can be traced back to the advent of the Miss America contest in 1921, although the first beauty contest had been organized as early as 1854 by showman P.T. Barnum. In 1854, women could not display a great deal, but by 1921, female bathers were to be seen and enjoyed on American beaches, wearing one-piece bathing costumes, displaying legs and necklines. As with later editions of the Miss America pageant, the contestants were judged in various categories but it was the one featuring the bathing costume for which the predominantly male audience was present.

When sixteen-year-old Margaret Gorman won that first contest, she was described as "the most beautiful bathing girl in America."

In later years, Miss America would be serenaded with the lyrics, "There She is, Miss America" by Bert Parks (1914-1997). Parks was the host of the Miss America Beauty Pageant from 1955 through 1979, when he was fired as being too old. It seems appropriate that politically incorrect ageism should have led to the brief demise of Bert Parks, who went on to host such politically incorrect pageants as Mother/Daughter, Miss Young International, Mrs. American, and, most outrageously, National Miss Indian USA. At least the guy had a sense of humor, parodying himself and singing "There She Is, Miss America" to a lizard in the Marlon Brando vehicle *The Freshman* (1990).

Beauty contests might upon initial consideration be ideal backgrounds for motion picture scenarios, but the basic problem is the Production Code's forbidding undue female body exposure, in particular cleavage. At no time could the "gap" between the breasts be visible. As the Code warned, "The effect of nudity or semi-nudity upon the normal man or woman and much more upon the young and upon immature persons, has been honestly recognized by all lawmakers and moralists." As a result, there are few films featuring beauty contests, with one of the first being *The Case of the Lucky Legs* (1935), in which Perry Mason, played by Warren William, defends the winner of a Lucky Legs contest.

Toward the end of the 20th century, with the demise of the Production Code, the beauty contest was utilized as the subject for a handful of films. It was parodied with the "Young American Miss" contest in *Smile* (1975); *Miss All-American Beauty* (1982) was a drama of a small-town Texas beauty pageant; Holly Hunter entered a local Southern beauty contest in *Miss Firecracker* (1989); the Ms Galaxy contestants were held hostage in *No Contest* (1994); and, of course, Divine had to get into the act and host the "Alternative Miss World" pageant in *I Wanna Be a Beauty Queen* (1985).

With the 1953 debut of *Playboy*, Hugh Hefner raised the exploitation of the female form to a new level, with more skin and far less visible talent. The entrepreneur moved from the printed page to the broadcast arena with the 1982 premiere of the Playboy Channel (a successor to the Escapade Channel) on cable television. "We take the staples out of the centerfold" was the claim of the channel, which offered no hard-core pornography, and which transformed itself into a pay-per-view offering in 1989. The centerfold came to the big screen with *The Centerfold Girls* (1974) and to television with *Katie: Portrait of a Centerfold* (1978), starring a young Kim Basinger. The tragedy of Dorothy Stratten, a *Playboy* centerfold murdered by an ex-lover, was the subject of a made-for-television movie, *Death of a Centerfold: The Dorothy Stratten Story*, in 1981 and a 1984 book by lover/director Peter Bogdanovich, *The Killing of the Unicorn: Dorothy Stratten, 1960-1980*.

The woman who sparked a sexual revolution with her bathing attire was Australian Annette Kellermann (1887-1975). Neither a great beauty nor a great entertainer in the typical manner, Kellermann (she later dropped the second "n" during World War I) came to fame as a swimmer. She swam the lengths of the best known of Europe's rivers—the Seine, the Danube, the Rhine, and the Thames—and then in 1907, she arrived in the United States to begin what was to prove a lengthy career in vaudeville. Kellermann appeared at Boston's Revere Beach, wearing a one-piece bathing costume and was promptly arrested by the police. The costume showed little of her body, apart from the neck, lower arms and lower legs, but it fitted snugly and provided voyeurs with a clear image of the contours of the lady's body.

On the vaudeville stage, Annette Kellermann appeared in a glass-enclosed tank, complete with mirrors above, thus providing the male audience with a very good view of her body. She was not the only underwater entertainer; there was also Blatz, the Human Fish, who ate, read a newspaper and played the trombone underwater, and Enoch, the Fish Man, who also played the trombone, as well as singing and, incredibly, smoking under water. In a nod of recognition to Blatz and Enoch, and also to add a slightly kinky appeal, Kellermann would sometimes eat a banana underwater. Annette Kellermann appeared in a handful of films before retiring in the 1930s, and was the subject of a film biography, *Million Dollar Mermaid*, starring Esther Williams who did for male audiences what Kellermann had done but three decades later.

It was not just female bathers who were of concern to the beach police. In the *New York Times* (May 27, 1921), the Long Island Chief of Police announced that he was also concerned about "bald-headed beach lizards" that came to stare. Men's bathing attire was also subject to censorship, and some beaches insisted that men must be covered down to the knees and that a skirt flapping over the thighs was essential. The latter was probably devised to hide the male genitalia that became instantly visible once the woolen bathing costume got wet. The wet t-shirt contests of seventy years later revealed far less than did those woolen bathing costumes!

The one-piece bathing suit gave birth to the jazz babies — featured in song in 1919 — and with the advent of the 1920s, the flappers. Described by the *New York Times* (July 16, 1922) as "shameless, selfish and honest," the flappers represented a new breed of liberated women who had little regard for housework and the hereditary obligations of the female sex, but rather craved fun, fun and more fun. If they were to marry, they would prefer their husbands be wealthy, and this search for the ideal and financially secure male led to many flappers being described as gold diggers. A sexual revolution was taking place perhaps, but one of which women could not be completely proud. With their interest in style over substance, wealth over power, flappers can hardly be designated feminists.

It was a 1919 Avery Hopwood farce *The Gold Diggers* that introduced the phrase into the American language. On screen, Hope Hampton was the star of the first adaptation in 1923, followed by Nancy Welford in 1929. Alice White typified the gold digger in a series of Hollywood films of the 1920s, and in the next decade, the stereotype was continued by Ginger Rogers and Joan Blondell in the *Gold Diggers* series from Warner Bros. (Ruby Keeler might be the star of the films, but in no way could this sweet, naïve little girl tapping out her soul be described as a gold digger.)

A typical gold digger was fifteen-year-old Peaches Browning, who embarked on a vaudeville career in 1926 after breaking up with her

51-year-old millionaire husband, Edward "Daddy" Browning, dubbed by the tabloid press as the "High Priest of the Daddy Cult." One of the least talented but best known of real-life gold diggers was Peggy Hopkins Joyce (1893-1957), with many husbands and many lovers, including Chaplin, and whose philosophy of life may be summed up in the newspaper headline, "Husbands Go, Jewels Stay." She was very much in the tradition of Evelyn Nesbit Thaw, "the girl in the red velvet swing," an artist's model whose 1905-1906 love affair with architect Stanford White led to his being killed by her millionaire husband Harry K. Thaw. There was less scandal in Joyce's life as she quickly came to fame as a showgirl in the 1917 edition of the *Ziegfeld Follies*. In 1931, Eddie Cantor sang of her, in just one of the many references to Peggy Hopkins Joyce in song and elsewhere,

> Take Peggy Joyce
> With little voice
> She soon became
> The nation's choice!
> I tell you, Buddy
> She's made a study
> Of makin' Whoopee.

Peggy Hopkins Joyce made a few films, of which the best known is the W.C. Fields vehicle, *International House* (1933). In one of the most outrageous moments on screen, Joyce asks Fields what she is sitting on. "It's a pussy," exclaims the comedian, holding up a cat.

The flappers dressed more lightly and more provocatively than their predecessors, and their bodies also underwent a subtle and under-reported change. Although female entertainers had long shaved their armpits, American women in general first became obsessed with the subject in 1915 as new, sleeveless evening dresses introduced the need to remove "objectionable hair." Manufacturers of women's razors and depilatories emphasized a new look that was hygienic and comfortable. In the 1920s, as skirt lengths shortened and bathing costumes became more revealing, women were subjected to increased advertising in regard to hair removal from the legs, although it was not until

World War II, the absence of nylon stockings and the bare-legged look that hair removal from the legs became standard for American womanhood. Manufacturers, acting up the attitude of the male, advertised to women that female body hair was "ugly," "morbid" and "disfiguring." Body hair was a masculine rather than a feminine trait.

As women became interested in cosmetic surgery in the 1920s, the 1927 song, "There's a Trick in Pickin' a Chick Chick Chicken," told its male listeners, "You must be wise, you must be gifted to recognize a face that's lifted." Vaudevillian Irene Franklin sang "Be Your Age" to an aging female colleague, pointing out that "A guy who had been drinking, shot at you and killed poor Lincoln." The song belongs to an era when Fannie Ward (1871-1952) was a major star of vaudeville and film, noted for the ageless quality of her looks, personality and talent. She was Marlene Dietrich before Marlene Dietrich appeared on the scene. Fannie Ward was the "Eternal Flapper," who claimed that at the age of 45 she could pass for fourteen on stage, and that at sixty, her legs were still slim and handsome.

Despite the glamour of the youthful Peggy Hopkins Joyce and the aged Fannie Ward, the entertainment industry still picked on women as ugly or stupid or both. In 1922, Billy Jones and Ernie Hare, "The Happiness Boys," sang of "Elsie Shulkz-en-heim," written by Cliff Friend and Frank Silver. Among the lady's attributes are that she is ten pounds less than any horse -- "she's my hippopotamus" — and that she has pearly teeth, one pointing North and one pointing South. "She had her nose done over — now she looks very gentile to me." Rudy Vallee sang of "Kansas City Kitty," written in 1929 by Jesse Greer and Billy Rose, again whom Vallee hopes won't get any fatter, and who was so dumb she thought July 4 was an English King and Babe Ruth a showgirl. "Sure was a pity, she wasn't pretty." In another song from the same period, "You'll Do It Someday, So Why Not Now," Rudy Vallee reminds his girlfriend that a young chicken is far more attractive than an old hen.

At the same time, The Record Boys told us "Sally's Not the Same Old Sally," written by Al Bernard and Sam Stept circa 1925. She had read Elinor Glyn's *Three Weeks* and,

INCORRECT ENTERTAINMENT

When I left home she had not been kissed.
Now there's not a boy in town that she's missed.

The bathing beauty, the showgirls and the dumb blondes are all representative of women as sexual objects, desirable but basically untouchable. This was not so much the placing of the female upon a pedestal but rather putting her on public display. The concept dates back as far as 1831, when the New York stage played host for the first time to "living statues" or "tableaux vivants." Women, and sometimes, men would pose, without moving, as modern-life equivalents of statues or famous moments in history. It helped to generate an audience in that many of the statues or painting represented were of semi-clothed women, such as in "The Three Graces," "Venus and Cupid" or "Adam and Eve." These "living statues" or "Tableaux vivants" gave rise to modern burlesque, and survive today in the Pageant of the Masters, held each year since 1932 in Laguna Beach, California.

Once audiences grew tired of just leering at women who did nothing but wear scanty attire, it was necessary for the entertainment industry to move the female image forward. All-girl orchestras came into vogue in the 1930s with Ina Ray Hutton, "the Blonde Bombshell of Swing," and Phil Spitalny and His All Girl Orchestra, featuring Evelyn and her magic violin. The all-girl orchestras, in fact, date back to the late 1880s and the Fadettes Woman's Orchestra in Boston; other female orchestras from the 1910s and 1920s include the Rita Mario Orchestra, Frankie Cramer and Her Melody Bandits, and the Ingénues, who were decidedly misrepresented in the late 1920s as "The Band Beautiful." Some of these all-girl combinations were led by women, but some of the most successful had a male conductor, billed first, and to whom the women on stage and in publicity were obviously subservient.

In that most film buffs are gay, fans of early film musicals have not paid too much attention to the "crotch shot" prevalent throughout. The camera lovingly moves along a line of chorus girls, concentrating not only their faces or even their breasts, but upon that forbidden area between the legs. Dance director Busby Berkeley knew exactly what erotic appeal could be derived from his chorus girls. In his films of the 1930s and 1940s, he uses the female body in a stylized abstract fashion. The women are sexual objects, as early as the "No More Love" number from *Roman Scandals* (1933), with its array of nude slaves, all with very long blonde hair. As she performs "We're in the Money" in *Gold Diggers of 1933* (1933), Gingers Rogers sports a coin-covered crotch, implying her vagina is for sale—or at least for rent. In "Shadow Waltz," from the same film, the violin-playing chorus girl meld into one gigantic lighted violin. They are human harps in *Fashions of 1934* (1934). In *The Gang's All Here* (1943), Carmen Miranda as "The Lady in the Tutti-Frutti Hat" appears to be wearing giant bananas balanced on her head—and the symbolism is all too obvious.

In the 1960s, beach and biker movies introduced a new generation of bimbos, with unmemorable faces, stunning bodies and forgettable names: Joan O'Brien, Diane McBain, Francine York, Jean Hale, Chris Noel, and Karen Jensen. The surfing sweetheart Gidget was a stereotypical bimbo of the era, played first by Sandra Dee, and later by Deborah Walley and Cindy Carol. As the series lost its appeal, its star changed from the relatively well known to the instantly forgettable.

The James Bond films featured their own type of bimbo, created to enforce the masculinity of their hero. Ursula Andress was the first Bond girl, emerging from the sea in a skimpy bikini in *Dr. No* (1962). She was beautiful but seldom as stupid as the label of bimbo might suggest, although Shirley Eaton's character in *Goldfinger* (1964) is foolish enough to allow herself to be covered in gold paint—and thus killed.

No matter how much women may have risen in their own esteem and that of others, spousal abuse has always been an often unacknowledged presence—except in popular entertainment. It was not until the 1985 made-for-television movie exposing wife-beating, *The Burning Bed*, starring Farrah Fawcett, and the 1993 feature, *What's Love Got to Do with It?*, concerning Ike's abusive relationship with Tina Turner, that the subject was taken seriously. In earlier years, it was the subject of humor. In 1915, vaudeville performer Ruth Roye sang,

INCORRECT ENTERTAINMENT

Cy's been drinking cider,
Better take his wife and hide her,
He'll treat her mighty cruel

British music hall comedian Gus Elen would sing in the 1920s and 1930s of his newly-married friend, while brandishing a hammer with which he planned to beat the offending wife:

It's a great big shame, and if she belonged ter me,
I'd let 'er know who's who,
Nagging at a feller wot is six foot three,
And 'er only four foot two.
Oh! They 'ad not been married not a month nor more,
When underneath 'er thumb goes Jim.
Oh, isn't it a pity as the likes of 'er
Should put upon the likes of 'im?

On January 2, 1937, Warner Bros. released the one-reel cartoon, *He Was Her Man*, a parody of the song "Frankie and Johnny," in which the former is beaten up for laughs from the audience and from Johnny. There is some slight satisfaction when the film concludes with Frankie's taking a gun and killing her man.

It was Hungarian playwright Ferenc Molnar who provided the most persuasive argument for wife-beating in *Liliom*, and it was Richard Rodgers and Oscar Hammerstein II who presented it to a far wider audience in their musical adaptation of the play, *Carousel*. As discussed elsewhere, *Liliom* and *Carousel* tell the story of Liliom, a carnival barker, renamed Billy Bigelow for the musical, who falls in love with a young factory girl named Julie. Unthinkingly, Billy abuses Julie after their marriage. He is killed in an attempted robbery, but permitted to return to earth briefly to see his daughter graduate from school. When the girl rejects him, he hits her, as he had done Julie, and when the daughter tells her mother what had happened, she compares the blow to a kiss. "It is possible for someone to hit you hard and not hurt you at all," remarks Julie, echoing the comments of battered wives throughout the world. As the lyrics to one of the songs go, "He's yer feller, and you love him, and there's nothing more to say." If this was not bad enough, somehow Billy's behavior on earth is sufficient to elevate him to heaven.

John Raitt played Billy opposite Jan Clayton in the original production of *Carousel*, which opened at New York's Majestic Theatre on April 19, 1945 to rave reviews. A 1956 film version starred Gordon MacRae and Shirley Jones. A 1995 production by Britain's National Theatre was a success both in London and New York, although director Nicholas Hytner did remove the line stating that the slap "felt like a kiss."

There might be slight changes in the libretto to *Carousel*, but has the attitude toward spousal abuse really changed? A joke circulating in the 1980s and later asks, "Why are there so many battered women?" and provides the answer, "Because they don't understand the phrase, 'Shut the fuck up!'"

There is a modern male equivalent of the bimbo, and that is the himbo. A name first used in the late 1980s, the label himbo is generally attached to men with good-looking bodies and questionably small brains. According to *The Washington Post* (February 26, 1994), "The 'himbo' shows up regularly in film, in calendars, in print ads from Calvin Klein." *The New York Times* (September 25, 1994) defined himbos as "straight, good-looking men who read *Hampton's* magazine and chase models around SoHo on their Harleys."

The name is often applied to muscular male models, including Lucky Vanous, who removed his shirt in a 1994 Diet Coca-Cola advertisement to the delight of a female audience, and Fabio, who posed endlessly, minus his shirt, for the covers of romance novels. Brian "Kato" Kaelin became an instant himbo after his performance on the witness stand at his landlord O.J. Simpson's murder trial and confirmed his status by stripping nude for *Playgirl*. On television, the himbo is best represented by David Hasselhoff on *Baywatch*, and in motion pictures, where there are many potential himbos, the most obvious is Keanu Reeves.

CHAPTER ELEVEN

The Male Body on Display

It might be as politically incorrect as overt admiration of the female breast, but the feminine gaze and the gay gaze have long been directed on screen to the most attractive aspects of the male anatomy, the penis, the buttocks and the chest. Neither Rudolph Valentino, the screen's first major matinee idol, nor his closest competitor, Ramon Novarro, can legitimately be designated himbos. Both were relatively intelligent if subject to a number of human failings. Certainly, Valentino knew his best feature was not his acting ability but his finely chiseled body, and he gladly displayed his naked chest while slowly donning his bullfighting attire in *Blood and Sand* (1922), while wearing a 18th century wig in *Monsieur Beaucaire* (1924), while having it whipped to the delight of sadomasochists in the audience in *The Son of the Sheik* (1926) and while in very brief bathing attire that also accentuated the length of his penis in *The Young Rajah* (1922). There is even a saucy and short promotional film in which the star, seated in his car at the beach, begins undressing only to draw the blinds after he has stripped to the waist.

As with most male stars up through recent years, the chest is hairless. Somehow, even a thin layer of hair is offensive both to the camera and the audience. The baby-smooth chests of the young gentlemen in the Calvin Klein advertisements are no recent phenomena. Other and lesser Latin lovers of the screen, including Antonio Moreno and Gilbert Roland, obviously viewed body hair as part of their ethnic persona; they retained it and, also, they retained their minority stature among Hollywood leading men. Playing a locker scene opposite the very clean-shaven Robert Stack in *The Bullfighter and the Lady* (1951),

Gilbert Roland was asked by director Budd Boetticher to remove all body hair. The request was an insult to Roland's Latino culture; he refused and never had a good word again for his director.

Shaving was a Hollywood ritual for its leading men. When English actor Henry Wilcoxon reported for work on Cecil B. DeMille's *Cleopatra* (1934), the director told him, "You'll have to shave, you know." When Wilcoxon responded, "I shaved this morning," DeMille explained the shaving involved the actor's chest, arms and legs.

Some actors varied their hirsute qualities. In 1952, Cornel Wilde had an extremely hairy chest in *At Sword's Point* and no hair, again perhaps at the request of Cecil B. DeMille, in *The Greatest Show on Earth*.

Edgar Rice Burroughs' creation Tarzan has no visible body hair in the illustrations accompanying the original novels, and on screen has no chest hair until the late 1950s. Gordon Scott was the first film Tarzan with chest hair in *Tarzan's Great Adventure* (1959), although he had earlier shaved for *Tarzan's Hidden Jungle* (1955) and *Tarzan and the Lost Safari* (1957). Beginning with *Tarzan and the Valley of Gold* (1966), the 14th screen Tarzan, Mike Henry, is the first to have chest hair in every film.

It was the film industry's self-regulating body, the Motion Picture Producers Association of America, which required Jeff Chandler to shave the hair off his chest for the 1952 production of *Yankee Buccaneer*. The Association had no objection to a bared chest but only if it was hairless. As the actor explained it to *The Hollywood Reporter* (August 25, 1952), chest hair was OK in advertisements for the film but not in the production itself: "I suppose if there were just a suggestion of it, it would be all right, but in this case there's quite a bit of hair on the chest." (In view of the actor's interest in cross-dressing, one would have assumed that he was quite familiar with chest shaving.)

Peter Gallagher waxed his chest for *The Idolmaker* and *Summer Lov*ers (1982). As late as 1983, John Travolta shaved and waxed his chest for *Staying Alive*, but times were changing if somewhat slowly. Led by Burt Reynolds and Alec Baldwin, a handful of actors were not merely hairy but positively gorilla-like. As one critic noted, if

Alec Baldwin did not shave his neck, "his chest hair would grow all the way to his eyebrows." That ridiculing of the hairy-chested, as also evidenced by the fake chest hair of the leading character in *Austin Powers: The Spy Who Shagged* Me (1999), was a warning to many leading men that it was better to be shaven than sorry. Those actors posing as gay icons, including Tom Cruise, Leonardo DiCaprio, Matt Damon, Keanu Reeves, and Brad Pitt, remained hairless, along with Calvin Klein model Marky Mark (later known as an actor under his real name of Mark Wahlberg) and the models on the covers of *Men's Fitness* and similar magazines. The Chippendale strippers, again with a large gay following, shave on a regular basis.

Head and body shaving has fetish appeal. Catering to the gay community, Barber Shop Video offered a number of video releases featuring young men having their heads (and sometimes more) sheared and shaved. A typical release, *Sir, Cut It All Off, Sir!*, features seven supposed Marine inductees enduring boot camp haircuts from two butch drill sergeants. Shaving cultists take the subject very seriously. They will willingly pay $53.70 for video footage of "a 23-year-old with medium brown hair sheared into a Mohawk and ultimately into a total head shave."

Head shaving has obviously replaced chest shaving as an entertainment craze, as television personality Matt Lauer and actor Bruce Willis underwent radical hair cutting and head shaving to cover up incipient baldness in the late 1990s. It was the new 1990s look in entertainment, pioneered in the basketball arena, embraced by rap stars such as Ice Cube and Tupac Shakur, and eventually used for social protest by singer Sinead O'Connor.

It might be argued that the most famous penis of recent years belongs to Jason Biggs, the star of *American Pie* (1999), which plays a prominent role in the production but which is encased in a freshly-baked pie and never presented to public gaze. There is another penis that generated considerable attention a few years earlier in the summer of 1993, and that belonged to an ex-marine named John Wayne Bobbitt. Bobbitt returned home drunk one night and after forcing his wife Lorena to have sex with him, she took a kitchen knife and severed his penis. Luckily for Bobbitt, two surgeons were able to reattach the organ—and then the fun really began. In November 1993, he was tried for rape and she was tried for malicious wounding. Both were acquitted. John Wayne Bobbitt embarked on a "world tour" to help pay his legal and medical expenses, while his wife was hailed by feminists as a folk hero. Earlier, a feminist group in Ecuador had threatened to castrate 100 men if Lorena was sent to prison.

The publicity the drama evoked was remarkable, and by January 1994, *US News and World Report* estimated that John Wayne Bobbitt had been the subject of more than 1,300,000 column inches of newspaper and magazine reporting, most of it derogatory. Typical was a November 22, 1993 editorial cartoon in *Newsweek*, depicting a Thanksgiving Day gathering at the home of Lorena and John Wayne Bobbitt, with relatives hiding under the table because of the knife the former is holding. On the same day, the *Nation* suggested that the story read like "a perverse postmodern novel."

With his penis the center of public attention, John Wayne Bobbitt embarked on a porno career, starring in *John Wayne Bobbitt Uncut*, which received its invitational-only premiere on September 29, 1994 at the Academy of Motion Picture Arts and Sciences. A spokeswoman for the latter assured the screening in no way involved the Academy, while Bobbitt's costar, Tiffany Lords, went on the Geraldo television show to claim that Bobbitt had made her pregnant. Lords told concerned viewers that she would have an abortion and continue her porno career. With America and the world at last having the opportunity to see what everyone had been talking about for the past six months, *John Wayne Bobbitt Uncut* became the best-selling adult video of all time. (The $50,000 he received from the film went as a one-time child support payment.)

From victim to freak was not a gigantic step for Bobbitt. *John Wayne Bobbitt Uncut* was followed by *Frankenpenis*, in which audiences had the opportunity to view augmentation surgery on Bobbitt's penis. By 1996, the poor guy was reduced to co-starring with porn diva Kym Wilde in S&M videos. After his first encounter with the dominatrix, he told the *L.A. Weekly* (March 15, 1996), "It's just like when I was in the [Marine] Corps. Adapt and adjust, adapt and adjust. And besides, it's not like I haven't felt pain before."

Male nudity on screen dates back to the silent era. There is a strongly homoerotic shot of a naked (and hunky) slave, chained with his back to the camera, in the galley scenes of *Ben-Hur* (1926). Publicity photographs from the period show the film's star, Ramon Novarro, displaying a remarkable amount of naked body, down to the thighs and with the genital area in shadow, and looking, coincidentally, a lot less flabby than on screen. You can retouch a still photograph, as Hollywood quickly discovered, but only in recent years can computers do the same thing to the moving image. There is full rear nudity from Lew Ayres and fellow actors at the start of the sound era in *All Quiet on the Western Front* (1930). Another wartime drama, *Wings* (1926), offers a peek-a-boo rear shot through an open door of a group of nude military recruits. Seventy years later, there was a similar scene in the 1993 Academy Award-nominated Welsh-language feature, *Hedd Wyn*, but this time, the shot was lengthy and frontal. Time had marched on.

The first major front male exposure on screen is, arguably, in *The Harrad Experiment* (1973), featuring leading man Don Johnson (who had yet to achieve major stardom) and Gregory Harrison (who was still an extra). It was Jan-Michael Vincent, unconcernedly facing the camera, who legitimized frontal male nudity in *Buster and Billie* (1974). There was not a major rush to follow his lead, with the most notable exceptions being Perry King in *Mandingo* (1975), Robert De Niro in *1900* (1977), Christopher Atkins in *The Blue Lagoon* (1980) and *A Night in Heaven* (1983), Richard Gere in (among others) *American Gigolo* (1980) and *Breathless* (1983), Gary Oldman in *Chattahoochee* (1990), Viggo Mortensen in *The Indian Runner* (1991), Tom Berenger in *At Play in the Fields of the Lord* (1991), Eric Stoltz in *Naked in New York* (1994) Ewan McGregor in *The Pillow Book* (1996) and *Young Adam* (2003) and Kevin Bacon in *Wild Things* (1998). A couple of Hollywood's older leading men were enthusiastic supporters of frontal nudity, although part of their audience might have asked why they did it: Dennis Hopper in *Tracks* (1976) and *Carried Away* (1996), and Harvey Keitel in *Bad Lieutenant* (1992) and *The Piano* (1993).

On March 17, 1988, the *Wall Street Journal* complained that it now seemed a requirement for men to prance naked on screen. The *Journal* noted that Rob Lowe's performance in *Masquerade* was no surprise, but it was difficult to understand Harrison Ford's motivation in *Frantic* or Sidney Poitier's feeling the urge at sixty in *Little Nikita*. The sightings were, of course, all from the rear. Generally, it was left to European actors to throw caution and modesty to the wind, with Malcolm McDowell the easy winner in the frontal nudity race.

Screenwriters often lack originality, and many have found that humiliation in the form of "depantsing" provides the perfect lead-in to rear total or semi-total nudity. Robert Taylor was perhaps the first Hollywood star to be depantsed, or as it is called in England "de-bagged," in the 1938 feature, *A Yank at Oxford*. A college setting was also the background for Robin Phillips' depantsing in *Decline and Fall of a Bird Watcher* (1969), based on the Evelyn Waugh novel titled simply *Decline and Fall*. Both Taylor and Phillips wore undergarments. In much later Hollywood, the underpants followed the trousers, and among those baring their buttocks for their art are Jack Palance in *The Mercenary* (1968), Charlton Heston in *Planet of the Apes* (1968), Roger Herren in *Myra Breckinridge* (1970), George Segal in *Born to Win* (1971), Ken Wahl in *The Wanderers* (1979), Robert Beltran in *Latino* (1985), Kevin Costner in *American Flyers* (1985), Marc Price in *Trick or Treat* (1986), Mel Gibson in *Lethal Weapon* (1987), Anthony Edwards in *Downtown* (1990), and Sean Patrick Flannery in *Powder* (1995).

In April 1934, a group of angry chorus girls on the set of *Murder at the Vanities* attacked director Mitchell Leisen and removed his trousers. The bisexual and somewhat effeminate filmmaker responded by hitting some of the girls—and then fainting.

French connoisseur Jean-Luc Hennig has noted, "If women are asked to assess an assortment of men, then muscles, mouth, strong build, nape, torso, Adam's apple, ears, ankles and penis, as well as height, are of absolutely no significance; what counts are the eyes and the bottom. They hold the promise. The advantage of a beautiful backside is evidently that you can admire its shape and hold it." The male bottom achieved its apotheosis with the sculptures of Michelangelo. The male attribute was then basically ignored by the art world for five centuries until rediscovered by Hollywood.

On stage, male nudity dates back at least to the 1890s, when strongman Sandow began appearing in American vaudeville and elsewhere. He would pose wearing nothing more than a very large fig leaf, obviously suggestive of a very large penis, and was also thus shot by theatrical photographer Napoleon Sarony. Postcards of the Sarony photograph were sold in their thousands to adoring women — and men. Sarony paved the way for other musclemen, including Bartolomeo Pagano, who appeared as the character of Maciste in Italian films from 1914 onwards, many of which were released in the U.S., for Steve Reeves in the 1950s, and for his imitators, including Mark Forest (a.k.a. Lou Degni), Mickey Hargitay, and Rock Stevens (a.k.a. Peter Lupus). All were very much sex icons, emphasizing brawn over brain.

Aside from Sandow, the female audience gained its first major opportunity to view semi-naked men courtesy of the sport of boxing. The boxing matches themselves were off-limits to respectable ladies, but the early films of them were not. And thanks to their female appeal, a large number of films of boxing events were made available; more than twenty between 1897 and 1910. At least two American boxing champions — Jack Johnson in 1909 and Jack Dempsey in 1922 — played vaudeville. Even in the early years of the 20th century, female audiences preferred "a bit of the rough" from their male entertainers. They would much rather look at a muscular boxer than, say, dancer Paul Swann, who in 1914 billed himself as "The Most Beautiful Man in the World," and was jeered for his effeminacy.

In recognition of an ever-growing, lascivious female readership, *Playgirl* began publication in May 1973. Intended as a feminist response to *Playboy*, the monthly magazine promised male centerfolds, beginning with Lyle Waggoner, well known at the time for his television appearances with Carol Burnett. In that first issue, Waggoner was cross-legged and revealing nothing, but in the next issue, former movie star George Maharis showed all. The selection of the gay Maharis was indicative of a major problem that *Playgirl* had (along with a lack of quality literary pieces that was comparable to those in *Playboy*). Not only were few heterosexual stars willing to pose frontally nude, but also the readership was becoming increasingly gay. The magazine survives, but makes little pretense to be anything more than a gay publication.

One of the first encounters with full frontal male nudity in a mainstream play came in 1971 with David Storey's *The Changing Room*, starring John Lithgow as a vulnerable, injured and naked football player. Cross-dressing and frontal nudity were issues in David Henry Hwang's 1988 play, *M. Butterfly* (filmed in 1993). Other classic male nudes (and occasional female ones) include *Oh! Calcutta!* (which ended its Broadway run in August 1989), *Angels in America, Equus, Six Degrees of Separation, Hair,* and the strongly gay-oriented *Naked Boys Singing*. In 1995, males were nude on stage in David Dillon's *Party* and Terrence McNally's *Love! Valour! Compassion!* (filmed in 1997). As the decade ended, two Australians, Simon Morley and David Friend, brought their imaginative, if rather boring, presentation, *Puppetry of the Penis,* to the United States after a triumphant run in London. The American publicity was slightly more subdued than the English, which promised, "Two Men, Two Dicks, No Pants." All that was required to perform "genital origami," they explained, was a large penis.

In the late 1990s, Canadian stand-up comic Craig Campbell would perform a routine about circumcision and then physically demonstrate what he was talking about by stripping nude. One woman in the audience was quoted in 1997 as saying, "He's hung like a bear." Nudity definitely helps sell seats, when the naked are Howard Hesseman (*Quills*) or Jude Law (*Indiscretions*).

As a result of the increased demand for male nudity on stage, Actors' Equity Association introduced strict rules, forbidding nudity at auditions until a final callback, no photography of nude scenes without written authorization, and no mingling of naked actors with audience members.

The Chippendales dancers, who fronted their own club in New York from 1982-1990, introduced nudity and male stripping to the average American female. What the Chippendales had done in person, the 1997 British movie *The Full Monty* did on screen for women throughout the world. Written by Simon Beaufoy, the film, which utilizes a slang expression meaning going all the way, is the story of a group of unemployed steel workers in the north of England city of Sheffield. In order to generate some income, they decide to put on a strip show. The leading man, Robert Carlyle as Gaz, is relatively attractive, but what makes *The Full Monty* so appealing is that the other members of the cast and their screen personae are not the usual handsome, virile, muscled studs of female and gay fantasy. Typical is the character of Dave, played by Mark Addy, who is 35 pounds overweight and borders on the obese. The men face a variety of emotional problems, including impotence and latent homosexuality, and the film reverses gender roles with the men stripping for money—and, thereby, prostituting themselves. Women in the audiences are seeing on screen their husbands, neighbors and co-workers putting on a strip show, while the male audience can empathize with the characters and their problems, as well as getting some satisfaction that men no different in appearance or mindset to them can strip and arouse a female audience to screams of delight.

So successful, and rightly so, was *The Full Monty* that it became a 2000 Broadway musical, with a new book by Terrence McNally, and a new setting of Buffalo, New York.

The male penis, particularly in package form, is the unspeakable obsession in American popular culture. It is the reason why the UPS drivers hold such a fascination for the housewives and office workers to whom they deliver and display their packages. What is it about that brown uniform that is so appealing compared, say, to the crisp white shirts and blue trousers of the Federal Express deliverymen? As *The Wall Street Journal* once noted, it is the "complete package" that is as provocative as the company's telephone number: 1-800-PICK-UPS.

CHAPTER TWELVE

Substance Abuse

Alcohol is the drug of popular American choice, followed, in what is probably a fairly tight race by cigarettes (legal) and assorted drugs from marijuana to cocaine (illegal). The manner in which office workers gather in vaguely sinister groups outside their workplaces, hastily puffing away on cigarettes, might lead any non-American to the conclusion that cigarettes are, in reality, illegal. All manner of drugs have been featured in all forms of 20th century entertainment. Some of its better-known names may have taken a different viewpoint, but Hollywood's corporate attitude toward drugs has almost always been a negative one (although the results sometimes have been so unintentionally amusing as to suggest the opposite).

That all-American genre, the film Western, could not escape the insidious reach of marijuana. As early as 1924, *Notch Number One* featured a scene in which the All-American hero goes berserk after smoking marijuana or "loco weed." The 1929 Yakima Canutt vehicle, currently in video distribution as *High on the Range*, but original released under a different title, implies that marijuana was firmly entrenched as part of American social behavior. At one point, a character comments, "There's too much marijuana smoking on this ranch." The anti-drug sentiment of the 1936 features, *Reefer Madness* and *Marijuana* (subtitled "The Weed with Roots in Hell") is so heavy-handed that the reissue of these films in the 1970s proved popular with marijuana-smoking American college students.

As early as 1894, Thomas Edison copyrighted *Chinese Opium Den*. The emphasis in this and other early films was on opium rather than other types of drugs, and generally they warned of the dangers of smoking. A notable exception is D.W. Griffith's *Broken Blossoms* (1919), in which the Richard Barthelmess character is seen enjoying opium as a blessed relief from the discrimination that he, as a Chinese immigrant, experiences in London's Limehouse district.

Another early Hollywood star, Douglas Fairbanks, Sr., demonstrates the effects of cocaine addition in *The Mystery of the Leaping Fish* (1916), in which he plays Coke Ennyday, a detective whose boundless energy and verve is the result of a daily dose of the drug. Ultimately, the film denigrates the recreational use of cocaine, and pictures foreigners, rather than Americans, as purveyors of the drug. Around the same time as the release of the film, composer W.C. Powell wrote two songs whose titles leave no doubt as to their subject matter: "Dope" and "The Dopey Rag."

One of the two leading ladies in *The Mystery of the Leaping Fish* was Alma Rubens, who died at the age of 33 in 1931 of drug addiction. Other silent stars whose early deaths were the result of over-indulgence in drugs include Olive Thomas, Barbara La Marr, Mabel Normand and Wallace Reid. Later Hollywood stars whose names were linked to drugs include John Belushi, Errol Flynn, Bela Lugosi, and River Phoenix. In 1948, Robert Mitchum was charged with possession of marijuana and served a brief jail term; in the 1960s he remarked disingenuously, "I've been smoking it since 1945 and it never got to be a habit with me." In 1960, Cary Grant, childless, discontented and apparently unable to fall in love, took to experimenting with L.S.D. He told the fan magazines that L.S.D. had made him "ready for life, ready for love," and *Modern Screen* (June 1960) avidly informed its readership, "The daring experiment with the drug called L.S.D. has proved to be a success."

In the 1920s, Hollywood was so linked to the use of drugs in the minds of American audiences that on January 22, 1922, the trade paper *The Moving Picture World* published a poem titled "In Hollywood the Poppies Blow":

In Hollywood the poppies blow,
Tall columns rise of poppy smoke.

INCORRECT ENTERTAINMENT

The correspondents snuff the "snow,"
Then write in dreams that come from "coke."

The hop pipes glow, the stories grow –
Old heroin provides the facts –
Imaginations slumming go,
And twist the simple, kindly acts.

And hemp, the hasheesh and the dope
Arrange that blameless folk bear blame.
Fake interviews with shadow ghosts
Are easy when you use no name.

The orgies that they write about
Are brain creations of their own,
The lethal fumes arising high
Come up in rings that they have blown.

It matters not how wild the lie,
If readable "it's fit to print."
The buzzards to their carrion fly
And gorge their public without stint.

In Hollywood the poppies blow;
They will continue so to do
Until the voice of truth prevails
And tells the liars they are through.

The two best-known propagandists for the drug craze of the 1970s were Cheech and Chong, a comedy teamed formed in January 1970 by Richard Marin (born 1946) and Tommy Chong (born 1938). Noted for their gags on the subject of pot, the couple told *Rolling Stone* (December 14, 1978), "We want to be the Bob Hopes of the doper generation, smoking onstage." Cheech and Chong appeared in live concerts throughout the United States and Canada, and were particularly popular with campus audiences. They released their first album, *Cheech & Chong*, in September 1971, and made their first feature film, *Up in Smoke*, for Paramount in 1978, under the direction of Lou Adler. *Up in Smoke* was the first major Hollywood feature since World War II with a sympathetic approach to marijuana use, as Cheech and Chong go in search of pot, pursued by narcotics detective Stacy Keach. Since 1985, Cheech and Chong have gone their separate ways, and both have mellowed as the political climate has turned to the right.

Drug use was virtually ignored by Hollywood in the 1940s, but was the subject of critical examination in the 1950s with *The Man with the Golden Arm* (1955), *Monkey on My Back* (1957) and *A Hatful of Rain* (1957). The drug scene of the 1960s led to a number of films promoting a positive approach to the subject, including *The Trip* (1967), *I Love You, Alice B. Toklas* (1968), *Easy Rider* (1969), *Bob & Carol & Ted & Alice* (1969), *Zabriskie Point* (1970), and *The Magic Garden of Stanley Sweetheart* (1970). Since then, the only individuals who have had fun with drugs have been the characters of Edina Monsoon and Patsy Stone, as played by Jennifer Saunders and Joanna Lumley, in the BBC television series *Absolutely Fabulous* (1992-1995).

The American tribal love-rock musical of the 1960s, *Hair*, emulated the youth culture of the decade, advocating free love and free drugs, and including in its repertoire a song titled "Hashish." With book and lyrics by Gerome Ragni and James Rado, and music by Galt MacDermot, *Hair* opened off-Broadway as a New York Shakespeare Festival Public Theatre (Joseph Papp) presentation at the Anspacher Theatre on October 17, 1967. With a cast including both Ragni and Rado, the show opened on Broadway at the Biltmore Theatre on April 29, 1968. It was filmed by director Milos Forman in 1979, and seems as dated as the hippy generation it glorifies.

"Hashish" was not the only song on the subject of marijuana. African American orchestra leader Cab Calloway popularized two similar numbers, "The Wail of the Reefer Man," by Ted Koehler and Harold Arlen, introduced in the 1932 New York revue *Cotton Club Parade*, and "Reefer Man" by J. Russell Robinson, first heard in the 1933 Paramount feature *International House*. Two other songs from the same period are "Smokin' Reefers" by Howard Dietz and Arthur Schwartz, introduced in the New York revue *Flying Colors* in 1932; and "Marahuna" [sic] by Sam Coslow and Arthur Johnson, introduced by Gertrude Michael in the 1934 Paramount feature *Murder at the Vanities*.

A country-and-western song from the 1930s, performed by the Memphis Jug Band, and with uncredited lyrics, is titled "Cocaine Habit." The Memphis Jug Band urges its listeners to "take a whiff on me," as well as pointing out,

> I love my whiskey and I love my gin,
> But the way I love my coke is a darn gone sin.
> [And]
> Since cocaine went out of style,
> You can catch me shooting needles all the while

Drug use is generally accepted in the recording industry, but drug dealing as a funding means is a little more difficult to document. In all probability, rapper Eazy-E, whose real name was Eric Wright (1963-1995), founded his record label, Ruthless Records, with drug money. Eazy-E certainly deserves recognition for a lack of political correctness in his friendship with one of the policeman accused of beating Rodney King and in donating $2,500 for the 1991 presidential election campaign of George Bush. On stage, prolific playwright Clyde Fitch was responsible for *The City*, in which drugs played a major role as a son discovers that his father has another, illegitimate, son, who is engaged to his sister. So profane was the production that two women in the audience fainted at the first performance at the Hyperion Theatre, New Haven, on November 15, 1909. First seen on the London stage in November 1924, Noel Coward's drama, *The Vortex*, dealt outrageously with the "vortex of beastliness" that traps a son and his drugs and a mother and her lovers, although later audiences would realize that it was homosexuality rather than drugs with which the son had a problem. Some British critics suggested that a Broadway production would be an insult to the people of England, but *The Vortex* opened in New York at the Henry Miller Theatre on September 16, 1925, starring Noel Coward as Nicky and Lillian Braithwaite as his mother.

Two major productions dealing with drug addiction were produced on the New York stage in the 1950s. Michael V. Gazzo's *A Hatful of Rain* opened at the Lyceum Theatre on November 9, 1955, starring Ben Gazzara as the likeable dope addict Johnny Pope. Tennessee Williams' drama of an aging movie actress with a drug and alcohol problem and her young gigolo, *Sweet Bird of Youth*, opened at the Martin Beck Theatre on March 10, 1959, starring Geraldine Page and Paul Newman. Don Murray starred in the film version of *A Hatful of Rain* (1957). Gavin Lambert extensively revised *Sweet Bird of Youth* for the screen, and provided Elizabeth Taylor with one of many opportunities for a performance verging on the camp.

Jeanne Eagels, one of the great theatrical stars of the 1920s, was a heroine addict whose life ended tragically in 1929 at the age of 39. She was portrayed on screen by Kim Novak in the 1957 film titled with a singular lack of originality, *Jeanne Eagels*. Neither the film nor Novak captured the appropriate period feel.

From the 1940s through the 1950s, black comedian Richard Buckley, billed as Lord Buckley (1906-1960), smoked marijuana on stage while discussing such politically incorrect topics as Jesus Christ and the Marquis de Sade.

No discussion of the power of drugs could fail to include Sherlock Holmes, whose drug of choice was cocaine in the stories and novels by Sir Arthur Conan Doyle. Only one classic Sherlock Holmes feature film makes reference to Holmes' chemical nemesis, and that is the 1939 version of *The Hound of the Baskervilles*, which ends with Basil Rathbone as Holmes saying to Nigel Bruce, "Watson—the needle!"

Holmes' drug use was first mentioned in the 1887 short story, "The Five Orange Pips." In *The Sign of the Four*, published in 1890, it is revealed that since July or September 1887, Holmes had been injecting himself with cocaine some three times daily, in an effort to reduce his melancholia. However, by 1896, and publication of the story "The Missing Three-Quarter," Dr. Watson was able to reveal that Holmes had been "weaned" of his "drug mania," and there is no reference to it in any of the Sherlock Holmes stories of the 20th century. The cocaine habit may have played only a minor role in the Sherlock Holmes saga, but it did lead George Bernard Shaw to dismiss the Baker Street detective as "a drug addict without a single amiable trait."

The use of cocaine in the 19th century was neither unusual nor illegal. When John Pemberton introduced Coca-Cola in 1886, it contained, as the name suggests, cocaine, acting as a both a stimulant and the origin of the bitter undertaste. It was not until 1903 that the use of cocaine in the soda was discontinued. A number of stimulant wines were marketed in the late 1800s, all containing cocaine. The most famous was Via Mariani, for which Charles Gounod wrote a song, and which was endorsed in 1898 by Pope Leo XIII.

As politically incorrect as it may be to endorse cigarette smoking today, it was once a standard commodity on American cinema screens. After all, Georges Bizet's 1875 opera, *Carmen*, is set in a cigarette factory. In 1897, the Edison Mfg. Co. produced a film advertising Admiral Cigarettes. Why shouldn't what was good enough for the 19th century be promoted as entertainment in the 20th? As early as 1907, Jean C. Havez and Louis Hirsch composed "The Land of Nicotine." Everyone smoked and American stars routinely endorsed their favorite brands in magazines and newspapers. In 1928, Lucky Strike (manufactured by the American Tobacco Company) began comparing its product to something somewhat less dangerous — candy. "Reach for a Lucky — instead of a sweet," the company advertised, utilizing endorsements from celebrities including Alice Brady, George Gershwin, John Gilbert, and Constance Talmadge. "I light a Lucky and go light on the sweets. That's how I keep in good shape and always feel peppy," explained Al Jolson. Amelia Earhart confessed that she carried Lucky Strikes with her on her record-breaking 1928 TransAtlantic flight. As late as the 1950s, Liggett & Myers advertised, "Rosalind Russell says L&M filters are just what the doctor ordered," while at the same time, Jack Webb was inviting Americans to join him in smoking L&Ms.

In the 1930s and 1940s, radio listeners were all too familiar with the various brands of cigarettes sponsoring their favorite programs, which often contained the brand name in their titles. There was *The Camel Caravan*, a comedy-variety show running from 1933-1954, and Camel also sponsored *The Screen Guild Theater* from 1947-1949. Described by one contemporary publication as "Lady Nicotine's newest baby," *The Chesterfield Quarter-Hour* of dance music was heard from 1931-1933. There was also *The Chesterfield Show*, with Andre Kostelanetz and His Orchestra from 1934-1939, *Chesterfield Time* with Fred Waring and His Orchestra from 1939-1944, and the music-variety show *The Chesterfield Supper Club* from 1944-1949. The theme song for the latter was the 1938 Charles Kenny and Nick Kenny number, "While a Cigarette Was Burning."

Lucky Strike sponsored two of the most popular programs on radio, *Your Hit Parade* (from 1935-1937), and, from 1944-1948, *The Jack Benny Program* was retitled *The Lucky Strike Program*. Philip Morris sponsored *Crime Doctor* from 1940-1947 and *It Pays to Be Ignorant* from 1944-1948. From 1939-1944, it also had *The Philip Morris Playhouse*, with four-foot midget Johnny Roventini, in pageboy uniform, reminding listeners "you get no cigarette hangover" with Philip Morris and urging them to "calllll for Philip Mor-raisss!"

The character of Carmen is obviously the basis for the Spanish cigarette maker portrayed by Geraldine Farrar in the 1920 silent film *The Woman and the Puppet*, and played by Marlene Dietrich in the 1935 production of *The Devil Is a Woman*. The North Carolina tobacco industry in the 1890s is the subject of *Bright Leaf* (1950), starring Gary Cooper and based on the 1948 novel by Foster Fitz-Simons.

"Cigarette smoking has ... long been one of the theater's most powerful means of expression," wrote critic Walter Kerr in the *New York Times* (January 30, 1981). A shared cigarette — two cigarettes lit by one male — is an integral part of *Now, Voyager* (1942), starring Paul Henreid and Bette Davis, with the former asking, "Shall we just have a cigarette on it?" That same concept had been the basis for the 1934 Paul Francis Webster and Lew Pollack song, "Two Cigarettes in the Dark." Robert Walker expresses his love for Jennifer Jones with a cigarette in *Since You Went Away* (1944). Humphrey Bogart is first seen smoking a cigarette in *Casablanca* (1942), and is seldom without one in *The Maltese Falcon* (1941) and *The Big Sleep* (1946). Cigarette smoking is the symbol of the liberated woman, with Lauren Bacall making her entrance in *To Have and Have Not* (1944) with the demand that Humphrey Bogart light her cigarette.

There was no clear-cut delineation between heroes and villains as far as cigarette smoking went on screen. Edward R. Murrow reported on the effects of Nazi bombing on wartime Britain with a cigarette in his hand. Erich von Stroheim was a symbol of perversity on screen in *Blind Husbands* (1918) and *Foolish Wives* (1921) with a cigarette always to hand. Peter Lorre symbolized Nazi tyranny—with a cigarette in his hand—in *The Cross of Lorraine* (1943). Representing both good and evil, Mary Astor, Humphrey Bogart and Sydney Greenstreet all enjoy a cigarette in *Across the Pacific* (1942).

Those opposed to cigarette smoking were ridiculed as in RKO's *What a Blonde!* (1945), in which Leon Errol, who is allergic to tobacco smoke, is practically asphyxiated in a railroad carriage filled with smokers. As the poor man attempts to open the carriage window and get air, he is subjected to both verbal and physical abuse.

In an industry that was carefully self-regulated by the Production Code Administration, the so-called Hays Office, cigarettes could serve as an obvious substitute for sex. When Joan Collins tells Ray Milland in *The Girl in the Red Velvet Swing* (1955) that she knows how to puff on a man's cigar, there is no doubt as to the phallic connotation.

William Holden chain-smoked in *The World of Suzie Wong* (1960). Tom Cruise lit up in *Rain Man* (1988). In *Lethal Weapon 2* (1989), Mel Gibson, who is obviously no supporter of political correctness, is a police detective lighting up in defiance of the "No Smoking" signs. *The Client* (1994) opens with a ten-year-old teaching an eight-year-old how to relax with a cigarette, and later Susan Sarandon does just precisely that with a cigarette.

The squeaky-clean Walt Disney Company has not been on the side of political correctness when it comes to smoking. Both Geppetto and Pinocchio puff on stogies in *Pinocchio* (1940). Captain Hook favors a cigar and Peter Pan a pipe in *Peter Pan* (1953). And, as late as *Aladdin* (1992), the genie is a cigarette smoker.

A study in the *American Journal of Public Health* (June 20, 1994) noted that tobacco use on screen had not declined despite a reduction in Americans who smoked. The journal pointed out that the adopted mother of *E.T. The Extra-Terrestrial* (1982) smoked, as did the crew of *Ghostbusters* (1984). Philip Morris paid $42,500 to have Lois Lane smoke in *Superman* (1978), despite the character's not smoking in the comic books. In 1989, Philip Morris paid $350,000 to have Timothy Dalton as James Bond smoke a Lark in *License to Kill*.

Just as with James Bond, cigarette manufacturers, while always striving to appeal to the female smoker, have tended to emphasize the masculine element in smoking. During World War II, Lucky Strike promoted its brand with the description, "So round, So Firm, So Fully Packed, So Free and Easy on the Draw." The phallic symbolism was such that smokers might be deceived into believing that a Lucky Strike could not only compensate for a woman but also calm masturbatory cravings. Philip Morris introduced Marlboro cigarettes in 1955, initially for the women's market. Very quickly, the company changed the impetus, and created the Marlboro Man, often depicted as a Western-style hero on horseback, and in its television advertising used sophisticated entertainer, Julie London, in a nightclub setting, singing, "You Get a Lot to Like with a Marlboro." In response, a 1963 advertising campaign from Lucky Strike promoted the theme that "smoking is a pleasure meant for adults," and that "Lucky Strike Separates the Men from the Boys."

Cigarette advertising has been banned on television since 1971, but while some series, such as *Cheers*, are smoke-free environments, others are not. The main exceptions are programs from the United Kingdom, such as the detective series, *Prime Suspect*, with Helen Mirren, which features an ongoing fight over cigarettes.

The Washington, D.C.-based Tobacco Institute is, in fact, unwilling to dictate to the film or television industry in regard to tobacco usage. There is, however, some censorship of older television programs. When Nickelodeon screens *I Love Lucy*, it removes the original openings by sponsor Philip Morris, in which Lucy and Desi in caricature are seen smoking.

As early as 1902, two of Chekhov's one-act plays, *Smoking Is Bad for You* and *The Evils of Tobacco*, had been translated and published for the American vaudeville stage; in both Nyukhin lectures the ladies of his wife's boarding school. It was not until 1973 that an American playwright, Frederick Feirstein, warned of the pollution of the environment as a result of smoking in *The Family Circle*. On radio in the 1930s, the popular comedy series *Vic and Sade*, starring Arthur Van Harvey and Bernadine Flynne, featured a couple of episodes on smoking; in "Vic Breaks in Mr. Ruebush's Pipe" (1934), the son takes up pipe smoking after seeing how much his father enjoys it, while in "Harold (Rotten) Davis Takes Up the Tobacco Habit" (1937), a teenager brags of smoking while his friend faints away.

On record, Vaughn Monroe had sung "The Story of Two Cigarettes" by Mickey Stoner, Fred Jay and Leonard K. Marker in 1945; the Sons of the Pioneers had introduced "Cigareetes, Whisky and Wild, Wild Women" by Tim Spencer in 1947; and Peggy Lee had warned "Don't Smoke in Bed" in 1948. Taking a comment from Rudyard Kipling as their basis, Harry B. Smith and Victor Herbert had pointed out in the 1905 musical, *Miss Dolly Dollars* that "A Woman Is Only a Woman but a Good Cigar is a Smoke." While in 1930, Rube Bloom and Harry Woods had written of "The Man from the South (with a Big Cigar in His Mouth)."

Introduced by Ruth Etting in the 1931 edition of the *Ziegfeld Follies*, Mack Gordon and Harry Revel composed "Cigarettes, Cigars," which must be the anthem for the girls who once circulated around nightclubs selling cigarettes from a tray slung around their shoulders and across their front:

> Chesterfields, Camels, Luckies, cigars!
> I peddle my wares to "coked" millionaires,
> Rough guys and hoboes, street girls with no beaux—
> Penniless phonies who figure the ponies
> And try to be men of affairs.

The cigar is the classic trademark of a number of comedians, including George Burns, Alan King and Ken Murray. Among major characters who sported cigars are those played by Orson Welles in *Citizen Kane* (1941), Sydney Greenstreet in *The Maltese Falcon*

(1941), Henry Hull in *Lifeboat* (1944), Charles Laughton in *Witness for the Prosecution* (1957), and Jeff Bridges in *Jagged Edge* (1985). In the 1990s, cigar smoking was taken up by a number of female personalities, including Whoopi Goldberg, Madonna, Demi Moore, and Sharon Stone. In 1996, game show host Alex Trebek introduced a line of celebrity cigars, and the characters in Wayne Wang's *Smoke* (1995) are defined by the cigars they prefer.

In 1995, the video *Paula* provided the ultimate tribute to smoking with thirty minutes of nothing more than a woman enjoying a cigarette.

In the early years of the 20th century, a number of songs praised beer with a strong German accent. In 1902, Vincent P. Bryan and Harry von Tilzer wrote "Down Where the Wurzburger Flows," whose lyrics spoke of rivers of beer. Harry von Tilzer also provided the music to Andrew B. Sterling's lyrical "On the Banks of the Rhine with a Stein" (1905). In 1903, Vincent Bryan and J.B. Mullen wrote "Over the Pilsner Foam" and Andrew B. Sterling and Harry von Tilzer (yet again) could be found "Under the Anheuser Busch." That same year, Dan McAvoy wrote and performed "The Beer That Made Milwaukee Famous" and in 1907, Grace LaRue introduced in the *Ziegfeld Follies* "Budweiser's a Friend of Mine" by Vincent Bryan and Seymour Furth.

The joys of alcohol were endorsed in songs such as "Vodka," from the Otto Harbach, Oscar Hammerstein II, Herbert Stothart and George Gershwin musical, *Song of the Flame* (1926); "What's the Use of Getting Sober" by Busby Meyers (1938) and popularized in 1943 by Louis Jourdan and His Tympany Five; "Rum and Coca-Cola" by Morey Amsterdam, Jeri Sullavan and Paul Baron (1944) and made famous by the Andrews Sisters; "More Beer" by Julian H. Miller (1948); and "Bubbles in My Beer" by Tommy Duncan, Cindy Walker and Bob Wills (1948), and first recorded by Bob Wills and His Texas Playboys. "Cocktails for Two," written in 1934 by Arthur Johnson and Sam Coslow, was ridiculed in a popular 1946 recording by Spike Jones and His City Slickers.

Ted Koehler and Harold Arlen contributed "Hittin' the Bottle" to the 1930 version of the *Earl Carroll Vanities*. Al Dubin and Harry

Warren were responsible for "Good Old Fashioned Cocktail (with a Good Old Fashioned Girl)," sung by Ruby Keeler in the 1935 film, *Go into Your Dance*. And in the 1940 Broadway hit, *Panama Hattie*, Ethel Merman requested "Make It Another Old-Fashioned, Please," courtesy of Cole Porter.

In 1950, Amos Milburn had a hit with Thomas Maxwell Davis' "Bad, Bad Whiskey," and three years later with Rudolph Toombs' "One Scotch, One Bourbon, One Beer." Johnny Ray's first recording in 1951 was "Whiskey and Gin." Since 1939, many otherwise conservative and straight-laced Americans have been dancing to the "Beer Barrel Polka" (also known as "Roll out the Barrel") by Lew Brown and Jaromír Vejvoda, which is based on the Czech song, "Skoda Lásky" and was popularized by the Andrews Sisters.

With the passing of the 18th Amendment, the Volstead Act, better known as Prohibition, came into force in 1919 and was as hated in American popular culture as it was in American society. A year earlier, Edgar Leslie, Grant Clarke and George W. Meyer had written a song parodying New York's Blue Laws prohibiting alcohol on Sundays with a reference to the well-known preacher Billy Sunday: "I Love My Billy Sunday But Oh, You Saturday Night." In 1918, William Jerome and Jack Mahoney composed "Every Day Will Be Sunday When the Town Goes Dry." "What'll We Do on Saturday Night When the Town Goes Dry," asked composer Harry Ruby in 1919. That same year, Edward Laska and Harry von Tilzer wrote "The Alcoholic Blues" and Ring Lardner and Nora Bayes offered "Prohibition Blues." On the vaudeville stage in 1919, Belle Baker popularized "America Never Took Water and America Never Will" by J. Keirn Brennan, Gus Edwards and Paul Cunningham. The 1919 musical comedy *Oh, My Dear!* parodied the typical drinking song of the genre with "Sasparilla, Women and Song" by Alfred Bryan and Jean Schwartz. A hillbilly classic, "When the Roses Bloom Again," was parodied by Earl Shirkey and Roy Harper as "When the Roses Bloom Again for the Bootlegger" (no author credited), in which the revenue men discover the singers' still. In the 1919 edition of the *Ziegfeld Follies*, African American entertainer Bert Williams complained "You

Cannot Make Your Shimmy Shake on Tea," written by Rennold Wolf and Irving Berlin.

Flappers invented their own language for alcohol, referring to "giggle water" and "hooch." The Speakeasy was also the "gin mill." A haunting story of the soldiers returned from World War I is told by Johnny Marvin in "I'm the Man That's Been Forgotten," recorded circa 1930 or 1931 and with no author credited. In it, Marvin sings sadly, "I remember days of cheer when we had our stein of beer; can't we have it back again?" Like the man of the title, the song has been forgotten in comparison to "Brother, Can You Spare a Dime?" and "Remember My Forgotten Man."

In the 1920s, songwriters reminded Americans that there were neighboring countries where alcohol was legally available. Irving Berlin's 1920 hit, "I'll See You in C-U-B-A," was one such number that also advised its listeners that the country also had to offer "dark-eyed Stellas [who] light their fellas' panatelas." Yes, in 1920, Cuban cigars were legal. If not Cuba, there was always a quick trip across the St. Lawrence River and the greeting, "Hello Montreal" (written in 1928 by Harry Warren, Billy Rose and Mort Dixon). The notion that alcohol was strictly for medicinal purposes—"The alcohol sold nowadays is for external use"—was ridiculed by Harry von Tilzer, Arthur Terker and William H. Heagney in the 1925 song, "Pardon Me While I Laugh."

Cecil B. DeMille illustrates the hypocrisy of Prohibition in his 1921 film *Forbidden Fruit*, which compares a speakeasy with it limited supply of alcohol to the home of a wealthy family, where cocktails and other alcoholic beverages are readily available. Upton Sinclair's 1931 novel, *The Wet Parade*, provided a highly personal view of the effects of the Volsted Act on one family, and was adapted for the screen by Metro-Goldwyn-Mayer the following year.

The enforcers of Prohibition became public celebrities. Two leading Prohibition agents of the 1920s, Isadore Einstein and Moe Einstein, were dubbed Izzy and Moe, "the clown princes of Prohibition."

Alcohol consumption has always been prominently depicted on screen, and Prohibition certainly had little impact in Hollywood.

Just as each studio had its own bootlegger, selling to star and extra alike, so did the screen readily depict bootlegging and speakeasies as a natural part of American life. No speedy end to Prohibition was expected, as in 1920, the ever-busy Harry von Tilzer composed "Oh! By Jingo," promising "We'll have a lot of little liquor beggars—They'll grow up and be bootleggers."

Many film imports from France and Italy between 1904 and 1909 warned of the dangers of alcoholism. It was the subject of more than forty feature films in the 'teens, including the first version, in 1916, of *Madame X*. Based on a 1908 French play of a divorced woman who becomes an alcoholic and drug addict, *Madame X* was filmed in 1929 with Ruth Chatterton in the title role, in 1937 with Gladys George, in 1966 with Lana Turner, and in 1981 as a made-for-television movie with Tuesday Weld.

More than ninety feature films in the 1920s dealt with the subject of alcoholism, including the first version in 1921 of *Ten Nights in a Bar Room*, based on the classic 1890 melodrama by William W. Pratt. There were more than forty feature films in the 1930s, including *The Drunkard*. This 1935 film was based on an 1843 melodrama of unknown authorship; it ran incredibly for 9,477 performances in Los Angeles from 1933-1959, with audiences going to laugh rather than to learn of the dangers of alcohol.

The industry has always had a drinking problem, on and off screen, and *Daily Variety* (March 26, 1996) provided an interesting survey of actors and actresses who have won Academy Awards for their portrayal of heavy drinkers, beginning with Lionel Barrymore in *A Free Soul* (1931), and continuing with Wallace Beery (*The Champ*, 1931), Bette Davis (*Dangerous*, 1935), Thomas Mitchell (*Stagecoach*, 1939), Van Heflin (*Johnny Eager*, 1942), Ray Milland (*The Lost Weekend*, 1945), James Dunn (*A Tree Grows in Brooklyn*, 1945), Anne Baxter (*The Razor's Edge*, 1946), Claire Trevor (*Key Largo*, 1948), Dorothy Malone (*Written on the Wind*, 1956), Lee Marvin (*Cat Ballou*, 1965), Elizabeth Taylor (*Who's Afraid of Virginia Woolf?*, 1966), Gig Young (*They Shoot Horses, Don't They?*, 1969), Jason Robards (*Julia*, 1977), Maggie Smith (*California Suite*, 1978), Jessica Lange (*Tootsie*, 1982), Dianne

Wiest (*Bullets Over Broadway*, 1994), and Nicolas Cage (*Leaving Las Vegas*, 1995). Shirley Booth won an Oscar for her screen role and a Tony for her New York stage performance as a housewife dealing with her drunken husband (Burt Lancaster) in William Inge's *Come Back, Little Sheba* (1952). Similarly, Grace Kelly won an Oscar for her role as the wife of alcoholic singer Bing Crosby in *The Country Girl* (1954).

It is not always easy to take alcoholism seriously, as proven by the oft-hilarious screen adaptation of Jacqueline Susann's *Valley of the Dolls* (1967), and the even more outrageous "sequel" by critic Roger Ebert, *Beyond the Valley of the Dolls* (1970).

In the mid-1930s, the Production Code Administration tried desperately to restrict depiction of alcohol in films. It had little impact. The problem was that if alcohol was so bad, why was it as popular with movie heroes as with movie villains? There were actors such as Leon Errol, Harry Myers (a brilliant drunk in Chaplin's *City Lights*), Jack Norton, and Arthur Housman, who specialized in portraying drunks on screen, and, apparently, at least Arthur Housman, if not the others, was quite partial to a drink in real life. William Powell and Myrna Loy, as Nick and Nora Charles, were seldom parted from a cocktail in MGM's *Thin Man* series (1934-1947). There have been comic drunk scenes in *Ruggles of Red Gap* (1935), *The Philadelphia Story* (1940), and, of course, in more recent times, *Arthur* (1981), with Dudley Moore as a perpetually drunken millionaire. From its first incarnation as *What Price Hollywood?* in 1932, the story of *A Star Is Born* (1937, 1954 and 1976) relies on alcohol for its plotline. The male stars of the first three, Lowell Sherman, Fredric March and James Mason, are superb drunks. James Stewart can see his six foot, three-and-a-half-inch rabbit, *Harvey* (1950), thanks to his frequent imbibing. The character of Elwood P. Dowd, created by Mary Chase, was introduced on stage at New York's 48th Street Theatre on November 1, 1944, by Frank Fay, who had been an alcoholic but by this time was a coffee addict, drinking as many as 77 cups in a five-hour period.

There have been sympathetic portrayals of alcoholism, notably Claire Trevor, as already noted, in *Key Largo* (1948) and James Cagney, as a newspaperman with a drinking problem, in *Come Fill the Cup* (1951).

Alcohol gives meaning to the marriage of Elizabeth Taylor and Richard Burton in *Who's Afraid of Virginia Woolf?*, and what could be more attractive than Tom Cruise as a bartender in *Cocktail* (1988)?

Real-life battles with alcohol have been featured in *I'll Cry Tomorrow* (1955), with Susan Hayward (who had earlier played an alcoholic singer in *Smash-Up: The Story of a Woman* in 1947) as entertainer Lillian Roth, *The Buster Keaton Story* (1957), with Donald O'Connor as the title character, *Too Much, Too Soon* (1958), with Dorothy Malone as Diana Barrymore, Mickey Rourke as writer Charles Bukowski's alter ego in *Barfly* (1987), and Albert Finney as novelist Malcolm Lowry's alter ego in *Under the Volcano* (1984).

The problems of his parents—alcohol and drug addiction—were influential in the serious, later plays of Eugene O'Neill. *The Iceman Cometh*, a Theatre Guild production that opened at New York's Martin Beck Theatre on October 9, 1946, concerned the "whisky-ridden derelicts" of Harry Hope's bar who are confronted by the "iceman," the reformed alcoholic, originally played by James Barton. While *The Iceman Cometh* was playing New York, the world premiere of O'Neill's *A Moon for the Misbegotten*, again produced by the Theatre Guild, took place in Columbus, Ohio, on February 20, 1947. (It had been finished some seven years earlier.) James Dunn starred as alcoholic landlord James Tyrone, Jr. Completed in 1941, *Long Day's Journey into Night*, featuring a dope-addicted mother and an alcoholic son, eventually received a public presentation on February 10, 1956 in Stockholm, Sweden. *The Iceman Cometh* was filmed in 1973 and *Long Day's Journey into Night* in 1962.

With his first novel, *The Lost Weekend*, Charles Jackson gained instant fame with his depiction of a five-day binge of alcoholic Don Birnam, who also had problems with his latent homosexuality (as did Jackson). The latter problem was scrupulously avoided in Billy Wilder's 1945 film version, starring Ray Milland. The storyline was modernized in *Days of Wine and Roses* (1962), with Jack Lemmon leading his new bride, Lee Remick, down the pathway to alcoholism. In *The Morning After* (1986), Jane Fonda, playing an actress, wakes up in bed with a dead body after a drunken night she cannot recall.

In *Whiskey Galore* (released in the U.S. as *Tight Little Island* in 1949), it is good Scotch whiskey from a sinking ship that is as much the star as any actor. Whiskey can often be "casually" noted on screen, as with Macallan in *Two Deaths* (1995), Glenlivet in *The Birdcage* (1996), Dewars in *Swingers* (1996), and Johnnie Walker in *Donnie Brasco* (1997). When Seagram took over Universal, there was no discernable promotion on screen of its products, Glenlivet and Chivas.

Because the label never seems to change with the decade or even the century, champagne always seems to hold a special, semi-sentimental appeal on screen. In the 1890s, vaudeville and musical comedy star Anna Held toasted audiences with a glass of champagne in a little film that is only a few seconds in length, but is still vibrant with her personality and those expressive eyes. In *The Great Gabbo* (1929), Erich von Stroheim orders Veuve Clicquot—"very cold"—with which to seduce leading lady Betty Compson. Veuve Clicquot was the champagne of choice for Sean Connery as James Bond, although a later Bond, Timothy Dalton, favored Bollinger.

In 1934, Con Conrad, Ben Oakland and Milton Drake composed "The Champagne Waltz," sung by Gladys Swarthout in the 1937 film of the same name, and in 1951 Johnnie Ray recorded "The Lady Drinks Champagne" by Jack Wilson and Alan Jeffreys. In 1939, Evelyn Laye reminded listeners that "All thro' a Glass of Champagne," a poor girl was led into sin, and in the 1958 film, *Gigi*, Leslie Caron enthused about "The Night They Invented Champagne." Champagne has also been known to cause indigestion, as younger listeners of Lawrence Welk and his Champagne Music have discovered.

In all truth, alcohol is a potent—literally—link to the past. In *Cheers for Miss Bishop* (1941), Martha Scott and the married man she loves drink Orvieto wine and he talks of the golden sunshine of Italy represented by its texture. In *Arch of Triumph* (1948), Ingrid Bergman and Charles Boyer may not have Paris, but they do have the Calvados brandy in which to share.

Alcohol on television somehow lacks appeal. It is obviously there—an integral part of *Cheers* (NBC, 1982-1993) with its bar setting. The two stars of *Laverne and Shirley* (ABC, 1976-1983) live in

Milwaukee and work at an unidentified brewery. Everyone on *Dallas* (CBS, 1978-1991) seemed to have a drinking problem — even if they would not always admit it. Larry Hagman, as J.R. Ewing, was seldom without a glass of whiskey in his hand, and in a curious case of life reflecting art, the actor's mother, Mary Martin, was almost killed in 1982 when the car in which she was traveling was hit by a drunken San Francisco driver.

In 1999, in time for the new millennium and a new era of political correctness, the Entertainment Industries Council announced plans to encourage scientifically based depictions of drug, alcohol and tobacco use on the screen and television.

CHAPTER THIRTEEN

The Songs of a Nation

Topical, seldom enduring and often tasteless, the popular song has never been without an enthusiastic if somewhat deluded writer and a performer whose appeal is often questionable.
In the first two decades of the 20th century, presidential campaigns were celebrated in many songs: J.B. Robinson and T.C. O'Kane campaigned for William McKinley and Theodore Roosevelt in 1900 with "Mack and Teddy." "Would You Rather Be a Tammany Tiger than a Teddy Bear" wrote Jeff Branen and W.R. Williams, belittling Theodore Roosevelt, in a 1908 campaign song for William Howard Taft. "Step into Line for Taft" was J.M. Hagen's precise comment. In 1912, Henry D. Kerr and Alfred Solman announced "We're Ready for Teddy Again" and C.H. Congdon's one word title, "Roosevelt," said it all in support of Roosevelt's Progressive Party, while Ballard MacDonald and George Waller Brown announced simply "Wilson — That's All." By 1916, George Fairman was announcing, "We've Got Another Washington and Wilson Is His Name" in readiness for the 1916 presidential campaign.

In the 1910s, the politics heated up. In 1915, Edward M. Zimmerman and Marie Zimmerman composed the anthem, "Votes for Women." The I.W.W. ("Wobblies") had its own anthem in Rudolph von Liebich's "We Have Fed You All for a Thousand Years," published in 1918 and protesting the unequal distribution of food and land.

The 1928 presidential campaign pitted New York governor Al Smith against Herbert Hoover, and Billy Jones and Ernie Hare, "The Happiness Boys," made a recording endorsing both. On one side, they sang, "He's Our Al," written by Harry von Tilzer and Lew Brown, and on the other, "Mr. Hoover and Mr. Smith" by Robert King and Herb Magidson. The latter is obviously based on the classic vaudeville song, "Mr. Gallagher and Mr. Shean." "Mothers dream of having a son like him," sang Jones and Hare of Al Smith. "His guiding light to make thing right is honesty and truth." In "Mr. Hoover and Mr. Smith," the one asks the other if he's dry (i.e., supports Prohibition). The response is that he'll know in November (i.e., after the election).

The fight for Irish independence produced at least one anti-British ballad in 1919, shortly after the end of World War I: "Let's Help the Irish Now" by Bernie Grossman and Billy Frisch. Almost thirty years later, as Jews were fighting the British in Palestine, Jack Yellen and Sammy Fain came up with "The Jews Have Got Their Irish Up." The 1947 ballad has an Irishman supporting the Israeli cause and announcing, "Instead of singing 'Eli, Eli,' they are swinging the shilalee." He continues,

> They're fighting for their home, and, be it Finkelstein or Flynn,
> The man who's fighting for his home is the man who's got to win!

Jewish humor could be found in some early songs, including "My Yiddische Colleen" by Edward Madden and Gus Edwards, featured in the 1911 edition of the *Ziegfeld Follies*, and "My Yiddische Butterfly" by Al Dubin and Joseph Burke, published in 1917 and featured in the revue *The Show of Wonders*. A parody of the popular hit "Poor Butterfly," the song lyrics included "flutter, flutter, flutter, 'round your Abie Perlmutter."

Popular songs could and did promote products. The number of songs referencing beer companies is discussed elsewhere. In the 1901 musical, *The New Yorkers*, Dan Daly introduced a song by George V. Hobart and Ludwig England titled "The Kodak Girl." In 1905, Vincent Bryan and Gus Edwards wrote "In My Merry Oldsmobile," but it was, in reality, a song about dating, and its use as a commercial theme did not occur until decades later.

Walter Michael O'Keefe is not a familiar name in the annals of popular music, but he was the author of such memorable songs as "The Man on the Flying Trapeze," "The Tattooed Lady" and "I'm

Gonna Dance wit' de Guy Wot Brung Me." O'Keefe is also responsible for the 1928 hit, "Henry's Made a Lady out of Lizzie," which celebrates Henry Ford's introduction of a new Model A car to replace his famous Model T or "Tin Lizzie" from 1908. In lyrics that are topical, the song jokes that the Model T had "shaken the hell out of more people than evangelist Billy Sunday ever saw," that the new model has sex appeal or "It" and that it is guaranteed to "live as long as Fannie Ward," the legendary actress whom it was jokingly claimed had heard the cannons boom on the battlefields of Gettysburg. Henry Ford was no stranger to controversy, being the country's leading exponent of anti-Semitism. However, "Business is business," we are reminded and Ford has changed the nose of the car "so she looks like Abie's Irish Rose," a reference to the long-running Broadway show of the 1920s by Anne Nichols in which Jewish Abie marries his Irish girlfriend.

In 1927, Colonel Charles Lindbergh was the first aviator to fly nonstop from New York to Paris, and L. Wolfe Gilbert and Abel Baer celebrated the event with "Lucky Lindy," dedicated to the mother of "the hero of the day." There were other similar songs, including "Lindbergh (The Eagle of the U.S.A.)" and "When Lindy Comes Home," written and introduced by George M. Cohan.

The classic response of popular culture to the Wall Street crash was the October 30, 1929 headline in the trade paper *Variety*, "Wall St. Lays an Egg." A year earlier, the composers of "I Faw Down and Go Boom," had predicted, "I played the market on Wall Street," and "I faw down and go boom." The 1920 hit "Ain't We Got Fun" had promised "The rich get rich and the poor get laid off," and that was the outlook for the decade following the Wall Street Crash

Far more so than their modern equivalents, with the dishonorable exception of recent patriotic ballads, the songs of the past are generally the most outrageous. "Sing us the old ones," the handful of fans would yell at Arthur Tracy, billed as the Street Singer in 1931 and still performing fifty years later. Sentimentality was rife as Tracy serenaded audiences with "Trees," "It's My Mother's Birthday Today," "In a Little Gypsy Tea Room," and his theme song, "Marta, Rambling Rose of the Wildwood." As Noel Coward remarked, there is something terribly potent about cheap music, and this was never more evident than in Tracy's recording of "Pennies from Heaven" as used in the 1981 MGM film of the same title.

While Arthur Tracy was singing about Marta, Nick Lukas was tiptoeing through the tulips. The song was resurrected in January 1968, when a tall man with shoulder-length hair, white makeup, a beaklike nose, an effeminate walk, and a ukulele appeared on Rowan and Martin's *Laugh-In,* singing "Tip-Toe through the Tulips." His name was Tiny Tim, and he became an instant American celebrity, a freak who was apparently as innocent as his talk suggested and who believed in what he was saying to the media. He spoke of a vanished America, of an era which to him was still real: "I just wish I were the RCA Victor dog hearing His Master's Voice." To Tiny Tim, all men were Mister and all women Miss. "I believe in a sense of purity with women. I have to be pure because they're pure," he commented. And to that end, he explained that he took a ninety-minute "big shower" each day, followed by several little showers after "nature calls." Americans by the million watched the *Tonight Show,* starring Johnny Carson, on December 17, 1969, when Tiny Tim married on live television a Philadelphia teenager named Vicki Budinger. Tiny Tim was, in the words of *Time* (May 17, 1968), "the most bizarre entertainer this side of Barnum & Bailey's sideshow," but as pop critic William Kloman wrote in the *New York Times* (March 2, 1969), he was also "a grotesque mirror of our times."

Tiny Tim always refused to reveal his age, telling interviewers, "I really believe I'm nineteen." In reality, he was born Herbert Khaury in New York on April 12, 1933, and had been performing in New York in amateur concerts and nightclubs since the 1950s, calling himself variously Larry Love and Darry Dover. As early as 1954, Khaury used a falsetto voice at the Lion's Club in Greenwich Village. And *Laugh-In* was not Tiny Tim's first television exposure; he had appeared on the Merv Griffin show a number of times since 1966.

In 1968, Tiny Tim appeared in the documentary feature *You Are What You Eat*—he is also featured in the 1987 film *Blood Harvest*—and made his first album, "God Bless You Tiny Tim," which sold more than 100,000 copies. The following year, Doubleday published his book of *Beautiful Thoughts*, and in 1970, he was the subject of a *Playboy* interview. But by 1971, Tiny Tim's career was in decline. "People say I've come back," said the performer in 1979. "I've never been away. I never retired. It's just that since 1970, I've played in places that you probably haven't heard of too often."

Despite the pronouncement after his wedding that the honeymoon would begin with "a three-day fast from S-E-X, not even a kiss," Tiny Tim and his wife were the proud parents of a daughter, Tulip, born in 1971. The couple split up in 1972, and Tiny Tim later married Jan Alweiss in 1984 and Susan Gardner in 1995. The entertainer returned briefly to fame in 1993 when he auditioned, unsuccessfully, for the role of an old woman in the film *Naked Gun 33 ⅓: The Final Insult* (1994). With his last wife, Tiny Tim moved to Minneapolis, and there he died on November 30, 1996 as he performed his signature tune, "Tip-Toe through the Tulips," for the Women's Club of Minneapolis.

Some popular singers lead freak-like existences despite a seemingly staid public presence. One such example is the British recording star Cliff Richard, who was born Harry Webb in Lucknow, India, on October 14, 1940. A major presence in British entertainment, Richard has recorded more than 100 hit records, including "Summer Holiday" (1963), "Congratulations" (1968) and his first American hit, "Devil Woman" (1976).

In 1966, Cliff Richard made a highly publicized conversion to Christianity, changing his image and, surprisingly, reviving his career. He wrote a number of books, and in 1995, he became the first pop singer to be knighted. He is a curious character, beloved of the late Queen Mother, and in denial in regard to sex. Richard has admitted to having sex on only two occasions, once in 1958 and once in 1964. In a 1962 song, co-written with Bruce Welch, he sang of being "a bachelor boy until my dying day," and it is that bachelor boy label that has resulted in his often having to defend himself against charges of being homosexual. The singer has repeatedly stated that he has an updated Sherlock Holmes and Dr. Watson relationship with his live-in companion Bill Latham, and in his 1988 book, *Single-Minded*, he wrote with incredible naiveté, "If every middle-aged man who's single is automatically gay, where does that leave the Pope?"

Cliff Richard's middle-aged and female admirers seem to care little as to his possible sexual orientation. They are reminiscent of the fans who adored those two gay darlings of British musical theatre, Noel Coward and Ivor Novello. To them, like the *Sunday Times* (June 18, 1995), Cliff Richard is "a national treasure."

An American and female equivalent might be Doris Day, born Doris von Kappelhoff in Cincinnati on April 3, 1924. She is certainly not gay, but has become something of a gay icon. A major star from 1948-1968, the singer/actress is inexorably linked to the virginal, all-American image. Freckle-faced and with hair the color of butter that would not melt in her mouth, Doris Day seems almost over-zealous in seeking a virginal image, far removed, apparently, from her early private life; as Oscar Levant once said, "I knew her before she was a virgin."

Doris Day is the star of turgid bio-musicals such as *I'll See You in My Dreams* (1951), in which she plays the wife of lyricist Gus Kahn (best line: "There is more in a man's heart than appears on a cardiogram"); or insipid comedies such as *Do Not Disturb* (1965), in which she stares down a pack of fox hounds and rescues the fox. All in all, she looks less of an artificial creation in black and white. But she can never escape that coldness, that Aryan quality; she is Sonja Henie without the ice skates yet with an unrecognized ill-defined quality.

In direct counterpoint to Doris Day—and from an earlier era—are Sophie Tucker, Mae West and the young Ethel Waters. To most audiences, Sophie Tucker was a "big fat mamma," but earlier in her career, she was the "red-hot momma," with suggestive songs such as "I'm the 3-D Momma with the Big Wide Screen," "I May Be Getting Older Every Day (But Getting Younger Every Night)," "There's More Music in a Grand Baby Than There Is in a Baby Grand," and "There's No Business Like That Certain Business—That Certain Business Called Love." When anti-Semites in a Paris audience hissed her, and when her recordings were banned by the Nazis, Sophie Tucker actually wrote a letter of complaint to Adolph Hitler! Tucker never shied away from jokes about her weight or her age, unlike Mae West who seemed honestly to believe that she was ageless and slim—thanks to heavy makeup and what must have been iron corsets and girdles. She sang of "Any Kind of Man," "Oh, What a Moanin' Man" and reminded her audience, "I'm a Night School Teacher." With her sex was a joke—often a tasteless one. She wrote plays that were "depraved" and dull: *Sex* (1926), *The Drag* (1927) and *Diamond Lil* (1928). The titles and the police efforts to close them are what made them famous not their storylines.

That "camp," homosexual quality was always there. As early as 1916, *Variety* suggested that Mae West would be better in male attire when appearing in a double act with her sister. In the late 1920s, she was talking about the "Pleasure Man" bunch that the police referred to as "fairies." In old age, she was appearing in a nightclub act with a group of loincloth-clad musclemen.

In her later years, Ethel Waters went the opposite way to Mae West. She ceased worrying about her figure and took up religion in heavy-handed fashion. Seeing her in *The Member of the Wedding* (1952), one might be forgiven for forgetting that Ethel Waters once gyrated in almost nothing in the 1928 revue *Africana*, and that some of her best songs are some of the dirtiest ever recorded: "You Can't Do What My Last Man Did," "Shake That Thing" and "My Handy Man."

Arthur Tracy's heart-warming, or perhaps more accurately heart-wrenching, song "It's My Mother's Birthday Today" is typical of a curiously perverse genre in popular music that flourished from the turn of the 19th century through into the late 1920s. When George Jessel ponders whether to sing a fifth reprise of "My Mother's Eyes" in the 1929 film *Lucky Boy*, an old stagehand reminds him that a song about a mother is never old-fashioned. In reality, songs about mother are very antiquated, with dated lyrics open to ridicule even by those to whom the words are dedicated. "My Mother's Eyes" was written by L. Wolfe Gilbert and Abel Baer in response to "Mother of Mine, I Still Have You," the hit song from Al Jolson's film *The Jazz Singer* (1927), written by Grant Clarke, Al Jolson and Lou Silver. A third film of the period, MGM's *The Hollywood Revue of 1929*, features "Your Mother and Mine," written by Joe Goodwin and Gus Edwards, and introduced by Charles King.

One of the earliest Mother songs is Paul Dresser's "Your God Comes First, Your Country Next, Then Mother Dear," published in 1898. It was followed by James R. Horner's "Mother's Hymn to Me" (1901) and George O. Poole and Hattie Starr's "My Onliest Little Dolly" (1901), which tells the tale of a small child who pawns her doll in order to buy bread for her sick mother. In 1903, John McCormack popularized "Mother o' Mine," from the poem by Rudyard Kipling, with music by Frank E. Tours. "Mother o' Mine" should not be confused with the later Al Jolson song or the 1919 "Mammy o' Mine," written by William Tracey and Maceo Pinkard.

There were some comic numbers. In 1906, Arthur Gillespie wrote "Mother Has Got the Habit Now," in which mother joined father in the decision to stop work, and in 1908, Vesta Victoria explained divorce in "Mother Hasn't Spoken to Father Since" by William Jerome and Jean Schwartz. A few years later, both Al Jolson and Nora Bayes had success on the vaudeville stage with "Mother's Sitting Knitting Little Mittens for the Navy," written by R.P. Weston and H.E. Darewski, and published in 1915.

That Southern surrogate mother, the Negro "mammy," was of course not forgotten with "Mammy's Chocolate Soldier" by Sidney Mitchell and Archie Gottler (1918), "I'd Love to Fall Asleep and Wake Up in My Mammy's Arms" by Sam M. Lewis, Joe Young and Fred A. Ahlert (1920), "My Mammy" by Joe Young, Sam M. Lewis and Walter Donaldson (1920), and that paean of praise to Oedipal love, "I'm Missin' My Mammy's Kissin' and I Know She's Missin' Mine" by Sidney Clare and Lew Pollack (1921).

The start of the World War One in Europe and the potential that American might enter the conflict and draft its young men led to a rash of mother songs. Jack Crawford, billed as the poet scout of the Grand Army of the Republic, wrote "My Mother Raised Her Boy to be a Soldier." Far more popular, however, and dedicated to the Mothers of America, Alfred Bryan and Al Piantadosi's "I Didn't Raise My Boy to Be a Soldier" urged America to keep out of the War, and

American sons responded with such affectionate ballads as "M-O-T-H-E-R, a Word That Means the World to Me" by Howard Johnson and Theodore F. Morse (1915), "What a Wonderful Mother You'd Be" by Joe Goodwin and Al Piantadosi (1915), "My Mother's Rosary" by Sam M. Lewis and George W. Meyer (1915), "Ireland Must Be Heaven, for My Mother Came from There" by Joe McCarthy, Howard Johnson and Fred Fisher (1916), "Mother" by Rida Johnson Young and Sigmund Romberg (1916), "Little Mother of Mine" by Walter H. Brown and H.T. Burleigh (1917), "My Mother's Lullaby" by Charles Louis Ruddy and Harold Brown Freeman (1917), and "That Wonderful Mother of Mine" by Clyde Hager and Walter Goodwin (1918). To thank American mothers for ignoring the 1914 plea of Bryan and Piantadosi, Harry A. Ellis and Lew Porter wrote "Mothers of America, You Have Done Your Share" (1919).

The flow of mother songs slowed down but did not abate in the 1920s. It changed pace with Alfred Bryan and Fred Fisher contributing "Daddy, You've Been a Mother to Me" in 1920. It was followed that same year by "That Old Irish Mother of Mine" by William Jerome and Harry von Tilzer. Two Broadway shows introduced mother songs: *Little Nellie Kelly* featured "You Remind Me of My Mother" by George M. Cohan (1922) and *My Maryland* offered simply "Mother" by Dorothy Donnelly and Sigmund Romberg (1927).

As Oedipus Rex proved, we love our mothers, but by the 1950s tastes had changed, it was the father getting the attention with "Oh! My Pa-pa" by Paul Burkhard, John Turner and Geoffrey Parsons (1953), and mothers regarded with a jaundiced eye in "I Saw Mommy Kissing Santa Claus" by Tommie Connor (1952). Only the Country and Western field still found a place for mother love, with Willie Nelson's enjoying considerable success with a new rendition of "My Mother's Eyes."

CHAPTER FOURTEEN

Hollywood's Fascist Follies

In 1934, Metro-Goldwyn-Mayer publicized the latest honor received by contract star Wallace Beery. The award, for Beery's portrayal of Pancho Villa in *Viva Villa!*, was the Gold Medal of Italy's National Fascist Association of Motion Picture and Theatrical Industries. In 1933 and 1934, two Hollywood filmmakers produced features displaying strong fascist undercurrents, Cecil B. DeMille's *This Day and Age* and Harold Lloyd's *The Cat's Paw*. Hitler's favorite filmmaker, Leni Riefenstahl, had difficulty in finding an audience for her 1936 film of the Berlin Olympic Games. Everywhere that is except for Nazi Germany and Los Angeles. One month before the film received its world premiere in Berlin, *Olympia* was given an unofficial world premiere at the Jonathan Club in Los Angeles. The official U.S. premiere of the film took place, perhaps not surprisingly, at another city institution whose membership restrictions against African Americans and others continued to stir controversy well into the last decades of the 20th century, the California Club in downtown Los Angeles.

From a political viewpoint, Hollywood in the 1930s is generally remembered as a fairly liberal community, where the Hollywood Anti-Nazi League and the Motion Picture Democratic Committee flourished, and where producers generated such anti-Nazi, pro-Allied subjects as *Confessions of a Nazi Spy*. The heroes of the day, as of the present in Hollywood, were the liberals, represented back then by Fredric March, Eddie Cantor, Melvyn Douglas, Lillian Hellman, Dalton Trumbo, and Budd Schulberg. The reactionaries are forgotten and might never have existed.

There was, however, another side to that period in Hollywood history, a hypocritical one that saw film studios headed by prominent Jewish businessmen, striving to maintain cordial relations with Nazi Germany and putting economics above human life. The 1930s was also a decade of considerable Fascistic activity within the film industry, with the formation of right-wing, quasi-military squads by at least two Hollywood stars, a fervor for filmmaking within Mussolini's Italy, and a general consensus of opinion that the blessing of the German consul in Los Angeles was more important to a film's success than approval by the Hays Office.

The British blackshirts of Sir Oswald Mosley had their Hollywood counterparts in two private armies, one led by Victor McLaglen and the other by Arthur Guy Empey and Gary Cooper. British-born McLaglen won the 1935 Academy Award for Best Actor for his performance in *The Informer*. Two years earlier, he had become an American citizen and began organizing the California Light Horse Regiment to uphold what he perceived as the values of "Americanism." "Sure, we're organized to fight," he told the Associated Press. "We consider an enemy anything opposed to the American ideal, whether it's any enemy outside or inside these borders. If that includes the Communists in this country, why, we're organized to fight them, too."

The California Light Horse Regiment was modeled after the California Lancers, created by two of Hollywood's "Russian Princes," David and Sergei Mdivani, with backing from their wives, former actress Mae Murray and Mary McCormick. The Mdivanis planned to utilize the California Lancers as part of an attempt to regain their native Georgia from Soviet control.

McLaglen's group was able to establish additional units in Pasadena, Long Beach and Oakland, and claimed to be in touch with similar outfits in Brooklyn, New York, and Washington, D.C. Its biggest show of strength came in December 1934, when McLaglen led his cavalry to William Randolph Hearst's *Examiner* Building in downtown Los Angeles, where a "goodwill serenade in honor of the newspaper" was staged. Subsequently, McLaglen marched his brigade to the American Legion's Olympic Stadium, at which he made a speech on the subject of "America for Americans," looking—according to one contemporary report—"like a combination of a Canadian Mounted Policeman, General Goering and Mussolini."

The actor stoutly defended his regiment against charges of Fascism. In the midst of a 1935 lawsuit involving gambling losses, McLaglen replied to critics, "Some say I'm a Nazi, and some say I'm a Fascist, but here it is straight: I'm just a patriot of the good old-fashioned American kind."

World War I hero Arthur Guy Empey (author of a once popular book titled *Over the Top* which was turned into a silent film) had been a member of the California Light Horse before forming his own regiment, the Hollywood Hussars, in the spring of 1935. As reported in the trade press at the time, the Hollywood Hussars were "armed to the teeth and ready to gallop on horseback within an hour to cope with any emergency menacing the safety of the community—fights or strikes, floods or earthquakes, wars, Japanese 'invasions,' Communistic 'revolutions,' or whatnot."

Co-founder of the Hollywood Hussars was Gary Cooper, who explained the reasons behind the group's creation: "Americanism is an unfailing love of country; loyalty to its institutions and ideals, eagerness to defend it against all enemies; undivided allegiance to the flag; and a desire to secure the blessings of liberty to ourselves and posterity. Therefore, Americanism is the foundation upon which we are building the American Hussars. We are solemnly pledged to uphold and to protect the sacred principles and ideals of our country."

Cooper's involvement with the Hussars was brief. Exhibitors protested the actor's participation in such a group, and in June 1935, Paramount issued a formal statement that its contract star was withdrawing his support and endorsement. Noting that the Hollywood Hussars was now being promoted as a national organization of a semi-military-political nature, Paramount quoted Arthur Guy Empey that "the organization has outgrown the purpose for which Cooper organized it ... The Hussars, however, are not a Fascist or a political group."

On April 2, 1938, the British fan magazine *Film Weekly* announced that the screen's best-known vamp, Theda Bara was to return to filmmaking. She was about to leave for Italy, where her productions would be directed by her husband Charles Brabin, and sponsored by Mussolini.

"Italy has been hurt that we have an unfair attitude towards Fascism, that we don't understand that Italy wants to help the Ethiopians, that the Ethiopians welcomed the Italian armies and went gladly over to their side. We only hear the other side of the picture over here. Mussolini? He's marvelous! Marvelous! Plain! Simple! Sympathetic! Marvelous Man! Knows everything!"

The speaker was not a politician from the extreme right, but Hollywood producer Walter Wanger, announcing plans to make between one and three features a year in Italy beginning in the fall of 1936. The first production was to be *Three Times Loser*, starring Sylvia Sidney and Henry Fonda, and directed by either Gregory LaCava or William K. Howard. Supporting Wanger's plans was distributor United Artists on whose board were Charlie Chaplin (who voiced no disagreement with the plan) and the Bank of America's Dr. A.H. Giannini. It was the latter who welcomed Carlo Roncoroni, president of Italy's Fascist National Confederation of Builders and member of the Joint Executive of the Fascist Confederation of Industrials, to Hollywood to discuss filmmaking ventures between Hollywood and Rome.

A year later, in September 1937, the *New York Times* reported Mussolini's arrival in Munich for a meeting with Hitler, at which "all stage and film stars and some of Germany's prettiest girls were assembled by Leni Riefenstahl, feminine arbiter of the Nazi picture world." While his father was enjoying a visit with Hitler, Vittorio Mussolini was arriving in New York en route to study film production in Hollywood at the invitation of Hal Roach, the man responsible for the comedy successes of Laurel and Hardy, Harold Lloyd and Our Gang. Greeting the Duce's son were Roach and Charles Pettijohn, general counsel for the Hays office.

Hal Roach announced plans for a new production company, Mussolini-Roach-RAM Pictures, which was to make musicals and operas in Italy. Conspicuously absent was any representative of Roach's American distributor, Metro-Goldwyn-Mayer, which was initially announced as one of the financial sponsors of the scheme. MGM's president, Nicholas M. Schenck, made it very plain to Roach that his company would not be associated with Mussolini. Nevertheless, Hal Roach was full of enthusiasm for his new project. He told *Motion Picture Daily*, "Mussolini wants his son to go into business. Vittorio decided on the film business and I'm sort of a chaperon. I think Benito Mussolini is the only square politician I've ever seen."

The dictator's son was taken before the newsreel cameras, and the children from the *Our Gang* series were introduced to him, and expressed their enthusiasm at his visit. Less enthusiastic was the Hollywood Anti-Nazi League and the Motion Picture Artists Committee, both of which organized protests and forced curtailment of Vittorio Mussolini's visit to Hollywood. Neither Wanger nor Roach produced any Italian films. When I challenged Roach about the partnership, he maintained that it would have gone forward had it not been for World War II and the problem that "The Jewish people in the picture business didn't like it."

Hal Roach was not the only comedy producer with a streak of anti-Semitism. It was quite prevalent among his contemporaries. Mack Sennett was notoriously anti-Semitic. *Sunset Magazine* (August 1923) published a glowing profile of comedian Harold Lloyd, and ended its piece with the most astonishing comment: "One of the most important experiments the cinema has ever known is being conducted at the Lloyd workshop. Nowhere in the offices, on the stages or in the dressing rooms can be seen a Semitic countenance. As everyone knows, the lost tribe of Israel has turned up in the rich field of the movies. Where there is honey there are bees. But the bees buzzeth not on the Lloyd lot."

Mussolini was not the only dictator interested in the Hollywood film industry. In March 1938, Herbert J. Yates, the head of Republic Pictures, told *Motion Picture Herald* that the Japanese government had offered to purchase his company, intending to use it and, presumably its best-known leading man John Wayne for "propaganda purposes." A year earlier, reports had circulated that the German government was planning a circuit of nineteen theatres to be located in New York, Chicago, San Francisco, Philadelphia, and Detroit.

Olympia, Leni Riefenstahl's feature-length film of the 1936 Olympic Games held in Berlin, is not simply a documentary of a historic event, but more precisely a paean of praise to National Socialism, with abundant shots of Hitler, swastikas and Fascist salutes (erroneously identified as Olympic salutes). Much of the civilized world regarded *Olympia* as little more than Nazi propaganda, and the Hollywood Anti-Nazi League worked strenuously to prevent the film's release in the United States.

The German government financed a trip to America by Leni Riefenstahl in November 1938 in the hope that the filmmaker might be able to persuade an American distributor to handle the production. Riefenstahl arrived in New York, aboard the *Europa*, on November 4, 1938, and quickly enjoyed the pleasures of New York's nightspots. As reported in *The Hollywood Tribune* (June 2, 1939), she visited an all-black revue, commenting, "It is all breath-taking jungle ability, but no brains and no inspiration. Did a Negro ever make a great invention?" As an afterthought, Riefenstahl opined, "The Jews are backing the Negroes politically. Under their influence the Negroes will become Communists, and so the Jew and the Negro will bring bolshevism to America." Despite such remarks, the filmmaker was generally welcomed during her stay at the Hotel Pierre. *The New York Daily News* called her "charming," and columnist Walter Winchell considered her "as pretty as a swastika."

John E. Otterson, who had served as president of Paramount Pictures from 1935-1936, and was regarded in Germany as being anti-Semitic, promised to help Riefenstahl in selling her film in the United States. She was feted at a private dinner party by John Abbott of the Museum of Modern Art and his wife, Iris Barry, founder of the Museum's Department of Film.

However, events outside of the United States caught up very quickly with Leni Riefenstahl. In Germany, on the night of November 11, 1938, Kristallnacht, the anti-Jewish pogrom, including the burning and looting of synagogues and Jewish stores and the torture, beating and rounding up for removal to concentration camps of vast numbers of Jews, took place. The German consul in New York urged Riefenstahl to return to Germany, but instead she moved on to Chicago, where she was entertained by such well-known members of the American anti-Semitic community as Avery Brundage and Henry Ford. Buoyed by news from Los Angeles that the pro-Nazi skating star Sonja Henie might be willing to help release the film, Leni Riefenstahl decided to visit California.

She arrived on the *Super Chief* on November 24, 1938, intending to stay at the Garden of Allah Apartments in West Hollywood. However, demonstrations outside the complex made her change plans and rent a bungalow at the Beverly Hills Hotel. The Hollywood Anti-Nazi League published a full-page advertisement in *The Hollywood Reporter* for November 29, 1938, announcing, "THERE IS NO ROOM IN HOLLYWOOD FOR LENI RIEFENSTAHL." The following day, *Daily Variety*'s front page announced, "Hitler 'Girl Friend' Barred at Studios." However, both trade papers were somewhat incorrect. There was room for Leni Riefenstahl at the home of 20th Century-Fox executive Winfield Sheehan, Hal Roach gave a dinner in her honor, and Walt Disney accompanied her on a three-hour tour of his studio.

Although *Olympia* had supposedly not been seen in the United States, such is not the case. Riefenstahl had earlier shipped a rough cut of the film to her friend in Los Angeles, Hubert Stowitts, and, a month before the official Berlin premiere, he screened the film — on March 13, 1938 — at the Jonathan Club, at a dinner attended by a group of Olympic athletes. While Riefenstahl was on her Los Angeles visit, Harrison Chandler, the son of the publisher of the *Los Angeles Times*, was able to arrange for a screening of the film at the California Club, on December 14, 1938. Everyone attending the screening was sworn to secrecy as to Chandler's involvement in organizing the event and the California Club's participation. However, the film was reviewed — favorably — in both the *Hollywood Citizen-News* and the *Los Angeles Times*.

Early in January 1939, Riefenstahl returned to New York, without finding an American distributor for *Olympia*. "I hope next time it will be different when I come, yes?" she said, as she waved farewell from the train.

Leni Riefenstahl returned to the Los Angeles area in 1997 to receive a lifetime achievement award at the film buff convention, Cinecon. The event was held in the city of Glendale, and the filmmaker might have felt right at home there had she taken a close look at the design on the bases of the community's lampposts. Installed between 1924 and 1926, 930 lampposts in Glendale boast swastika-like designs. Irv Rubin of the Jewish Defense League tried to have the symbols removed in August 1995, but was unsuccessful when it was pointed out that the swastika-like designs were actually Native American symbols.

Had Irv Rubin checked a little more closely, he would have found many examples of such designs in American popular culture. Filmmaker Marshall Neilan used the swastika as a production logo in the 1920s and it may be seen on the titles and subtitles of many of his films. In 1908, the vaudeville team of Carter & Bluford introduced the popular song, "Swastika Sue," about a Native American who wears a swastika around her neck:

> Swastika Sue! Sue! I love-a you!
> Give me for keeps your talisman true.
> With it to guide me, I'll be true blue.
> Good luck and long life, Swastika Sue.

Producer Stanley Kramer could not resist using a swastika as part of the design of his stationary during production of *Judgment at Nuremberg* in 1961.

Irv Rubin's attack on the city of Glendale is typical of Hollywood hypocrisy. When Riefenstahl received her award in 1997, there were virulent attacks on her by the Jewish community writing in the *Los Angeles Times*. The following year when she sat down at a *Time* magazine luncheon at Radio City Music Hall, celebrating the magazine's 75th anniversary, she shared a table with Steven Spielberg. Neither Spielberg nor the Jewish community offered one word of condemnation of Riefenstahl or *Time* magazine.

Conspicuous during Riefenstahl's 1939 arrival at and departure from Los Angeles was Dr. George Gyssling, German consul in Los Angeles. Gyssling kept a close watch on the Hollywood film industry, determined to ensure that nothing anti-Nazi appeared on screen. Gyssling's censorship operation first came to public attention in June 1938, when it was revealed that he had sent threatening letters to the cast of Universal's *The Road Back*. The film, based on the novel by Erich Maria Remarque, is a post-war sequel to *All Quiet on the Western Front*, and was considered "unfriendly" to the Hitler regime. Barbara Read, Louise Fazenda, John King, Andy Devine, Slim Summerville, and John Emery were some of the actors who received a registered letter which read:

"With reference to the picture, 'The Road Back,' in which you are said to play a part, I have been instructed by my government to issue to you a warning in accordance with Article 15 of the German decree of June 28, 1932, regulating the exhibition of foreign motion pictures.

"Copy and translation of this article are enclosed herewith. You will note that the allocation of permits may be refused for films with which people are connected who have already participated in the production of pictures detrimental to German prestige in tendency or effect in spite of the warnings issued by the competent German authorities."

The inference was clear. Once a performer worked in an anti-German production, the studios would be warned that any future films featuring that performer would be subject to a boycott in German-controlled territories. A blacklist was in effect.

Actor John Emery was so angered by his letter that he approached the State Department, demanding, "Advise me whether, as a citizen of the United States, if in future it will be incumbent upon me in seeking my livelihood to yield to the pressure which is brought to bear upon me by a foreign consul."

As a result of Emery's protest, the State Department lodged a formal complaint with the German government, which assured the U.S. that no threatening letters would be sent in the future to Hollywood actors and actresses. In fact, the German Consul did not need to send such letters in regard to *The Road Back*. J. Cheever Chowdin of Universal reportedly met with Joseph Goebbels, who agreed to permit the film's German release on the understanding that Universal would change the ending to glorify Hitler. Although Universal subsequently denied that such a meeting had taken place, the company did alter the film with the addition of romantic scenes and the deletion of political ones. "Politics and fear had nothing whatever to do with it," maintained Universal's president R.H. Cochrane. However, on June 6, 1937, Universal shipped a print of *The Road Back* to German Ambassador Hans Luther in Washington, D.C. for his approval, and the joke around Hollywood was that the film's editing credit should have gone to George Gyssling.

Despite the State Department's warning, Consul Gyssling continued to interfere in the production of anti-Nazi films. He told Warner Bros. that "he could not foretell the consequences" of the studio's producing *Confessions of a Nazi Spy*, and he "hoped they would not make it." Gyssling was, however, able to tell any studio personnel with relatives in Germany of the consequences to their loved ones of their participating in anti-Nazi films. Such relatives would promptly be shipped to concentration camps.

Paramount's Foreign Department brought up an interesting point in advising against production of *Confessions of a Nazi Spy* in a confidential letter to Joseph Breen, head of the Production Code Administration, dated December 10, 1938:

"I think the big mistake Warners are making in this matter is that they have not heeded the action taken by Charlie Chaplin in dropping his plan to make a burlesque of Hitler [subsequently produced as *The Great Dictator*]. Chaplin announced, and we think very rightly, that in making a picture of this kind he would be devoting his moneymaking talents to a film which could only have horrible repercussions on the Jews still in Germany. The same charge will be leveled by Germany on Warners in making this picture and I feel sure that if the picture is made and is in any way uncomplimentary to Germany, as it must be if it is to be sincerely produced, then Warners will have on their hands the blood of a great many

Jews in Germany. If they are willing to call this showmanship then I imagine that they must know what they are about."

The most blatant example of threats by Gyssling relates to the 1936 production of *I Was a Captive of Nazi Germany*. Proposed cast members of German origin were summoned to the consul's office, and all either quit the production or asked the producer not to list their names in the credits. Indeed, at the film's release, only Isobel Lillian Steele, the star upon whose experiences the story was based, was credited on the production. Not even the director dared to reveal his identity. The Hays Office deliberately delayed issuing a Production Code certificate for the film in an effort to appease the Germans. On August 8, 1936, Joseph Breen wrote the film's producer, asking that he withdraw his application for the approval of the Production Code Administration, adding, "The official protest filed with us by the Consul for Germany at Los Angeles could not, we feel, be passed over lightly." Earlier, on July 22, 1936, Breen had pointed out that, "We would have to reject your picture as a violation of the Production Code which directs 'The history, institutions, prominent people and citizenry of other nations shall be represented fairly.'"

Mayor Bill Thompson of Chicago went one step further. He described Chicago as "the sixth German city," and refused permission for the film to be screened there on the basis that it might create demonstrations by German residents.

In Germany itself, American film companies tried wherever possible not to compromise their business dealings. When Hitler came to power, Universal was ordered to cease its non-Aryan film production in Germany. The company simply moved production head Joseph Pasternak to Budapest, where German-language filmmaking continued. Universal's general manager for Europe, Max Friedland, was able to work out an agreement with the German authorities, permitting the release of the company's German-language films despite Jewish participation in their production.

Despite the blatant (and widely publicized in the United States) anti-Jewish activities of the Hitler regime, at least three major studios with Jewish heads, Fox, Paramount and Metro-Goldwyn-Mayer, were still operating within Nazi Germany as late as April 1937. These same studios maintained offices in Vienna, following the 1938 German annexation of Austria. Yet again, in an effort to appease the German authorities, all Jewish executives and employees in Vienna were dismissed. Manager Flemminger of 20th Century-Fox and Bernstein of MGM were at least able to leave the country. Other employees were not as lucky and perished in concentration camps as a result of the actions of their Jewish bosses in Hollywood.

The relationship between the major Hollywood studios and Nazi Germany up to the end of 1938 was very much a matter of compromise. Louis B. Mayer, Adolph Zukor and Carl Laemmle were not so naïve and uninformed as to be unaware of what was happening to their fellow Jews in Germany. A filmscript of *The Road Back* was prepared by R.C. Sheriff as early as 1933, but suppressed by Carl Laemmle, concerned that its production would hurt his German interests. When the film was eventually made in 1937, it was because Universal's German interests were almost non-existent, and not because the studio was concerned with the spread of German militarism or German treatment of the Jews and other minority groups.

If the Jewish studio heads could claim ignorance of what was happening in Europe, they were certainly aware of what was taking place in Hollywood. In 1938, the Anti-Communist Federation of America circulated a flyer that read, "Christian Vigilantes Arise! Buy Gentile. Employ Gentile. Vote Gentile. Boycott the Movies! Hollywood is the Sodom and Gomorrha [sic] where International Jewry controls vice-dope-gambling, where young gentile girls are raped by Jewish producers, directors, casting directors, who go unpunished. The Jewish Anti-Nazi League controls Communism in the Motion Picture Industry."

To gossip columnist Hedda Hopper, Dore Schary, who was later to head MGM, revealed a 1940 plot to place the body of a dead child on Louis B. Mayer's front lawn the night of Passover. The story was to be put around that this was the child whose blood was used in the Passover. Schary also recalled the invention of an instrument called a "kike killer." As described by the producer/writer, "On one end was a round ball; on the other end a spike. You hit the kike in the stomach with the spike; when he doubles up, you take the round part and hit him over the head."

Fascism would never again advance this close to the Hollywood film community, and its presence was felt in large part because of failings within the industry. A decade later, it was those same failings that made the industry incapable of stifling or overcoming the House UnAmerican Activities Committee investigations.

CHAPTER FIFTEEN

Hedda Hopper's Hollywood

Hedda Hopper had a file on J. Edgar Hoover. She also had a file on Richard M. Nixon. In fact, she had a file of correspondence on every Republican president from Hebert Hoover through Ronald Reagan. These and hundreds of other files on just about every Hollywood star of the 1940s, 1950s and 1960s are housed in the Margaret Herrick Library of the Academy of Motion Picture Arts and Sciences. They reveal the political power that Hedda Hopper wielded through her column and the manner in which she was used by the conservative element in the United States during a period of anti-Communist hysteria.

Hedda Hopper was born Elda Furry in Hollidaysburg, Pennsylvania, on June 2, 1890. She wanted to be an actress, and gradually built herself up from chorus and show girl to playing second lead in a touring version of *The Quaker Girl*. (Noted in later years for her salty, explicit language and her own lack of interest in sex, Hopper was once described by her manager, Dema Harshbarger, as a Quaker from the neck down.) In 1913, Elda Furry married DeWolf Hopper, a veteran actor more than thirty years her senior, who was best known for his rendition of "Casey at the Bat." She bore him a son, DeWolf Hopper, Jr. who, as William Hopper, was featured on the *Perry Mason* television series. The couple divorced in 1921.

She adopted the name Hedda Hopper in 1918, after beginning her film career two years earlier. Usually playing distinguished-looking and well-dressed society women, Hedda remained busy on screen through the early 1930s. However, as she got older, parts got fewer. She needed a new career, and in 1937, she got one when MGM publicist Andy Hervey and Louis B. Mayer's assistant Ida Koverman suggested Hedda as columnist for the Esquire Feature Syndicate. When her column was picked up by the *Chicago Tribune* syndicate, Hopper's readership was to be the largest of any gossip columnist in the United States. She turned out not only six daily columns and a Sunday feature, but also wrote feature articles for popular and fan magazines and made regular radio broadcasts—and she never stopped working until the day she died, on February 1, 1966.

While there were many gossip columnists in the 1930s through 1950s, Hedda Hopper's only rival and the dominant figure in the field until she came along was Louella Parsons (1884-1972). Parsons had entered the newspaper industry in 1916 and became motion picture editor of the *New York Morning Telegraph* in 1918. When William Randolph Hearst gave her a syndicated movie column in 1926, she became the most powerful commentator on the motion picture industry, literally able to make or break Hollywood stars. Parsons continued in power until she wrote her last column on November 30, 1966. *New Theatre* (August 1935) called her "Hearst's Hollywood stooge," as, in column after column, Louella would comment in reference to the newspaper tycoon's mistress, "Marion [Davies] never looked lovelier." Louella Parsons' columns were strictly businesslike, written with little style, finesse or consideration of the world beyond Hollywood. Typically, on April 2, 1939, when Europe was on the verge of war, with Britain and France attempting to appease Hitler, Parsons wrote, "The deadly dullness of the past week was lifted yesterday when Darryl Zanuck admitted he had bought all rights to *The Bluebird* for Shirley Temple."

Described by the *Saturday Evening Post* (July 15, 1939) as "The First Lady of Hollywood," Louella Parsons was anything but attractive, being both fat and ugly, but she yearned to be more than just a writer and desperately sought outlets for herself on radio and in motion pictures. "Louella is a reporter trying to be a ham," said her rival. "Hedda Hopper is a ham trying to be a reporter."

In 1930, Louella married urologist Dr. Harry Watson Martin—"Doc" as she called him—and they were together until his death in 1951. As well as being noted for his treatment of Hollywood stars with VD, Doc Martin was also a notorious drunk. Legend has it that when he fell asleep after drinking too much at a Hollywood party, Louella said to let him sleep as he had surgery at seven the next morning. Once, Martin forgot to fasten his trousers and his penis was exposed, leading a wag to comment, "There's Louella Parsons' column."

Like her rival, Hedda was a Republican, and there was never any doubt as to her political leaning. Back in 1932, her friend Ida Koverman, also a staunch Republican, had urged Hedda to run (unsuccessfully) for public office. She supported Senator Robert Taft over Dwight D. Eisenhower and Senator Barry Goldwater over Richard M. Nixon as Republican nominees for president. On June 18, 1964, she wrote to one of her readers, "I wouldn't vote for Dick Nixon if he were running for dog catcher ... Barry Goldwater has guts, principle and conscience, and that is why he won't vote for the Civil Rights Bill. It gives the Negroes supremacy over the Whites."

Hopper's attitude toward Nixon was subject to change. To Mamie Eisenhower, she recalled how the Nixons met their first movie stars at her home: "I can still remember how thrilled they were." After opposing Nixon's nomination as Eisenhower's vice-president, she changed her opinion of him, and in 1958 wrote to Bernard Baruch, "Things in Washington are getting worse and worse. If only Ike would step aside and give the reins to Dick Nixon, I believe we would be in a much better situation much faster. But Ike could never get out of the clutches of Sherman Adams, Milton Eisenhower and Paul Hoffman; they seem to have a noose around his neck."

Harry Truman was tolerated. John F. Kennedy and Franklin D. Roosevelt were not. Hopper shed no crocodile tears at Kennedy's assassination, denouncing the president as "a cocky millionaire." "I thought we would never get rid of the Roosevelts," fumed Hedda, "but the Kennedys are worse, and there are more of them!" On being shown a photograph of Eleanor Roosevelt riding a camel, the columnist retorted, "That's the first good hump Eleanor has had since she married Franklin."

To be a good American, however, it was not enough to vote Republican; it was also very necessary, as Hedda constantly reminded her readers, to fight communism. "I love my country," she wrote Bernard Baruch, "I love our ancestors who fought for freedom and I am going down fighting for it even if I am stoned." The freedom for which Hedda Hopper was fighting, and for which she expected her 35 million readers to fight, was the freedom to live in a country where "Godless Communism" was outlawed.

Hedda had little doubt that the film industry was communist-controlled. To Hedda there was no question that the members of the Screen Writers Guild covertly sowed the seeds of communism through the storylines and the characters in the films that they wrote. She was most anxious to appear in a 1947 debate to be broadcast on ABC's *Town Meeting of the Air*, on which she would list films that reflected communist propaganda. There were objections to her plan by fellow anti-communists such as director Sam Wood and actor Adolphe Menjou. Perhaps they were concerned that Hedda would make a fool of herself in view of some of the films she had already denounced in her column as anti-American, including Frank Capra's *Mr. Smith Goes to Washington* and *Meet John Doe* and the Loretta Young vehicle *The Farmer's Daughter*. The last, according to Hedda, "managed to hold up to ridicule our whole process of free elections." *A Song to Remember* was denounced because it suggested Chopin was a revolutionary rather than a Polish nobleman.

In the end, it was left to Lela Rogers—Ginger's mother—and state senator Jack Tenney to lead the anti-communist attack, while actor Albert Dekker and Screen Writers Guild president Emmet Lavery opposed the motion that "There really is a Communist threat in Hollywood." Because of Hopper's interest in the broadcast, the trade papers reported that studios advised their actors not to appear in opposition to the motion for fear of antagonizing Hedda and being blacklisted from her column.

(Years later, Hedda reported to one of her readers that "Dekker, whether he knew it or not, played ball with many organizations that have been cited by the Attorney General as Communist, Communist dominated, and/or subversive." The ever-watchful Hopper also noted that Mrs. Dekker was chairman of a meeting of the Congress of American Women which "voted to oppose the shipment of arms and supplies by the United States to Greece which was then fighting Red Revolution within its borders.")

On August 22, 1957, Frank Sinatra called Hedda "a nice old broad," and although she professed horror at the singer's involvement in politics, Hopper was kindly disposed toward the singer. Basically, however, celebrities whom she interviewed for her column were expected to toe the anti-communist line. It is fascinating to read the transcripts made by Hopper's secretaries of interviews with stars desperately trying to extricate themselves after the columnist had accused them of participation in a left-wing film. Some, such as Tony Randall and Olivia de Havilland, argued back and stood their ground. Most did not, and never was there more Hollywood hypocrisy on display. In a November 1965 letter Candice Bergen reported on the horrors of life in Communist Czechoslovakia. "I know now that we must fight this to the very, very end," wrote Bergen in a letter signed, "Conservatively Yours."

"If we back down in Vietnam, the Commies will take all of Asia," opined Nick Adams in a June 13, 1965 interview. "They are taking over — gradually ... it will be socialism and then communism," said Lillian Gish in a June 5, 1963 interview. "I'm glad I'm as old as I am," replied Hedda, "I don't want to live under communism."

Some Hollywood stars did stand up to Hedda, most notably Joan Bennett, whose liberalism was in stark contrast to the ultra-conservative viewpoint of her older sister, Constance. When journalist Harry Crocker ran a piece demanding higher standards in Hollywood reporting, Joan Bennett reprinted the article in a paid Valentine's Day advertisement in the trade papers, alongside an attack on Joan Fontaine by Hedda. Around the Hopper piece was outlined a heart with the words, "Can This Be You Hedda." Bennett followed up on her initial attack with the delivery of a live skunk to the columnist, with a note,

> Be my filthy Valentine
> Little peas in a pod, oh, how divine,
> For just like you, I am "de trop"
> And also leave a horrible scent wherever I go.

In response, Hedda gave the skunk, which she christened Joan, to James Mason and his wife, Pamela. She also pondered how Joan Bennett could have afforded the advertisements in view of the commercial failure of her husband Walter Wanger's current film, *Joan of Arc*.

While deploring the fact that ZaSu Pitts "couldn't get into pictures because she fought the Communists," Hedda Hopper denounced pro-Communist actors from abroad — notably Yves Montand and Simone Signoret — who were being courted by the American film industry. The one actor whose presence in the United States proved particularly distasteful to Hedda Hopper was Charlie Chaplin. It was Hedda who had championed the cause of Joan Barry in her 1943 paternity suit against the comedian. As early as 1947, the columnist was discussing plans for the deportation of Chaplin with J. Edgar Hoover. She discussed the Chaplin problem with Richard Nixon, who, on May 29, 1952, wrote her,

"I agree with you that the way the Chaplin case has been handled has been a disgrace for years. Unfortunately, we aren't able to do too much about it when the top decisions are made by the likes of Acheson and McGranery. You can be sure, however, that I will keep an eye on the case and possibly after January we will be able to work with the Administration which will apply the same rules to Chaplin as they do to ordinary citizens."

Chaplin was never out of Hedda's column. In November 1965, while the comedian was making *The Countess from Hong Kong*, she wrote, "I don't know about the rest of you, but personally I feel better when an ocean separates Charlie and the land of the free. Let's keep it that way." According to George Eells in his dual biography, *Hedda and Louella*, Hopper telephoned fellow newspaperwoman Florabel Muir only days before her death, to say, "I hear that son-of-a-bitch Chaplin is trying to get back in this country. We've all got to work together to stop him!"

J. Edgar Hoover first recognized the value of Hedda Hopper's column in the mid-1940s. To Hedda, the head of the FBI was "My dear Edgar," to whom she would appeal in August 1947, "Would you give me some facts to hurl back at the angry mob in the audience who is going to ask me very embarrassing questions? Naturally, I won't be able to accuse certain stars of being registered Communists, as even those who are deny it, always have and always will. But you're so wise and have so many facts at your fingertips that I feel that I can call upon your friendship for help. I know you're just as anxious to rid the country of our enemies as I am."

Almost ten years later, on March 6, 1958, Hopper praised Hoover: "You have been such a fighter against communism for so long and done such a marvelous job .... In Hollywood, I have a feeling there are more than ever and they work harder. All those idiotic decisions handed down by Earl Warren and the Supreme Court make me ashamed. A man like Earl Warren should never — never — never [have] been made Chief Justice of the United States ... Thank God we have a man like you to keep on fighting and one who never lowers his standards."

Hopper was unable to use some of the information provided by Hooper. However, it did not go unwasted as she passed material on to the American Legion for its magazine. Typical of Hopper's letters to Robert B. Pitkin, managing editor of *American Legion Magazine*, is one dated December 9, 1955, in which the columnist writes, "I believe you would also like to know that the man who wrote the novel from which *The Man with the Golden Arm* motion picture was taken is Nelson Algren. He has a long Commie record going back to 1935, and extending up to the time of [the] Ethel and Julius Rosenberg defense in which he participated. He was also a writer on the *Daily Worker*."

Judge Irving Kaufman, who sentenced the Rosenbergs, was another of Hedda's correspondents. "Mine is a hard position in this jungle of Hollywood," she wrote him, "because I am fighting almost single-handed, but I shall go down fighting just as you are doing." Kaufman belonged to a hard-core group of Hopper's readers and supporters that also included Major Arch E. Roberts (who provided data on the Pro Blue Foundation), General Edwin A. Walter ("a symbol of militant Christian patriotism") and General A.C. Wedemeyer (a hardliner against North Korea, to whom Hedda wrote in March 1965, "I think our pictures are getting worse and worse, but then all decency in our lives is going out of the window ... I believe it all started with the infiltration of communism into the writing guilds of the motion picture industry").

Not surprisingly, Senator Joseph McCarthy was one of Hopper's correspondents, and he enjoyed her support. On a 1953 trip to Europe, she was shocked to find that McCarthy was not too well regarded, and that the American propaganda machine was not supportive of his actions. On July 30, 1953, Hedda reported her findings to President Eisenhower, noting, "McCarthy can take nothing from you; nor should he. He was appointed to do a job. It's an unpleasant, dirty job; but he's doing it. And in my opinion he deserves the support of everyone who calls himself a Republican and an American. Otherwise the kind of America for which our forefathers fought, bled, and died is gone."

At the same time, Hedda was disturbed by McCarthy's criticism of Eisenhower. She pointed out to him that she, he and the president of the United States were working for the same cause but that all should agree that the Communists would not be out of the government or the film industry by 1954. "You've got people thinking you're running for President," Hedda told McCarthy, "and I want to warn you now that if you split the Republican party, the Commies and the Democrats are going to have the last laugh, because Mr. Stevenson, and not Ike, and not you, will make it in 1956."

Daily, Hedda Hopper received anonymous letters from readers naming Communists within the industry. One of the most devastating was a letter from the "Faithful Employees" of RKO Radio Pictures, dated November 7, 1947, enclosing a list of more than seventy RKO personnel who were accused by their colleagues of being Communists.

"How much longer must we endure Adrian Scott, Ed Dmytryk, Paul Jarrico, Waldo Salt, Leonardo Bercovici, John Paxton, Nat James, as well as innumerable pinkos," asked the faithful RKO employees. As she passed the letter on to RKO president Paul Rathvon, Hopper commented, "All of this Red menace could have been forestalled if some of our biggest producers had listened to reason as long as seven years ago."

Hedda's column was a natural outlet for organizations such as the Anti-Communism Voters League, the Committee to Proclaim Liberty and the Americanism Educational League. However, one organization for which Hopper had no time was Myron Fagan's Cinema Educational Guild, publisher of *Red Channels*, a listing of Communists within the entertainment industry. She was furious that one of her friends, Groucho Marx, had been "named" by Fagan, and, with remarkable irony, told a reader that one should be careful whom one accused of being a Communist.

There were those whom Hopper defended. Despite angry letters from her readers, she stood by Lucille Ball when she was accused of having been a member of the Communist Party in the 1930s. Despite pressure from the American Legion, Hedda remained friendly with Carl Foreman, and when he announced the end of his long exile in Europe, she wrote him, "Wonderful to know you will be coming home ... you have been away too long."

However much criticism one may level again Hedda Hopper, she was a woman who remained true to her beliefs and her friends. When the Federated Women's Clubs of America went against Hedda and named *Spartacus* as Picture of the Year, the columnist took out a paid advertisement in *Variety* (February 13, 1961), expressing her opposition, and adding, "*Spartacus* was one of the worst pictures I've ever seen and the script was written by Dalton Trumbo" (one of the Hollywood Ten).

One of the oddest aspects of Hedda Hopper's personal and private lives was her love-hate relationship with gays and lesbians. In print, she denounced gays. When asked to write a piece for *Photoplay* on Rock Hudson, she told the editor, "Of course, we can't say that he's a faggot, but we can hint at it." After *Look* magazine published an article on Cary Grant, she wrote the editor, "Whom does he think he is fooling? He started with the boys and now he has gone back to them." She would hint that Noel Coward was Adlai Stevenson's speechwriter, and speculate at what happened when the two spent time together at Coward's Jamaican retreat.

In the second volume of her autobiography, *The Whole Truth and Nothing But*, published in 1963, Hedda suggested that Michael Wilding was less than a man and that he was overly friendly with Stewart Granger. Wilding sued for libel, and when her publisher reached an out-of-court settlement, she joked at a women's club meeting that Wilding would probably get all the exotic hats for which she was famous — "But then, of course, he'll enjoy wearing them."

While denouncing gays in public, Hedda's closest friend was her manager Dema Harshbarger, who was a well-known lesbian. Hopper would often host parties at which all the guests were gay. Hedda was fully aware that her rival Louella Parsons' daughter, Harriet, was a lesbian, and that her 1940 marriage to actor-writer King Kennedy was one of convenience in that Kennedy was gay. Not only did Hedda not reveal the truth, but when Harriet and Kennedy divorced in 1946, she hired the latter as her "leg man" or personal assistant.

Hedda Hopper never forgot the people who had been kind to her when she had been a struggling actress in the industry. Her first leading man, William Farnum, was always sure of a friendly word in her column, as was D.W. Griffith, who had hired DeWolf Hopper back in 1915, when both he and his wife desperately need the money. She went against the entire film industry in 1942 when she defended Lew Ayres for declaring himself a conscientious objector. "I'm defending the right of conscious," she told her radio audience, "one of the things we're fighting this war for, and it's no part of a brave and free people to brand as a coward a man who dares disagree with them."

Never did Hedda Hopper try and curry favor. She was as outspoken in private as in public. If she did not like the length of an actor's hair, she told him so. Perhaps the best caricature of Hopper is given by Ilka Chase in the 1955 screen adaptation of Clifford Odets' *The Big Knife*.

The columnist took delight in criticism from those that she opposed. She proudly told her readers that the communist party publication, *The Daily Worker* (August 23, 1950), in its review of *Sunset Blvd.*, had labeled both her and Cecil B. DeMille as "Two of the most bigoted, sybaritic, ostentatious, and fraudulent reactionaries in all filmdom." When Alvah Bessie wrote "An Open Letter to Hedda Hopper" in *People's Daily World* (August 14, 1952), criticizing her praise for Franco's Spain, Hopper replied with a savage attack on Bessie, accusing him of fighting a war against fascism in the green room at Warner Bros. rather than on the battlefield, as had men such as Audie Murphy.

It is a curious coincidence that Edward R. Murrow, who had played a crucial role in the downfall of Senator Joseph McCarthy, would also be responsible if not actually for Hedda's downfall, at least for making the columnist appear a fool on national television.

The date was December 6, 1959, and the program was *Small World*, broadcast over the CBS network. The concept was that of a four-way transatlantic conversation, in this particular instance with Murrow in London, Simone Signoret in San Francisco, Agnes de Mille in New York, and Hedda Hopper in Hollywood. Hedda used the occasion to attack *The Blackboard Jungle*, a film that she thought represented America in an unfavorable light, and which she had been instrumental in persuading her friend, Clare Booth Luce, to have withdrawn from the Venice Film Festival. Signoret pointed out that the film did not harm America, but on the contrary proved that America was free enough to tell things about itself. Agnes de Mille quickly sided with Signoret, and then brought up the "real horror walking this land" during the McCarthy era. An infuriated Hopper talked of brainwashing by the communist element that had led to the changing of the lyrics of "Ol' Man River" in order not to offend the Negro. As Signoret and de Mille argued with her, Hopper's responses became sillier and sillier. America suddenly saw Hedda Hopper for what she was — a foolish old lady out of touch with reality.

Of course, Hedda continued to attack communism in her column. She continued to detect subversive elements at work within the industry, but more frequently those portions of her column that dealt with the communist threat were excised by the two most important newspapers publishing Hedda, the *Los Angeles Times* and the *New York Daily News*. Sadly, Hedda wrote to Hanford MacNider on December 9, 1964, "I'm not permitted to write anything about politics in my column. The syndicate tells me they have their own political writers and I'm not one of them."

Hedda Hopper died suddenly on February 1, 1966. There were sufficient columns already prepared for her voice to continue to be heard for the remainder of the month. She closed her Sunday column for February 27, 1966, with the comment, "I still think that motion pictures are the greatest propaganda medium ever put into the hands of a man. We can show our way of life all over the world the same night. The Commies thought so too. That's the reason they moved into Hollywood and infiltrated the ranks of our writers. We're still suffering that infiltration."

CHAPTER SIXTEEN

The Porky's Trilogy

It would be very wrong to assume that the American film industry's fixation with body parts and bodily fluids began in the late 1990s. Neither *There's Something about Mary* (1998), written and directed by two brothers, Peter and Bobby Farrelly, nor *American Pie* (1999), also written and directed by two brothers, Chris and Paul Weitz, are particularly unique in the annals of American bad taste.

For a non-classic and somewhat dated example of crudity and vulgarity in modern American cinema, one need look no further than the *Porky's* trilogy. The emphasis is on sexual initiation and humiliation, which continue as prime ingredients in such productions. The humor is juvenile, with the scripts taking delight in the use of childish slang for various male and female body parts. A character, who calls himself "Meat," goes around offering to show the female students at his high school why he is so named. It is all "tits and ass," as demonstrated by the opening of the final film in the trilogy, *Porky's Revenge*, which begins with Pee Wee's fantasy involving himself seen nude from the rear at graduation while a visiting female student from Sweden bares her breasts. Appropriately, the Swede is played by Kimberly Evenson whose biggest claim to fame, aside from her breasts, is that she was featured as the September 1984 *Playboy's* Playmate of the Month. As a matter of record, Pee Wee's breasts—or "man tits" as the Porky's gang would call them—at this point are as large of those of many of the female students on campus.

What differentiates the *Porky's* trilogy from later and better-produced films in the genre, such as *American Pie* (1999) is the quantity of male frontal nudity to be found here. In more recent, and obviously less liberal times, it is OK to discuss the penis but it should not be visible on screen.

Set in Fort Lauderdale in 1954, with a backdrop of the Angel Beach High School, *Porky's* was created by writer-director Bob Clark, and, supposedly based on his teenage memories. The first film was financed, at $4.2 million, by independent producer Melvin Simon, and subsequently picked up for distribution by 20th Century-Fox (which also released the two later features). The first two productions were identified as Canadian, with the United States film industry accepting credit for the last. The teenagers in the three films were all unknowns, and have remained so: Don Monahan (Pee Wee), Tony Ganios (Meat), Roger Wilson (Mickey), Wyatt Knight (Tommy), Mark Herrier (Billy), Cyril O'Reilly (Tim), and Scott Colomby (Brian). Much too old for the roles when the series began, the actors look positively thirty-something by the final production. The only casting criteria appears to have been the willingness of the performer to drop his pants on demand. Surprisingly, the casting director did not bother to check out Ganios's credentials prior to casting him as Meat, for as a fleeting, frontal nude show in the first film indicates, he is no better endowed than anyone else.

The basic storyline in *Porky's* (1981) concerns itself with the efforts to the teenagers to get even with Porky, a grossly overweight individual, who runs a bar-brothel, and his redneck sheriff brother after the pair have thrown the boys out of the establishment and badly beaten up Mickey. Much of the film involves Pee Wee's attempts at getting laid and the group's spying on the female students in the showers through the use of peepholes. One of the boys inserts his penis (a word unknown to the screenwriter) in one of the holes only to have it seized by an overweight, spinsterish gym teacher named Miss Ballbricker (played by Nancy Parsons). When the owner of the penis escapes, she tries to persuade the headmaster to organize an identification parade — a sort of privates on parade — but without success.

The film makes a vain attempt at political correctness in standing firm against anti-Semitism, just as the second film was to bring up the issue of Native American rights. But no amount of liberal underpinning can hide the fact that the entire series is alive with sexism. Throughout, Miss Ballbricker is humiliated because of her figure; in the third film, Porky's daughter is similarly insulted because she wears braces on her teeth. The Meat character is in fear of being forced to marry her, but no one makes the point that by this time, Meat is a far from attractive, overweight man and that braces can be removed far quicker than fat.

Ageism is equally at issue in the *Porky's* films. In the third episode, there is a humiliating sex scene between a biology teacher and her middle-aged suitor. In the second film, a group of Ku Klux Klan members have their heads shaved and is then forced to run around naked, the implication being that the young audiences for the film enjoy seeing their elders in such embarrassing, and frontally explicit, circumstances.

There is a strong undercurrent of homophobia in the first two features. In *Porky's*, there is a reference to "queer." In the second film, much humor is made of Billy's playing Oberon, "King of the Fairies," in a high school production of *A Midsummer Night's Dream*:

"So you're playing a big fairy?"

"Well, that's good casting."

And Pee Wee, playing Puck, is identified as "a little fairy."

Just as *Porky's* opens with Pee Wee's measuring his pajama-clad penis, *Porky's II: The Next Day* (1983) similarly finds Pee Wee employed, helping his penis (or "stiffy," as he calls it) get erect thanks to photographs in a *National Geographic* magazine. The plot here involves bigoted Reverend Bubba Flavel (played by Bill Wiley) attempting to shut down the school's Shakespeare festival because of the Bard's supposed lewdness. Unlike *Porky's*, where the frontal nudity is almost exclusively female, *Porky's II* includes a lengthy sequence of Pee Wee in the buff and facing the camera.

Director Bob Clark did not return for the final film but was replaced by James Komack when *Porky's Revenge* (1985) went into production. Chuck Mitchell returned as Porky, now operating his bar-brothel on a paddleboat. He is threatening the basketball coach over his gambling debts, and the "boys" agree to lose the state championship in order to cover the debt. Of course, they win and also, again, destroy Porky's. By this time, as Janet Maslin wrote in the *New York Times* (March 23, 1985), the characters had become "the oldest high school seniors in America." It is ironic that the film begins with Pee Wee's mother asking of him, "Do you intend never to graduate?"

In its first sixteen weeks of release, *Porky's* brought in more than $100 million, and despite being poorly produced, photographed and directed, it did garner praise of a kind. David Ansen in *Newsweek* (April 5, 1982) described it as "good clean dirty fun," while *Variety* (November 13, 1981) called it "one of the grossest [films] ever released by a major studio." Interest in the series had long waned by the release of *Porky's Revenge*, and 20th Century-Fox was reduced to hyping it with a "Pig Out at Porky's" party at which seven UCLA fraternities participated in a rib-eating contest. In its first outing, *Porky's* had owed something in concept, if not sophistication, to *American Graffiti*. At the trilogy's close, it was little more than a fraternity beer bust.

CHAPTER SEVENTEEN

Icons of Political Incorrectness

The majority of the icons of 20th century bad taste and political incorrectness are deserving of book-length studies. Most, in fact, have been the subjects of more than one. Others remain relics of a bygone age and culture, awaiting their moment of ridicule or reverence. The contributions of each are original; some remain lasting while those of one or two are definitely in need or resurrection. We live in a society that generally applauds the second-rate or the shoddy, especially in the television medium, why then do we ignore these icons of the past century? Let us perhaps not praise famous men. But let us at least acknowledge a few shadowy figures with sometimes murky careers.

For almost as long as the motion picture graduated from its infancy, there were state censorship boards in Kansas, Maryland, New York, Ohio, Pennsylvania, and Virginia. There was also at least one city censorship board—in Chicago—and it was ruled by a curious character about whom little is known except his name and title, Major Metallus Lucullus Cicero Funkhouser. The second deputy lieutenant of police in Chicago, Major Funkhouser was responsible for the censorship of all films shown in the city for a number of years in the 'teens.

Funkhouser, as his name suggests, was of German origin, born in St. Louis, Missouri, on January 17, 1864, and determinedly opposed to the screening of any films that might be considered anti-German propaganda. When he banned Mary Pickford's 1917 feature,

The Little American, because of its depiction of the heroine fighting German invaders in France and facing a firing squad as a spy, distributor Paramount took the unusual step of filing suit against the city; the company was successful, and *The Little American* became the first film to play Chicago without censorship cuts.

The Major's actions might have been OK while America was still neutral, but once the country declared war on Germany, it was obvious that Funkhouser was facing an insurmountable problem. He still continued to censor or ban anti-Germany films, and in May 1918, he was suspended from duty after he had cut scenes from two prominent World War I propaganda features, *My Four Years in Germany* and *Hearts of the World*, both of which "offended his pro-German proclivities." Charges were preferred against him by the Civil Service Commission. Funkhouser was accused of general insubordination, inefficiency and the employment of "persons of ill repute and character to investigate and report moral conditions and to regulate and suppress vice." His reign as the arbiter of public taste in Chicago came to an end. Curiously, his opposition to blatantly offensive anti-German propaganda suggests Funkhouser might be categorized as an upholder of political correctness.

Upholding not so much political correctness as Americanism in its purist form was Lawrence Welk. With his broken English — he was the son of German immigrants — the squeaky-clean image of his organization, his overt patriotism, which left no room for dissent of any kind, and music that can never really have been in style despite being played by Welk for more than half-a-century, Lawrence Welk continues to represent the best of bad taste on American television. As he explained it, "Music changes but I don't." He was first seen on local television in Los Angeles in 1951, then on the ABC network from 1955-1971, in syndication from 1971-1982, and now, despite his being dead for more than a decade, on public television.

His program is the American equivalent of an evening with the Red Army Choir. The numbers are carefully regimented. There is just the right amount (very small) of liberalism in the hiring of a token black entertainer in the person of dancer Arthur Duncan. (As Welk kept assuring his audience, Duncan, and by extension all African Americans, had rhythm.) The performers were paid at a fixed scale, too low to allow savings and thoughts of going solo. Their private lives and public persona were carefully choreographed; when the original Champagne Lady, Alice Lon, showed too much leg in 1959, she was fired. The tempo of the music and of the shows never changed, a constant for its aging audience. Welk's audience, as evidenced by the advertising on the syndicated shows, wore false teeth, used medicinal aids such as Geritol and skin creams like Oil of Olay.

Many talk show hosts might be considered icons of bad taste. The long, and rightly, forgotten Wally George might qualify, as could the arrogant Geraldo Rivera. Wally George (1931-2003) was on television from 1969, launching his *Hot Seat* program and what he described as "Combat TV" in July 1983. However, another true pioneer of greater fame is Morton Downey, Jr. (1933-2001), who was at one time the best-known exponent of confrontational talk-show television. He was the son of a popular Irish tenor of radio and nightclubs, and Barbara Bennett, whose better-known film star siblings are Joan and Constance. (Wally George also had a link to motion pictures in that his estranged daughter is Rebecca De Mornay.) Amazingly, Morton Downey, Jr. was knighted by Pope Paul VI in early 1970 for his work aiding Biafran war victims. Prior to his career as a talk show host, Downey, Jr. had some success as a singer.

A chain-smoking super-patriot, Morton Downey, Jr. hosted a program notable for the manner in which he would verbally assault his guests, telling them, to "zip it, fathead." Sometimes the attacks would progress beyond the verbal as when he tried to strangle artist Mark Kostabi with a telephone chord, and an ambulance had to be called when Kostabi had a heart attack. Morton Downey, Jr. was very much a precursor to Jerry Springer, and just as the latter's audience would chant "Jerry! Jerry! Jerry!" so did Downey's respond, "Mort! Mort! Mort!"

The Morton Downey, Jr. Show began as a live broadcast on WWOR-New York on October 12, 1987; it was first broadcast in syndication on May 30, 1988 and was cancelled in September 1989. Downey's abrasive and insulting style had quickly lost its appeal, and the program became, in the words of *Variety* (July 6, 1988), "a shouting match nobody's listening to." In a last ditch effort to interest the media, Downey claimed in 1989 to have been attacked and beaten by skinheads at San Francisco International Airport. The "attack" failed to elicit any sympathy, and a final comeback show, *Downey*, in 1994 was a flop. With the demise of his talk show career, Downey, Jr. made some screen appearance, beginning in 1990 with *Predator 2*, in which he played a television reporter.

Political incorrectness has been the stock-in-trade of Kinky Friedman in his career as both a rock singer and a mystery novelist. In the 1970s, the entertainer wrote and recorded songs guaranteed to offend both Native Americans and African Americans. For his best-known number, "Get Your Biscuits in the Oven and Your Buns in the Bed," he was named "Male Chauvinist Pig of 1974," and even the title of his theme song, written in 1974, is sure to send liberals into a frenzy: "They Ain't Makin' Jews Like Jesus Anymore." In reality, while the lyrics refer to a "country nigger" and to "wops 'n' micks 'n' slopes 'n' spics 'n' spooks," the song carries a positive message — that if you, as a redneck, make anti-Semitic remarks, you are going to get beaten up.

Kinky Friedman semi-retired from singing to embark on a new career as a writer of mystery novels, featuring himself and a friend called Larry "Ratso" Sloman. The books, notable for Friedman's tongue-in-cheek humor, are intended to outrage, and have been described by a critic in the *Chicago Tribune* as "a hip hybrid of Groucho Marx and Sam Spade."

Born Richard Friedman in Texas on October 31, 1944, Kinky joined the Peace Corps after graduating from the University of Texas. In 1964, he recorded his first single, "Schwinn 24," under the name of King Arthur and the Carrots. He became far better known with his group Kinky Friedman and the Texas Jew Boys, whose hits include "The Ballad of Charles Whitman" and "Waitress, Please Waitress, Come Sit on My Face." Writing in *The Illustrated Encyclopedia of Rock*, Nick Logan and Bob Woffinden note that Kinky brought "an irreverent and charmingly lunatic approach to his work," but that "his ritual slaughter of various sacred cows has possibly left him temporarily up a commercial cul-de-sac." In the early 1970s, Kinky Friedman and the Texas Jew Boys were well teamed as the opening act for Cheech and Chong.

Claiming to be tired of touring and nervous at appearing in front of large crowds, Kinky Friedman put his singing career on hold. After saving a woman during an armed robbery attempt, he turned to writing. "That was a real road to Damascus experience," he told an interviewer. "I went home to my loft and started writing. The first book that I wrote, *Greenwich Killing Time*, was written in just a matter of a few months and was passed over by 28 publishers." *Greenwich Killing Time* was eventually published by William Morrow in 1986, and has been followed by a large number of highly entertaining and often provocative volumes, including *Elvis, Jesus & Coca-Cola* (1993) and *God Bless John Wayne* (1995). In 2006, Friedman embarked on a political career, announcing his candidacy for governor of Texas.

The publisher of Chuck Barris' 1993 autobiography, *The Game Show King: A Confession*, notes that the author has "generally contributed to the fun of popular culture." He has, indeed, and also provided us with some of the most distasteful programming on American daytime television. Born in Philadelphia on June 2, 1929, Chuck Barris came to New York and was a page at NBC prior to becoming a management trainee. It was at ABC that he had his first success with *The Dating Game*, which first aired on December 20, 1965. It was followed by *The Newlywed Game* (1966-1990), *How's Your Mother-in-Law?* (1967-1968), *The Parent Game* (1972), *The New Treasure Hunt* (1974-1977), and *Three's a Crowd* (1979-1980).

One of Barris' most offensive ideas for a television game show came to fruition as *The Gong Show*, a parody of an amateur talent contest, on which individuals were invited to indulge in self-humiliation as they displayed their talent or, more often, lack of it. The contestants were judged by a panel of three minor celebrities who had the opportunity to stop the act by gonging it at any time during the proceedings. Acts with the highest score received $516.32 in the daytime version of the show and $712.05 in the nighttime edition.

The Gong Show was created by Barris and Chris Bearde, and the former served as host when the program was first aired by NBC during the day from June 14, 1976 through July 21, 1978. When *The Gong Show* went into nighttime syndication in 1976, Gary Owens took over as host, but Barris returned in 1977, and remained with the program until its demise in 1980. His loud, over-enthusiastic personality coupled with his diminutive size and cheeky grin made Chuck Barris a likeable yet obnoxious television personality.

Acts on the first syndicated program included a dancer with four arms, a woman who belched in time to the music and "The Pointless Sisters." Regular performers included a black stagehand named Gene-Gene the Dancing Machine and the Unknown Comic. The latter was played by Murray Langston, wearing a paper bag over his head; in 1985, he tried for a movie career, starring as a rookie cop in the supposed comedy, *Night Patrol*. Regular judges included Jaye P. Morgan, Jamie Farr, Phyllis Diller, and Rip Taylor, with music provided by the Milton Delugg Orchestra.

The show was briefly revived in 1988 with Don Bleu as host. In addition to *The Gong Show*, Chuck Barris also produced *The $1.98 Beauty Contest* (syndicated 1978), hosted by Rip Taylor, on which three judges selected an unfortunate and often talentless female to win the cash prize and a tiara. Overweight, very camp and sporting a blond toupee, Rip Taylor was noted for showering his audience with confetti. In his early years, with his woeful and tragic tales, he was billed as "The Crying Comedian," but later Taylor became famous for his speedy delivery of tasteless gags.

Along the way, Chuck Barris produced and starred in a 1980 film version of his biggest success, *The Gong Show Movie*, and also wrote a 1974 novel, *You and Me Babe*. In 1984, he published *Confessions of a Dangerous Mind*, in which he claimed that in 1963, he had been enlisted by the CIA, and subsequently infiltrated the Civil Rights Movement, met with militant U.S. Moslems and killed enemies of the United States abroad. The claims were as outrageous and as anything Chuck Barris had brought to television, and presented to a wider public in an amusing 2002 screen adaptation, directed by George Clooney, and starring Sam Rockwell as Barris.

The world of the motion picture has given us at least two directors deserving of recognition as icons of bad taste, Edward D. Wood, Jr. and John Waters. The latter was born in Baltimore on April 22, 1946, continues to live there, and has set a number of his productions in the city. Waters is a cult director with a waspish demeanor, making no effort to hide his homosexuality, setting out to shock his audience by combining underground cinema with a mainstream approach to filmmaking. His first major success, and his third feature, *Pink Flamingos* (1972), features 300-pound high school chum, Harris Glenn Milstead, better known as drag queen, Divine, eating dog shit. *Polyester* (1981) reintroduced scratch-and-sniff cards, allowing the audience to experience the smells that the characters on screen were privy to, and it also starred a darling of the gay filmgoing community, one-time pretty boy hero Tab Hunter. *Hairspray* (1988) was a nostalgia trip back to the days of teen dance competitions on local television, and made a star of Ricki Lake (who was later to slim down and become the female talk show answer to Jerry Springer). The days have gone since John Waters was able to shock audiences, and his later films generally promise more than they deliver; his approach to bad taste is positively old-fashioned today.

Thanks to Tim Burton's romanticized, but highly entertaining and loving, biopic, *Ed Wood* (1994), its subject has shed his cult status and gained world renown as the worst filmmaker of all time, a somewhat dubious claim to fame and, arguably, untrue. How can the creator of films that are so unintentionally funny and entertaining be totally bad? What is, of course, fascinating about Edward D. Wood, Jr. (1924-1978) is that he was a transvestite who made life imitate art in his best-known work, *Glen or Glenda* (1953). With former horror star Bela Lugosi as the host, *Glen or Glenda* transcends its camp label and becomes the sad and touching tale of a heterosexual transvestite desperately seeking happiness and society's approval. Under the name of Daniel Davis, Wood stars as the central character trying to tell his fiancée how much he wants to wear her clothes. One is far more moved and sympathetic to *Glen or Glenda* than one is to, say, the most famous account of a transsexual, *The Christine Jorgensen Story*.

Wood wrote a number of trashy novels, including *Death of a Transvestite*, first published in 1967, but it is for his films that he will always be remembered with affection. If *Glen or Glenda* is the best, then the worst is *Plan 9 from Outer Space* (1959), whose star, Bela Lugosi, died before its completion and was replaced by a chiropractor friend of the director's wife who bears no physical resemblance to Lugosi.

Edward D. Wood, Jr. is not the only American to find happiness in drag. Some of the most popular performers on the vaudeville stage were female impersonators, including Bothwell Browne, Herbert Clifton, Francis Renault, Malcolm Scott, and Julian Eltinge, who was so famous that a New York theater was named in his honor. The most outrageous of all female impersonators, and the only one who really "swished" on the vaudeville stage, was Bert Savoy. It was Savoy who influenced Mae West in her walk, the insinuation of her lines and provided her with her most famous line, "Come up and see me sometime."

Born Everett McKenzie in Boston in 1888, Bert Savoy teamed up with Jay Brennan (1883-1961) in 1915, and by 1920 Savoy and Brennan were two of the most popular entertainers in vaudeville and revue. Brennan always appeared in immaculate male attire, while his partner camped it up in outrageous female costumes and, unlike other female impersonators, never removed his wig at the act's conclusion. Savoy was vulgar, whereas Brennan, had he appeared in drag, would have been far more ladylike. Critic Edmund Wilson wrote, "When he used to come reeling on the stage, a gigantic, red-haired harlot, swaying her enormous hat, reeking with corrosive cocktails of the West Fifties, one felt oneself in the presence of the vast vulgarity of New York incarnate and made heroic."

Bert Savoy was as camp offstage as on. On a sultry Tuesday afternoon, on June 26, 1923, he and fellow vaudevillian, Jack Vincent, were camping it up on Long Beach, Long Island. A thunderstorm suddenly swept across that area of Long Island, and after a particularly strong clap of thunder, Savoy commented, "Mercy, ain't Miss God cutting up something awful?" Instantly, there was a bolt from the sky, and both Savoy and Vincent were killed instantly.

It was as if everything the religious right had said and continues to say had come to fruition. Forget about political incorrectness. Religious incorrectness would be punished. As Harpo Marx joked, from that day forth, all gay men in Coney Island walked around wearing lightning rods. Thank you, Bert Savoy, for living a life and dying a death without parallel in popular entertainment.

Pride of place in any study of political incorrectness in 20th century entertainment belongs to a Harvard College professor named Tom Lehrer, whose songs, dating from the early 1950s through the late 1960s, are unique examples of "sick" but truthful portraits of the time.

Born in New York on April 9, 1928, Tom Lehrer was a professor of mathematics at Harvard and MIT who composed strictly for his own entertainment and had such little regard for the commercial worth of his songs that he custom-recorded them for himself and as "something to have around as a souvenir." His earliest parody song, "Fight Fiercely, Harvard," was written at the age of seventeen in 1945. Basically shy, Lehrer performed in public only under duress; his last concert tour was to Sweden, Denmark and East Germany in 1967 and his final public performance at a 1972 rally for George McGovern. Lehrer avoided being photographed and was a quiet, even gentle, practitioner of his art. The songs tripped off his tongue with an acidity that matched neither his apparent personality nor the manner of his presentation. The only entertainers who came close to Tom Lehrer in writing and performance are the British duo of Michael Flanders and Donald Swann, who took up a number of the same themes but display decidedly more enthusiasm in their work.

To describe Tom Lehrer's songs as bad taste or politically incorrect is unfair in that they mirror the times so remarkably well, and have stood the test of decades far better than, say, the satirical and often cynical humor of comedians like Lenny Bruce or Mort Sahl. There is honesty and integrity behind what he sings of, but no malice, bitterness or hatred. You laugh and, at the same time, one feels depressed as

Lehrer sings of "The Old Dope Peddler," "I Wanna Go Back to Dixie," "It Makes a Fellow Proud to be a Soldier," "The Vatican Rag," "The Masochism Tango," or his salute to the atomic age, "We Will All Go Together When We Go." Cole Porter would have applauded Lehrer's use of lyrics, such as "When the air becomes uranious—we will all go simultaneous" in the last number. These are the songs of "the liberal consensus who agreed that Adlai Stevenson was a good guy and lynching was bad."

The songs are never quite what they would seem to be. As Lehrer sings of the dope peddler "spreading joy wherever he goes," he is as much attacking his profession as glorifying it. These are sentimental ballads with a cynical twist. In "My Home Town," Lehrer sings nostalgically of the little girl next door: "Now there's a charge for what she used to give for free." And when it comes to the guy who taught Sunday School and kindly Parson Brown, well, Lehrer can only comment, "I guess I better leave this line out just to be on the safe side."

The delivery was always deadpan, with the performer leaving it to the audience to find the sick humor in a song such as "Poisoning Pigeons in the Park." Often the bad taste was tinged with reality, as in "Be Prepared," he tells the boy scout "Don't solicit for your sister, that's not nice—Unless you get a good percentage of her price." In "Pollution," Lehrer parodied Oscar Hammerstein II with "Fish gotta swim and birds gotta fly—But they won't last long if they try." Tom Lehrer's songs could belong in almost any chapter in this book, covering subjects as diverse as religion, sex, racism, and substance abuse. They are as new as they are old. One of his little-heard numbers concerns VD and is titled "I Got It from Agnes." Today, it might equally apply to AIDS. In the 21st century Lenny Bruce and Mort Sahl might have nothing to offer us, but we can still learn, we can still laugh and silently cry at the songs of Tom Lehrer.

The songs of Tom Lehrer are of such sophistication, such charm, that they transcend bad taste to become classics of political incorrect. They remain the goals for which all 21st practitioners of political incorrectness should aspire, but which none has yet achieved.

Bibliography

Abt, Vicki and Mel Seesholtz, "The Shameless World of Phil, Sally and Oprah: Television Talk Shows and the Deconstructing of Society," *Journal of Popular Culture*, vol. XXVIII, no. 1, Summer 1994, pp. 171-191.

Aman, Reinhold, ed. *The Best of Maledicta*. Philadelphia: Running Press, 1987.

Armstrong, Richard B. and Mary Willems Armstrong. *The Movie List Book: A Reference Guide to Film Themes, Settings, and Series*. Jefferson, N.C.: McFarland, 1990.

Barrios, Richard. *Screened Out: Playing Gay in Hollywood from Edison to Stonewall*. New York: Routledge, 2003.

Barris, Chuck. *The Game Show King: A Confession*. New York: Carroll & Graf, 1993.

_____. *Confessions of a Dangerous Mind*. New York: St. Martin's Press, 1984.

Beard, Henry and Christopher Cerf. *The Official Politically Correct Dictionary & Handbook*. London: Grafton, 1992.

Billington, Monroe, "The New Deal Was a Joke: Political Humor during the Great Depression," *Journal of American Culture*, vol. V, no. 3, Fall 1982, pp. 15-21.

Blanche, Tony and Brad Schreiber. *Death in Paradise: An Illustrated History of the Los Angeles County Department of Coroner*. Los Angeles: General Publishing Group, 1998.

Boskin, Joseph, ed. *The Humor Prism in 20th Century America*. Detroit: Wayne State University Press, 1997.

Bourdon, David. *Warhol*. New York: Harry N. Abrams, 1989.

Brottman, Mikita. *Offensive Films: Toward an Anthropology of Cinéma Vomitif*. Westport, Ct.: Greenwood Press, 1997.

Bruns, Roger A. *Preacher: Billy Sunday and Big-Time American Evangelism.* New York: W.W. Norton, 1992.

Burnett, R.G. and E.D. Martell. *The Devil's Camera: Menace of a Film-Ridden World.* London: The Epworth Press, 1932.

Campbell, Craig W. *Reel America and World War I: A Comprehensive Filmography and History of Motion Pictures in the United States, 1914-1920.* Jefferson, N.C.: McFarland, 1985.

"Carry On Camping," *Films and Filming,* May 1983, pp. 23-25.

Chung, Sue Fawn, "From Fu Manchu, Evil Genius, to James Lee Wong, Popular Hero," *Journal of Popular Culture,* vol. X, no. 3, Winter 1976, pp. 534-547.

Cohen, Karl F. *Forbidden Animation: Censored Cartoons and Blacklisted Animators in America.* Jefferson, N.C.: McFarland, 1997.

Cohen-Stratyner, Barbara, ed. *Popular Music: 1900-1919.* Detroit: Gale Research, 1988.

Cook, Jim and Mike Lewington, ed. *Images of Alcoholism.* London: British Film Institute, 1979.

Core, Philip. Camp: *The Lie That Tells the Truth.* New York: Delilah Books, 1984.

Corenthal, Michael G. *Cohen on the Telephone: A History of Jewish Recorded Humor and Popular Music, 1892-1942.* Milwaukee, Wi.: Yesterday's Memories, 1984.

Corliss, Richard, "Hollywood Goes on the Wagon," *Time,* August 22, 1988, p. 76.

Crew, Danny O. *Ku Klux Klan Sheet Music: An Illustrated Catalogue of Published Music, 1867-2002.* Jefferson, N.C.: McFarland, 2003.

Crisafulli, Chuck, "Uneasy Laughs in Simpson Humor," *Los Angeles Times,* March 6, 1996, pp. F1, F9-F10.

Cromer, Mark, "Cut!!," *L.A. Weekly,* March 15, 1996, p. 32.

Dalzell, Tom. *Flappers 2 Rappers: American Youth Slang.* Springfield, Ma.: Merriam-Webster, 1996.

Di Pietro, Robert J., "On the Defamation of Italian Americans," *Maledicta,* vol. VII, 1983, pp. 75-84.

Dittmar, Linda and Gene Michaud, ed. *From Hanoi to Hollywood: The Vietnam War in American Film.* New Brunswick, N.J.: Rutgers University Press, 1990.

Doherty, Thomas. *Projections of War: Hollywood, American Culture and World War II.* New York: Columbia University Press, 1993.

Dolan, Jill, "What No Beans?: Images of Women and Sexuality in Burlesque Comedy," *Journal of Popular Culture*, vol. XVIII, no. 3, Winter 1984, pp. 37-47.

Dorinson, Joseph, "The Gold-Dust Twins of Marginal Humor: Blacks and Jews," *Maledicta*, vol. VIII, 1984-1985, pp. 163-192.

Dunning, John. *The Encyclopedia of Old-Time Radio.* New York: Oxford University Press, 1998.

Dutka, Elaine, "Force of Habit," *Los Angeles Times*, September 5, 1996, pp. F1, F10, F11.

Dyer, Richard. *The Dumb Blonde Stereotype.* London: British Film Institute, 1979.

Erenberg, Lewis A. and Susan E. Hirsch. *The War in American Culture: Society and Consciousness during World War II.* Chicago: University of Chicago Press, 1996.

Ergenbright, Eric L., "The Most Startling Confession Any Star Ever Made," *Photoplay*, January 1937, pp. 24-24, 110.

Erickson, Hal. *Religious Radio and Television in the United States, 1921-1991.* Jefferson, N.C.: McFarland, 1992.

Felchner, William J., "Alcoholism in America ... The Hollywood Version," *Alcoholism & Addiction*, September-October 1985, pp. 24-25.

Frank, Robert, "In the UPS Man, Some Women Find a Complete Package," *The Wall Street Journal*, February 5, 1995, pp. A1, A6.

Gaddis, Pearl, "He, She, Or It," *Motion Picture*, July 1917, pp. 27-33.

Gary, Juliann, "Blame It on Bizet," *Los Angeles Times Calendar*, June 17, 1994, pp. 25, 27, 28.

Gidal, Peter. *Andy Warhol: Films and Paintings.* New York: E.P. Dutton, 1971.

Gilliatt, Penelope. *To Wit: Skin and Bones of Comedy.* New York: Charles Scribner's Sons, 1990.

Gilstrap, Peter, "Tread on Me," *New Times Los Angeles*, April 9, 1998, p. 6.

Greenberg, Harvey R., "Cinna the Poet: The Morton Downey, Jr. Show," *Journal of Popular Film and Television*, vol. XVII, no. 3, Fall 1989, pp.123-125.

Hall, Dennis, "No Laughing Matter: Values, Perception, and the Demise of AIDS Jokes," *Journal of American Culture*, vol. XVI, no. 2, Summer 1993, pp. 25-30.

Hope, Christine, "Caucasian Female Body Hair and American Culture," *Journal of American Culture*, vol. V, no. 1, Spring 1982, pp. 93-99.

Howard, Jay R., "Vilifying the Enemy: The Christian Right and Novels of Frank Peretti," *Journal of Popular Culture*, vol. XXVIII, no. 3, Winter 1994, pp. 193-206.

Ireland, Norma Olin. *Index to Full Length Plays: 1944-1964*. Boston: F.W. Faxon, 1965.

Isherwood, Christopher. *The World in the Evening*. Minneapolis: University of Minnesota Press, 1999.

Johnson, Glen M., "Sharper Than an Irish Serpent's Tooth: Leo McCarey's *My Son John*," *Journal of Popular Film and Television*, vol. VIII, no. 1, Spring 1980, pp. 44-49.

Johnson, Reed, "Bare Truths of Character," *Los Angeles Times* Calendar, April 21, 2002, pp. 8-9, 80-81.

Jones, Marvin. *Movie Buff Checklist: Male Nudity in the Movies*. Los Angeles: Campfire Productions, 1996.

Kern-Foxworth, Marilyn. *Aunt Jemima, Uncle Ben, and Rastus: Blacks in Advertising, Yesterday, Today, and Tomorrow*. Westport, Ct.: Praeger, 1994.

"Klu Kluxers See Own Robes in Pictures," *Motion Picture News*, August 5, 1922, p. 642.

Lamb, Chris, "The Popularity of O.J. Simpson Jokes: The More We Know, the More We Laugh," *Journal of Popular Culture*, vol. XXVIII, no. 1, Summer 1994, pp. 223-231.

Lane, Anthony, "Where There's Fire," *The New Yorker*, March 21, 1994, pp. 203-206.

Latham, Angela J., "Packaging Woman: The Concurrent Rise of Beauty Pageants, Public Bathing, and Other Performances of Female 'Nudity,'" *Journal of Popular Culture*, vol. XXIX, no. 3, Winter 1995, pp. 149-167.

Laufe, Abe. *The Wicked Stage: A History of Theater Censorship and Harrassment in the United States*. New York: Frederick Ungar, 1978.

Lentz, Robert J. *Korean War Filmography: 91 English Language Features through 2000*. Jefferson, N.C.: McFarland, 2003.

Leonard, John, "Phallus Interruptus," *Nation*, November 22, 1993, pp. 617-619.

Lighter, J.E. *Historical Dictionary of American Slang*. New York: Random House, 1994.

Logan, Nick and Bob Woffinden. *The Illustrated Encyclopedia of Rock*. London: Harmony Books, 1977.

MacDougall, Robert, "Red, Brown and Yellow Perils: Images of the American Enemy in the 1940s and 1950s," *Journal of Popular Culture*, vol. XXXII, no. 4, Spring 1999, pp. 59-75.

"Marjoe Apostate," *Penthouse*, February 1973, pp. 86-90, 108, 126.

Martin, Olga J. *Hollywood's Movie Commandments: A Handbook for Motion Picture Writers and Reviewers*. New York: H.W. Wilson Company, 1937.

Maslin, Janet, "When a Movie Serves a Mickey," *New York Times*, August 14, 1988, pp. 1, 21.

McAllister, Matthew P., "Comic Books and AIDS," *Journal of Popular Culture*, vol. XXVI, no. 2, 1992, pp. 1-24.

"Mirrors of Hollywood No. 2 Just a Nice Boy," *Sunset Magazine*, August 1923, pp. 15, 58.

Morago, Greg, "Furry-Chested Males: An Endangered Species?," *Los Angeles Times*, July 5, 1999, p. F12, F14.

Morrow, Patrick D., "Those Sick Challenger Jokes," *Journal of Popular Culture*, vol. XX, no. 4, Spring 1987, pp. 177-184.

Morsy, Soheir A., "The Bad, the Ugly, the Super-Rich, and the Exceptional Moderate: U.S. Popular Images of the Arabs," *Journal of Popular Culture*, vol. XX, no. 3, Winter 1986, pp. 13-29.

Muller, Adrian, "The Kinkster Writes Again," *The Armchair Detective*, vol. XXIX, no. 1, Winter 1996, pp. 38-42.

Nelson, Richard Alan. *A History of Latter-Day Saint Screen Portrayals in the Anti-Mormon Film Era, 1905-1936*. Master of Arts Dissertation. Brigham Young University, 1974.

O'Pray, Michael, ed. *Andy Warhol Film Factory*. London: British Film Institute, 1989.

Parish, James Robert. *The Encyclopedia of Ethnic Groups in Hollywood*. New York: Facts on File, 2003.

Nicholson, John, "Screen Spirit," *Scotland on Sunday*, October 12, 1997, p. 22.

Paul, Elliot and Luis Quintanilla. *With a Hays Nonny Nonny*. New York: Random House, 1942.

Phillips, Chuck, "As Associates Fall, Is 'Suge' Next?," *Los Angeles Times*, August 1, 2003, pp. 1, 26-27.

Provenzano, Tom, "Controversy and Contradiction: Morton Downey, Jr.," *Drama-Logue*, September 20, 1990, p. 7.

"Race Ridicule," *The Moving Picture World*, October 15, 1910, p. 872.

Radclyffe, Megan, "3 Fat Ladies," *Gay Times*, October 1997, p. 16.

Reuter, Donald F. *Shirtless!: The Hollywood Male Physique*. New York: Universe Publishing, 2000.

Richards, Jeffrey, "The Invasion of Bad Taste," *Weekend Telegraph*, November 28, 1987, p. X1.

Rockoff, Adam. *Going to Pieces: The Rise and Fall of the Slasher Film, 1978-1988*. Jefferson, N.C.: McFarland, 2002.

Rosenblum, Constance. *Gold Digger: The Outrageous Life and Times of Peggy Hopkins Joyce*. New York: Metropolitan Books, 2000.

Rozas, Diane and Anita Bourne Gottehrer. *American Venus: The Extraordinary Life of Audrey Munson Model and Muse*. Los Angeles: Balcony Press, 1999.

Sampson, Henry T. *That's Enough Folks: Black Images in Animated Cartoons, 1900-1960*. Lanham, Md.: Scarecrow Press, 1998.

Schechter, William. A *History of Negro Humor in America*. New York: Fleet Press, 1970.

Segal, Lewis, "The Thrill Is Gone," *Los Angeles Times Calendar*, September 28, 2003, p. E43.

Shaheen, Jack G., "The Hollywood Arab: 1984-1986," *Journal of Popular Film and Television*, vol. XIV, no. 4, Winter 1987, pp. 148-157.

_____, "Arab Images in American Comic Books," *Journal of Popular Culture*, vol. XXVIII, no. 1, Summer 1994, pp. 123-133.

_____. *Reel Bad Arabs: How Hollywood Vilifies a People*. New York: Olive Branch Press, 2001.

Shain, Russell E., "Hollywood's Cold War" and "Cold War Films, 1948-1962: An Annotated Filmography," *Journal of Popular Film*, vol. III, no. 4, Fall 1974, pp. 334-350 and 365-372.

Shapiro, Nat, ed. *Popular Music: 1920-1929*. New York: Adrian Press, 1969.

_____. *Popular Music: 1930-1939*. New York: Adrian Press, 1968.

_____. *Popular Music: 1940-1949*. New York: Adrian Press, 1965.

_____. *Popular Music: 1950-1959*. New York: Adrian Press, 1964.

_____. *Popular Music: 1960-1964*. New York: Adrian Press, 1967.

_____. *Popular Music: 1965-1969*. New York: Adrian Press, 1973.

Silberman-Federman, Nancy Jo, "Jewish Humor, Self-Hatred, or Anti-Semitism: The Sociology of Hanukkah Cards in America," *Journal of Popular Culture*, vol. XXVIII, no. 4, Spring 1995, pp. 211-229.

Simon, Richard Keller. *Trash Culture: Popular Culture and the Great Tradition*. Berkeley: University of California Press, 1999.

Slide, Anthony, "Films and V.D. in 1919," *Films in Review*, November 1974, pp. 573-574.

_____. *Great Pretenders: A History of Female and Male Impersonation in the Performing Arts*. Lombard, Il.: Wallace-Homestead, 1986.

_____, "Hollywood's Fascist Follies," *Film Comment*, vol. XXVII, no. 4, July-August 1991, pp. 62-67.

_____. *Robert Goldstein and The Spirit of '76*. Metuchen, N.J.: Scarecrow Press, 1993.

_____. *The Encyclopedia of Vaudeville*. Westport, Ct.: Greenwood Press, 1994.

_____. *The Hollywood Novel: A Critical Guide to Over 1200 Works*. Jefferson, N.C.: McFarland, 1995.

Smith, Robert L. *Who's Who in Comedy*. New York: Facts on File, 1992.

Sobel, Bernard. *Burleycue: An Underground History of Burlesque Days*. New York: Farrar & Rinehart, 1931.

Sobel, Robert. *They Satisfy: The Cigarette in American Life*. New York: Anchor Books, 1978.

Sontag, Susan, "Notes on 'Camp,'" in *Against Intepretation*. New York: Farrar, Straus & Giroux, 1966, pp. 275-292.

Starr, Michael E., "The Marlboro Man: Cigarette Smoking and Masculinity in America," *Journal of Popular Culture*, vol. XVII, no. 4, Spring 1984, pp. 45-57.

Starr, Warren, "Lighthorse McLaglen: Professional Patriot," *New Theatre*, November 1935, pp. 14-16.

Thomson, Ruth Gibbons. *Index to Full Length Plays: 1926-1944*. Boston: F.W. Faxon, 1946.

_____. *Index to Full Length Plays: 1895-1925*. Boston: F.W. Faxon, 1956.

Thompson, Frank, "Vice Versa," *The Hollywood Reporter*, November 23, 1992, pp. 68-71.

Wice, Nathaniel and Steven Daly. *alt.culture: an a-z guide to the '90s—underground, online, and over-the-counter*. New York: HarperPerennial, 1995.

Starks, Michael. *Cocaine Fiends and Reefer Madness: An Illustrated History of Drugs in the Movies*. New York: Cornwall Books, 1982.

Stine, Scott Aaron. *The Gorehound's Guide to Splatter Films of the 1960s and 1970s*. Jefferson, N.C.: McFarland, 2001.

Suid, Laurence, "The Making of the Green Berets," *Journal of Popular Film*, vol. VI, no. 2, 1977, pp. 106-125.

Tracy, Jack, with Jim Berkey. *Subcutaneously, My Dear Watson: Sherlock Holmes and the Cocaine Habit*. Bloomington, In.: James A. Rock, 1978.

Wallace, Amy, "Movies ad Nauseum," *Los Angeles Times*, May 12, 1998, pp. F1, F4.

Weaver, Neal, "Grin and Bare It," *LA Weekly*, May 11, 2001, p. 49.

Wheen, Francis, "Swish of the Big Stick," *The Guardian*, Part 2, October 31, 1996, pp. 2-3.

Wloszcyna, Susan, "Hollywood Answers the Call of Nature," *USA Today*, January 4, 1994, p. D1.

Zoller, Robert, "Rituals of Death in Postwar American Film," *New Orleans Review*, Winter 1999, pp. 80-87.

Index

African Americans, 1, 7, 30-31, 69-74
AIDS, 35-36, 97, 104, 230
AIDS-related comic books, 35-36
Alcohol, 172-179
All-Girl Orchestras, 14
American Civil War, 41-43
Amos 'n' Andy, 71
Angels, 66
Annie Get Your Gun, 74
Anstey, F., 15
Anti-Semitism, 5, 64, 183, 195, 202-203, 218
Aoki, Tsuro, 76
Arabs, 82-84
Arbuckle, Roscoe "Fatty," 8, 96
Arlen, Michael, 110
Arsenic and Old Lace, 129
The Avengers, 120

Baby Face, 73
Baker, Josephine, 93
Bakker, Jim and Tammy Faye, 60-61
Baldwin, Alec, 152-153
Ballet, 118-119
Banana Skins, 93
Bananas, songs about, 94-95
"The Band Played Nearer My God to Thee," 127

Bankhead, Tallulah, 21
Bara, Theda, 140-141, 193-194
Barber Shop Video, 153
Barbette, 116
Barnard, George D., 46
Baron, Paul, 172
Barris, Chuck, 225-227
Baskett, James, 72
Bathing Beauties, 147
Beach and Biker Movies, 148
Beauty Contests, 142
Beban, George, 80
Beer, 172
Behind the Door, 134
Bennett, Joan, 209-210
Bennett, Richard, 111-112
Berg, Gertrude, 64
Bergman, Ingmar, 130
Berkeley, Busby, 147
Bestiality, 119
Beyond the Valley of the Dolls, 176
Biggers, Ear Derr, 78
Bimbos, 139-150
Blackface, 71
Blonde jokes, 140
Bobbitt, John Wayne, 153-155
Bourne, Matthew, 118-119
Boxing, 157

The Brave, 136
Brendel, El, 80, 117
Broken Blossoms, 79
Brookside, 120-121
Browning, Peaches, 144
Browning, Tod, 134
Bruce, Lenny, 27-28, 66, 229
Buckley, Richard, 166

Camel Cigarettes, 167-168
Camille, 130
Camp, 2-3, 11-24, 187
Campbell, Craig, 158
Cannibalism, 99-100
Cardinals on Screen, 56
Carousel, 149-150
Carry On films, 13
Casablanca, 73
Caste System, 73
Cemeteries, 125-126
Challenger Disaster jokes, 36-37
Chamber Pots, 103
Champagne, 178
Chaplin, Charlie, 131, 93, 96, 200, 210-211
Charlie Chan series, 78-79
The Cheat, 76-77
Cheech and Chong, 163-164, 225
Chesterfield Cigarettes, 168
Chinese, 76-80
Chippendale Dancers, 158-159
Christian Science, 58
Cigarettes, 167-172
Cigars, 171-172
Cisco Kid, 76

Coca-Cola, 8, 150, 167
Cody, Iron Eyes, 75
"Cohen on the Telephone," 66
Cold War, 47-49
Condoms, 115
Confessions of a Nazi Spy, 200
Confidential magazine, 118
Convention City, 115
"Coon" songs, 1, 70
Cooper, Gary, 193
Cosmetic Surgery, 146
Coughlin, Father Charles, 5, 61-62
Crane, Bob, 124
Crouch, Paul and Jan, 61
Culver City, 90

Damaged Goods, 111-112
Daughter of the Dragon, 77, 118
Davis, Sammy, Jr. jokes, 39
Day, Doris, 186
Death, 123-137
Death Cults, 124-125
Death Culture, 137
"Death Films," 136-137
Death Row, 131
Death Takes a Holiday, 128
DeMille, Cecil B., 53-54, 76, 87, 152, 191
"Depantsing," 156
Devil, 66
The Devil's Camera: Menace of a Film-ridden World, 87-88
Dial-a-Joke, 25
Dietrich, Marlene, 20, 55, 146
Dr. Fu Manchu, 77-78

Dodd, Rev. Neal, 57-58
The $1.98 Beauty Contest, 226
Downey, Morton, Jr., 5, 223-224
Doyle, Sir Arthur Conan, 166

Eating, 93-96, 99-101
Empey, Arthur Guy, 193
Ethiopian Jokes, 36
Evangelists, 58-63
Excrement, 105

Fascism in Hollywood, 191-20
Female Impersonation, 19-20, 44, 116
Food, 93-96, 99-101
Freak Acts in vaudeville, 97
Frederick's of Hollywood, 108
French Jokes, 31
Friedman, Kinky, 224-225
From the Manger to the Cross, 53
The Full Monty, 159
Funkhouser, Major Metallus Lucullus Cicero, 221-222

The Garden of Allah, 55
Gay jokes, 27, 219
Gay Men, 13, 16, 48, 116-119, 211-212
Gein, Ed jokes, 34-35
George, Wally, 223
"Gloomy Sunday," 126-127
Glyn, Elinor, 109-110
Gold Diggers, 144-145
The Goldbergs, 64
"Golden Showers," 104
Goldstein, Robert, 45

Gollywogs, 8
The Gong Show, 225-226
Gortner, Marjoe, 62
Grant, Bob, 7
Gyssling, Dr. George, 199-201
The Green Berets, 49-51

Hadji Ali, 102
Hair, 164
Hampton, Hope, 140
Hayakawa, Sessue, 76-77, 79
Himbos, 150
Hispanics, 74, 75-76
Hollywood, 89-91
Hollywood Madams, 115-116
Home Shopping Network, 6
Homosexual, see Gay
Hoover, J. Edgar, 16, 211
Hopper, Hedda, 17, 202, 205-216
Horton, Edward Everett, 18
"The House I Live In," 47

I was a Captive of Nazi Germany, 201
"In the Baggage Coach Behind," 127
Incest, 120-121
Irish, 81-82
Italian-Americans, 80-81

Japanese, 76-77
Jennings, Al, 89
Jewish-American Princess jokes, 30
Jewish jokes, 29-30, 65-66, 182
Jews in Popular Entertainment, 64-66
Johnson, Martin and Osa, 99
Joyce, Peggy Hopkins, 145

Keller, Helen, 28-29
Kellermann, Annette, 143-144
Kerrigan, J. Warren, 17
Kinison, Sam, 97
Korean War, 49
Ku Klux Klan, 5, 41-43, 219

L&M Cigarettes, 167
Lehrer, Tom, 229-230
Liberace Jokes, 35
Life of Brian, 54
Liliom, 128, 149
Lingerie, 108
Little People, 98
Lucky Strike Cigarettes, 167, 170

MacLane, Mary, 108-109
Mafia, 80-81
Mama's Boys, 17-18
Mapplethorpe, Robert, 24
Marlboro Cigarettes, 170
Masterson, W. B. "Bat," 89
Maxwell, Elsa, 16
McAuliffe, Christa jokes, 36-37
McDaniel, Hattie, 72
McLaglen, Victor, 192-193
McPherson, Aimee Semple, 59
Mexicans, 75-76
Miss America, 141-142
Mr. Moto series, 79
Moral Re-Armament, 58
Mormon Church, 64
Morrow, Vic jokes, 40
"Mother" songs, 187-189

Mother-in-Law jokes, 26
Motion Picture Country House and Hospital, 86-87
Munson, Audrey, 107-108
Mutilation, 134
My Son John, 48-49

Native Americans, 74-75, 218
Nazimova, Alla, 14, 21-22
The Night Life of the Gods, 14-15
Noddy, 2
Nudity, 107-108, 151-159, 219
Nuns on Screen, 56

Obesity, 96-98
Oland, Warner, 78
Our Town, 129

Pangborn, Franklin, 15, 18-19
Parsons, Louella, 206-207
Patterson, Jennifer, 97-98
Peretti, Frank E., 5, 67-68
The Picture of Dorian Gray, 16-17
Pie Throwing, 93-94
"Piss Christ," 104
Playboy, 142-143
Playgirl, 157-158
Polish jokes, 30-31
Political jokes, 31-34
Political songs, 181-182
Popes on Screen, 56
Porky's Trilogy, 217-220
Presidential songs, 181-182
Press Releases, 85-86
Priests on Screen, 56-58

Product Placement, 89
Production Code, 15, 19, 88-89, 142, 152, 176
Prohibition, 173-175
Prostitution, 113-115
"Pussy" humor, 27

Quakers, 63-64
QVC, 6
Quayle, Dan, 139

Racism, 69-84
Rambo series, 51
Regurgitation, 102
Reincarnation, 132-133
Religion, 53-68
Reverend Ike, 60
Richard, Cliff, 185-186
Riefenstahl, Leni, 196-199
The Road Back, 199-201
Roach, Hal, 194-195
Roberts, Oral, 60
Robertson, Pat, 62, 68
Robeson, Paul, 126
Robinson, Anne, 120
Rogers, Will, 124
Rohmer, Sax, 77
Roland, Gilbert, 151-152
Roosevelt, Eleanor, 32-34
Roosevelt, Franklin Delano, 31-34, 124
Roseanne, 13, 96

S&M, 119
Salome (film), 21-22
Salome (stage), 22-23

Sanders, George, 16-17
Sapho, 111
Savage, Dan, 121
Savich, Jessica jokes, 39
Savoy, Bert, 228-229
Scottish jokes, 31
Serrano, Andres, 9, 104
Sex, 107-122
"Shaving," 145-146, 152-153
Sheen, Bishop Fulton, 60
Sherlock Holmes, 166-167
Shogun, 102
Simpson, O.J. Trial jokes, 37-39
Singer's Midgets, 98
"Sissies," 3, 19
Sisters of Perpetual Indulgence, 56
Sister Souljah, 56
Slasher Films, 133-134
Sloane Foundation, 89
Smith, Thorne, 14-15, 131
Snuff Films, 135-136
Song of the South, 72
Sontag, Susan, 2, 11
South Park, 105-106
South Park: Bigger, Longer & Uncut, 106
Southern Culture, 8, 41, 188
Spankings and Canings, 7-8
The Spirit of '76, 45
Spit, 4
Spousal Abuse, 148
Springer, Jerry, 6-7
Stallone, Sylvester, 51
Stuttering, 101
Sunday, Billy, 63
Swaggart, Jimmy, 60

Swanson, Gloria, 21
Swastikas, 198
Swedish-Americans, 80
Swearing, 4-5
Sweeney Todd, 100

"Tableaux vivants," 147
Tattoos, 6
Taylor, Rip, 226
"Thank You Mask Man," 27-28
Thaw, Evelyn Nesbit, 145
Tiny Tim, 184-185
Topper films and television series, 131-132
Tracy, Arthur, 183, 187
Tracy, Lee, 103-104
Trainspotting, 105, 115
Transsexuals, 119
Trinity Broadcasting Network, 6
Tucker, Sophie, 186-187
Turnabout, 15
Two Fat Ladies, 97-98

UPS, 159
The Unknown, 134
Urination, 102-103

Vamps, 140-141
Venereal Disease, 111
Vietnam War, 49-51
Viva Villa!, 75, 103-104

Vomiting, 101-102
The Vortex, 165

Wanger, Walter, 194
War, 41-51
Ward, Fannie, 146
Warhol, Andy, 14, 23-24, 89
Waters, Ethel, 187
Waters, John, 105, 227
Wayne, John, 50-51, 77, 105, 195
The Weakest Link, 120
Webb, Clifton, 17
Welk, Lawrence, 222-223
West, Jessamyn, 63
West, Mae, 187
Westheimer, Dr. Ruth, 121
Wife jokes, 25-26
Wisconsin Death Trip, 123
Women as sexual objects, 147-148
Wood, Ed, Jr., 227-228
Wood, Natalie jokes, 39
World War One, 43-45, 188-189
World War Two, 46-47
Wright, Clarissa Dickson, 97-98

Youngman, Henny, 25

About the Author

British-born Anthony Slide is the author of more than seventy books on the history of popular entertainment, and the editor of some 125 additional volumes in Scarecrow Press's *Filmmakers* series. He began his writing career with *Early American Cinema* in 1970, and among his other titles are *The Films of D.W. Griffith*, *Early Women Directors*, *The Cinema and Ireland*, *The American Film Industry: A Historical Dictionary*, *Great Pretenders: A History of Female and Male Impersonation in the Performing Arts*, *Nitrate Won't Wait: A History of Film Preservation in the United States*, *Lois Weber: The Director Who Lost Her Way in History*, *Eccentrics of Comedy*, *Silent Players: A Biographical and Autobiographical Study of 100 Silent Film Actors and Actresses*, and *American Racist: The Life and Films of Thomas Dixon*.

He is also a documentary filmmaker, with his best-known work being the 1993 feature-length production, *The Silent Feminists: America's First Women Directors*. He has also appeared on many television shows as a commentator, most notably E! Entertainment's *Mysteries & Scandals* series and has also provided a number of DVD commentaries. He is a former associate archivist of the American Film Institute and the former resident film historian of the Academy of Motion Picture Arts and Sciences, and in 1990, he was awarded a honorary doctorate of letters by Bowling Green University. At that time, he was hailed by Lillian Gish as "our preeminent historian of the silent film."

www.ingramcontent.com/pod-product-compliance
Lightning Source LLC
Chambersburg PA
CBHW062013220426
43662CB00010B/1318